Rules of the Game

Rules of the Game

Quiz Shows and American Culture

Olaf Hoerschelmann

State University of New York Press

Frontcover photos: Courtesy Wisconsin Center for Film and Theater Research.
Backcover photo: Courtesy University of Maryland/Broadcast Pioneers Library.

Published by
State University of New York Press, Albany

For information, address State University of New York Press,
194 Washington Avenue, Suite 305, Albany, NY 12210-2384

Production by Marilyn P. Semerad
Marketing by Anne M. Valentine

Library of Congress Cataloging-in-Publication Data

Hoerschelmann, Olaf, (date)
    Rules of the game : quiz shows and American culture / Olaf Hoerschelmann.
        p. cm.
    Includes bibliographical references and index.
    ISBN 0-7914-6809-7 (hardcover : alk. paper) — ISBN 0-7914-6810-0
    (pbk. : alk. paper)
    1. Quiz shows—United States. I. Title.

PN1992.8.Q5H64 2006
791.45'6—dc22
    # 61309364

2005024120

10 9 8 7 6 5 4 3 2 1

Contents

Illustrations

Acknowledgments

The development of this project mirrors my peculiar fascination with quiz shows over a long period of time, from its beginnings as a conference presentation to its final stage as a book. Many friends and a few colleagues have played an important role during this time. I would like to thank Shanti Kumar and Steve Fore as well as Diane Negra and Harry Benshoff for their collegiality and good humor in a sometimes difficult environment. Chris Anderson, Michael Curtin, and Beverly Stoeltje provided crucial intellectual and personal support throughout the writing of this book. Many thanks go to all of them.

This project also depended on the competent help of librarians and archivists. I would like to thank Michael Henry and Chuck Howell at the Library of American Broadcasting, University of Maryland, who helped me navigate their magnificent collection. Dorinda Hartmann at the Center for Film and Theater Research likewise provided crucial assistance during my work at the University of Wisconsin. Anna Yoon at the UCLA Film and Television Archives; Sam Brylawski at the Library of Congress; and the staff at the Museum of Television and Radio, Los Angeles, and at the Museum of Broadcast Communications, Chicago, made the holdings of these archives accessible and assisted me my greatly during my research. Finally, thanks go to Shanti Kumar not only for being a great friend and colleague, but also for hosting me during several research trips to Madison, Wisconsin.

My research assistants Caryn Murphy and Owen Pillion helped locate numerous articles in trade magazines, Laura Turner-Reed's transcriptions of many of radio programs made my research go much more smoothly and Jaime Sanchez provided crucial help in the creation of the index for this book. Eastern Illinois University and the University of North Texas provided financial support for this project. Particular thanks go to the staff at the State University of New York Press for their professionalism and support, especially to Interim Director James Peltz, my initial acquisitions editor Ron Helfrich, Marilyn Semerad, Director of Production, and Anne Valentine in the Marketing and Publicity Department. Thanks also go to two anonymous reviewers whose comments have helped me improve this book in some crucial areas.

Finally, my gratitude goes to Bettina Becker, who occasionally manages to explain the importance of life away from the keyboard and to Tristan and Leela who have dozens of reasons why playing hide and seek is more important than work and why watching children's television with them is much more exciting than watching quiz shows.

INTRODUCTION

Quiz Shows and American Culture

Some of the beginnings of this project lie in a paper I presented at a conference in San Antonio in 1994. When I explained to an interested conference participant that quiz shows were the subject of my paper, she said, "Oh,
I just hate those," and turned away. Luckily, this troubling experience did not
deter me from further investigating the genre. The public's attitude toward
quiz shows that such statements represent usually oscillate between two positions: disdain and dismissal. In the academic world, quiz shows are generally
regarded as a trivial cultural form that does not warrant scholarly attention.
Eric Barnouw's three-volume *History of Broadcasting in the United States*
devotes attention to the genre only in the context of the 1950's quiz show
scandals. The big-money quiz shows involved in the scandals are likewise dismissed or disdained. Barnouw quotes Charles Van Doren, the star contestant
of *Twenty-One*, regarding the history of the rigging of this program:

> [Producer Albert Freedman] told me that I would not have a
> chance to defeat [current champion] Herbert Stempel because
> he was too knowledgeable. He also told me that the show was
> merely entertainment and that giving help to quiz contestants
> was common practice and merely a part of show business.[1]

The phrase *mere entertainment* exemplifies the common strategy of dismissing quiz shows as inconsequential forms of public life. Their meaning
does not extend beyond immediate and ephemeral concerns over winners
and losers, ratings and shares. At the same time, the quiz show scandal is also
a popular focal point around which the vilification of the genre centers.
Newton Minow's well-known speech at the 1961 convention of the National
Association of Broadcasters implicitly responded to the scandals:

> I invite you to sit down in front of your television set when your
> station goes on the air and stay there without a book, magazine,
> newspaper, profit and loss sheet or rating book to distract you—
> and keep your eyes glued to that set until that station signs off. I
> can assure you that you will observe a vast wasteland. You will
> see a procession of game shows, violence, audience participation
> shows, formula comedies about totally unbelievable families,
> blood and thunder, mayhem, violence, sadism, murder, western
> badmen [*sic*], western good men, private eyes, gangsters, more
> violence, and cartoons.[2]

Although Minow does not single out quiz shows as the only television
genre of dubious quality, he nevertheless assigns them a prominent role in
the transformation of television into a vast wasteland. This speech, as well as
myriad other public expressions of disapproval, exemplifies the disdain that
the quiz show genre often invokes.

As my interest in quiz shows developed over several years, I quickly dis-
covered that the genre was a lot more than just the scandals. The historical
and cultural significance of quiz shows goes well beyond the 1950's big-
money quiz shows. As the following chapters demonstrate, quiz shows have
existed on U.S. radio and television for more than seventy years. They have
adopted a variety of distinct forms and they have represented a variety of ideological formations. *Rules of the Game* is the first comprehensive scholarly
study of the quiz show genre on radio and television. It sets out to answer
some of the challenges John Fiske posed in his landmark book *Television
Culture*. One of the few researchers to take quiz shows seriously, Fiske criticized the marginal position of the genre in scholarly discourse:

> Quiz shows...are widely devalued, they are excessive, they pro-
> duce a high degree of viewer participation, they make visible and
> validate many of the normally invisible everyday life-skills of
> women, they are primarily a daytime genre, though there are
> prime-time examples, and they appeal to the socially powerless.
> [The] reexamination of quiz shows and their audiences has
> hardly begun, but a...recovery of the genre and its audiences is
> not only theoretically possible, but also, I would argue, both prob-
> able and politically desirable.[3]

Throughout this book, my main interest lies in analyzing how ideological formations manifest themselves in this seemingly trivial cultural form. *Rules of
the Game* investigates how, throughout the history of the genre, quiz shows
have been used to animate a variety of conflicts in U.S. culture. However,
the genre does not necessarily articulate one narrow set of beliefs, but often
provides the opportunity for the subversion of dominant value systems. One
of the central theses of this book is that quiz shows create a discursive space

in which a reversal of cultural hierarchies is possible and in which the audience is at least symbolically involved in the production of a program.

My emphasis on the dialectic relationship between dominance and subordination in contemporary culture indicates the theoretical and methodological connection of this book to the field of British cultural studies. In its broadest definition, cultural studies uses humanist and interpretive methods to analyze cultural products and their meanings. British cultural studies specifically conceptualizes culture as a site of contestation and as an ongoing historical process. Its implicitly Marxist orientation directs attention toward the analysis of popular forms of culture and the practice of everyday life. In other words, a popular quiz show such as *Let's Make a Deal* is important for a cultural studies scholar because it is targeted toward a large, popular audience and because it attempts to invoke specific discourses of everyday life such as gambling and shopping.

As a cultural history, *Rules of the Game* goes beyond the study of radio and television texts in isolation. In *Selling Radio*, Susan Smulyan's exemplary history of the commercialization of radio, she emphasizes that a cultural history of the media should insist on "examining producers, texts, *and* audiences, as well as the economic and technological links among them."[4] Similarly, this project starts from the assumption that studying media texts without regard for the economic, institutional, and social forces that shape broadcasting as a cultural practice is inappropriate. To document the influence of some of the institutional forces in broadcasting, *Rules of the Game* makes extensive use of radio and television programs and industry documents available in various broadcasting archives in the United States. *Rules of the Game* approaches quiz shows from a historical and critical perspective, providing close textual analyses of radio and television programs from the 1930s to the present and locating the genre within larger social and industrial structures. The primary analytical concerns of this book are the connection of the genre to the production of knowledge in U.S. culture, the construction of text-audience relationships on quiz shows and their significance for the practice of broadcasting, and the rethinking of media genre theory.

QUIZ SHOWS, KNOWLEDGE, HIERARCHIES

Quiz shows are often involved in debates over the role of education in broadcasting, especially the social responsibility of networks to provide "uplifting" programs. The politics of education and knowledge in U.S. culture often exert a significant influence on the production of knowledge and cultural authority in the quiz show genre. This becomes obvious when we compare the use of these categories in the genre throughout its history: Early radio programs such as *Vox Pop* frequently used interviews with "the man on the street" as the core of the show without using "expert panels" or specialized knowledge. In contrast, the big-money quiz shows of the 1950s, such as *Twenty-One* or *The $64,000 Question*, were closely connected to discourses of knowledge and education through their use of upper-class contestants and forms of high cultural distinction. They are part of the hegemonic project of cold war educational policy with its focus on Anglo-European elite culture. Programs of the 1960s and 1970s, on the other hand, do not articulate a similarly unified set of beliefs. In the process of restructuring the genre after the scandals, the industry redefined quiz shows as *game shows*, entertainment forms with low prestige. These shows increasingly incorporated stylistic elements of the counterculture, leading to a destabilization of cultural authority in shows such as *Let's Make a Deal* or *The Price Is Right*. Similarly, dating shows in the 1990s also tend to display the instability of discourses of family, gender, and sexuality.

The preceding paragraph gives some indication of the longevity and popularity of the quiz show genre. However, despite the fact that quiz shows have been one of the stock genres of U.S. broadcasting since its beginning, they are also one of the least studied genres in the disciplines of mass communication and media studies. This book focuses on the history of quiz shows on U.S. radio and television and the ways in which this genre is articulated to various ideological positions.

Referring to Geraldo Rivera, Wayne Munson illustrates the dominant view of the value of quiz shows:

> [Geraldo Rivera] sees his show as additional to a daytime television environment formerly dominated by soap operas and game shows. Unfortunately, he cannot support his genre without attacking the others: even the tawdriest talk show teaches something, he implies, but "you can't say that about the game shows they replace."[5]

Game shows are generally perceived as being "just entertainment": They do not teach their audience anything and have no other redeeming value.

Even the most common forms of popular culture, however, have pedagogical implications. Henry Giroux, Peter McLaren, and others involved in critical pedagogy define *pedagogy* as any form of social life that is instrumental in the production of knowledge and the formation of social identities. Thus, popular culture is a particularly important site for investigation from the perspective of critical pedagogy:

> When one practices pedagogy, one acts with the intent of creating experiences that will organize and disorganize a variety of understandings of our natural and social world in particular ways.[6]

All forms of popular culture are involved in the organization of understandings of our natural and social world, in the construction of social identities for their audiences, and in the validation and invalidation of different forms of knowledge.

Quiz shows have always been in a particularly close relation to the sphere of education and knowledge. At different points in time, specific shows used a set imitating a schoolhouse, included professors or licensed psychologists as authorities, and featured contestants who held their Ph.D.s or were professors themselves. However, knowledge on quiz shows is neither limited to "serious," "educational," or "elite" definitions of the terms, nor is the scope of this book limited to these definitions either. The historical shifts occurring within an overall genre that incorporates education-oriented quiz shows; quiz shows focusing on everyday life, gambling, or physical activity; and dating shows focusing on knowledge of people are significant in themselves as indicators and instigators of change as well as agents of reproduction.

Overall, quiz shows can be regarded as symbolic forms that produce and naturalize discourses on a variety of forms of knowledge. By presenting these discourses in the form of play, quiz shows become a powerful tool to naturalize and validate specific forms of knowledge. They form part of the field of cultural distinction that Pierre Bourdieu describes.[7]

Bourdieu's notion of a field describes the existence of organized systems of practices, artifacts, and meanings (for example, art), which have their own internal logic. As a member of a culture, one is socialized into a habitus, that is, a specific position within the various fields of culture. Although cultural distinctions ultimately might be arbitrary to the outside observer, they are governed by an internal logic that possesses a high degree of common sense for an insider. However, one's position within a field remains flexible and therefore, not fully determined by the field's internal logic. Individual practices retain a certain amount of freedom within a field and can ultimately redefine a field to some extent. The interactive relation between structure and practice in a field that Pierre Bourdieu theorizes, allows us to consider the quiz show genre as a specific practice that is both structured by and the structuring of the field of cultural distinctions. Nevertheless, quiz shows also tend to naturalize the practices within a field and ultimately create a strong belief in their common sense character. Whereas specific shows will tend to reproduce dominant hierarchies of taste and knowledge, other shows in other contexts can also attempt to rewrite the field in many ways. At the same time, Bourdieu does not argue that the field completely determines individuals or their habitus. The position of audience members within the field of cultural distinctions is not predefined, but, rather, has to be negotiated in the process of watching a quiz show as well as in the context of everyday life. Although the field attempts to structure practices such as the decoding of a quiz show, it does not do so in a determined way, so that an individual's habitus becomes an element that is both structured by and structuring of the field. Bourdieu explains the possibility for and resistance to change in a stratified cultural

system that heavily relies on elements of taste and education for its maintenance. At the same time, the centrality that Bourdieu ascribes to these issues
also illustrates the subversive potential of quiz shows as representatives of the
field of cultural distinction. By maintaining and (re)defining the validity of
specific forms of knowledge and authority, quiz shows can exert a significant
influence over culturally central discourses such as education and taste.

Quiz shows are not just marginal to social life as an inconsequential
form of entertainment. They are a unique site where the validity of different
forms of knowledge and practice is negotiated and are a central tool for the
maintenance or disruption of educational and cultural hierarchies. Quiz
shows are ultimately also an important site for the construction of social
identities, a place where people can start to negotiate their position in the
field of culture, a place where social subjects can negotiate, challenge, and
understand their position in a stratified society.

QUIZ SHOWS, INSTITUTIONS, AUDIENCES

Much of the significance of this book lies in the way in which quiz shows are
related to developments in the broadcast industry and its institutional practices. Historically, audiences for popular forms of entertainment—and for
broadcasting in particular—have been defined as passive receivers of
prepackaged media messages. Instead of reproducing a clear separation of
performer and spectator, of text and audience, quiz shows provide a space in
which broadcasters attempt to redefine the relation between programs and
their audiences. Detailed analysis of industry records and of quiz shows in
various historical periods reveals the hidden assumption that the participatory character of quiz shows is a defining feature of the genre. This book
demonstrates how the genre enables the development and articulation of
social fantasies of interactivity and immediacy in mass communication.
Throughout their history, but especially in periods of instability in the broadcast industry, quiz shows reveal how assumptions about the practice of broadcasting and the role of the audience in mass communication change both in
the industry and in U.S. culture.

The analytical outlook of this book runs counter to some analyses of
popular culture that have tended to isolate texts from their social conditions
of production and reception. I use Tony Bennett's concept of reading formations,[8] theorizing a complex system of relations that develop between a media
text, its readings formations, and its audience(s). Consequently, my notion of
the field of cultural production is highly inclusive and does not limit itself to
the discussion of one isolated cultural phenomenon.

Similar to Bourdieu, I argue for the incorporation of quiz shows in a
larger, structured system of meanings that exerts influence on both production and reception. In contrast, John Fiske's theory of popular culture tends

to ignore the structuring elements inherent in the larger system of culture.[9] Fiske, however, rightfully points to the fact that the observation that capitalism alone produces cultural artifacts does not explain their significance or the role they play in a lived culture. Popular culture is consequently a form that comes into existence only through the audience's engagement with it. Although this engagement in its immediate context indeed happens on the audience's terms, Fiske is not willing to consider fully the influence of larger social and cultural contexts. Thus, Fiske's claim that television is a producerly text accurately describes the audience's engagement with the text, actively producing meanings that the dominant encoding institutions do not intend or condone, but it does not conceptualize the audience's position within the field of culture.

To move beyond Fiske's microlevel discussion of text-audience relationships, addressing the macrolevel process of the production of culture as well seems necessary. Whereas research on the political economy of mass communication has always been centrally concerned with these issues, it has often done so in a reductive manner.[10] In contrast, Patrick Hughes attempts to focus the study of mass communication on different levels of analysis.[11] Following Hughes's suggestions, quiz shows need to be understood on at least two levels: First, they need to be understood in terms of the textual structures that enable audiences to engage with them in a variety of ways that are not determined by the texts, but that are also not independent from them. Second, quiz shows need to be understood within a larger system of cultural production that exerts an influence above the level of a narrow text-audience relationship. This can be done by using notions such as a reading formation or by referring to the even wider concepts of *field* and *distinction* that Bourdieu proposes. The interactive relationship among institutions, texts, and audiences theorized herein needs to be understood as a historically specific relationship and as such includes elements of dominance and subversion in numerous ways.

QUIZ SHOWS, GENRE, POWER

The final key concern of *Rules of the Game* is the redefinition of the concept of genre in radio and television. As previous works on the history of talk shows and the history of soap operas demonstrate[12] only a comprehensive study of a genre can further an understanding of the larger historical shifts within genres that provide crucial analytical connections between media texts and their larger cultural environment. The development of quiz shows from the 1930s to the 1990s demonstrates the high degree of flexibility and instability of genres under changing industrial and cultural conditions. This book showcases several instances in the history of quiz shows that provide particularly interesting sites for a redefinition of the concept of genre in radio and television: the emergence of quiz shows and the concept of audience participation in the 1930s, the redefinition of the genre in the wake of the quiz show scandal in the late 1950s, and the remaking of quiz shows prompted by the rise of cable television and narrowcasting in the 1980s.

One of the main appeals of quiz shows is that they create repetitive, ritual performances that deal with issues of central concern to U.S. culture, such as competition, success, and knowledge. Consequently, Fiske attempts to define the genre according to its relation to knowledge.[13] He starts out with a basic split between factual knowledge and human knowledge and divides the genre further into "academic" knowledge and everyday knowledge as subcategories of factual knowledge, and knowledge of people in general and of specific individuals as subcategory of human knowledge. Whereas Fiske does not clearly distinguish between the phrases *game show* and *quiz show*, his categories of knowledge reflect principles that to some extent define a program and that can serve as a starting point to accentuate some of the driving forces that actively shape the genre. The quiz principle primarily drives all shows that deal with competitions between individuals or groups, based primarily on the display of factual knowledge. The game principle drives shows dealing with human knowledge (general knowledge of people or specific knowledge of individuals) or those based primarily on gambling or on physical performances.[14]

The relationship between a genre and the individuals and institutions that develop and maintain it is, of course, highly complex. The way in which genres are organized through these influences is very similar to the ways in which anthropologists have theorized the organization of ritual in a culture.

Although many anthropologists primarily link the term *ritual* to religious practices, Roy Rappaport sees it as:

> the performance of more or less invariant sequences of formal acts and utterances not encoded by the performers. . . . Ritual is understood to be a form or structure, that is, a number of features or characteristics in a more or less fixed relationship to one another. Events conforming to this definition occur outside of religious contexts.[15]

Quiz shows are, of course, not primarily encoded by the performers or contestants. A contestant appearing on *The Price Is Right* has to play pricing games in a highly specific form which the institutions and producers creating the program predetermine. The only elements on *The Price Is Right* or any other quiz show that are not predetermined are the actual winners on the individual program and their success at winning the available prizes. Importantly, however, the producers of a quiz show have the power to make succeeding harder or easier for a contestant.

Although Rappaport's work clearly establishes the role of a genre such as quiz shows as a ritual form, Victor Turner emphasizes the importance of ritual as a transitional form. Turner attributes particular importance to the liminal phase of a ritual, a transitional stage between two social positions that places its participants temporarily outside of social rules.[16] He regards rituals as instances in which "new symbols, models, and paradigms arise" and as "the seedbeds of cultural creativity."[17] A program such as *Let's Make a Deal* thus gains some of its effectiveness and popularity from the fact that it introduces a new ritual form, new and unusual patterns of behavior, and rules of play that are new to the genre.

Strong structural limitations govern ritual in tribal or agrarian societies, thereby offering limited opportunities for creative challenges to dominant discourses. In contrast, Turner claims that ritual in industrial society is connected to the spheres of leisure and play, which in turn rely much more on experimental forms capable of subverting or criticizing dominant culture:

> The genres of industrial leisure, the theater, poetry, novel, ballet, film, sport, rock music, classical music, art, pop art, and so on, play with the factors of culture, sometimes assembling them in random, grotesque, improbable, surprising, shocking, usually experimental combinations.[18]

Turner thus introduces the possibility of subversion in ritual, which is otherwise often assumed to have highly rigid and static properties. He also describes ritual genres in industrial societies as unstable and constantly changing, that is, as shifting and fragmented both in terms of their meanings and in terms of their audiences. Although Stoeltje differentiates between ritual and festival, her observations on the ideological function of these forms are similar to those of Turner.[19] In particular, Beverly Stoeltje points out that these two forms are differently articulated to power and authority:

> The most recent modern religions, such as Protestantism, completely dissociate festival from religion, and it then becomes a secular event. As a result ritual is associated with official religion, whereas festival designates occasions considered to be pagan, recreational, or for children. Like play and creativity, festival explores and experiments with meaning, in contrast to ritual, which attempts to control meaning.[20]

Because festival does not operate with rigid structures, it can incorporate dissenting voices and articulate social conflict.

Both Stoeltje's discussion of festival and ritual and Turner's discussion of ritual connect to the notion of the carnivalesque in at least two ways: The centrality of the grotesque and play connect to Bakhtin's discussion of the carnivalesque element in Rabelais, and the emphasis on the instability of meaning in these forms connects to Peter Stallybrass and Allon White's notion of the ambivalence of carnival.[21]

Stallybrass and White argue that carnival cannot be essentialized as conservative or progressive, but point out that carnival can serve as a site of conflict in a social environment that is already characterized by a degree of instability:

> The only thing that can be said in the abstract is that for long periods carnival may be a stable and cyclical ritual with no noticeable political transformative effects but that, given the presence of sharpened political antagonism, it may often act as catalyst and site of actual and symbolic struggle.[22]

Although Stallybrass and White insist on the centrality of the binarism between high and low social and cultural forms[23] in their discussion of carnival, thinking about the potential of carnival to address social change and transcend existing cultural categories altogether seems to be as important.

Consequently, Mikhail Bakhtin emphasizes the nonofficial character of carnival as an event that incorporates the audience as a whole and refuses spectator-participant splits.[24] It is opposed to the official feast that is focused on ideological reproduction, stability, and the status quo. Carnival is a liberation from established orders and often reverses official ritual and official logic. However, carnival is not necessarily limited to perform reversals of cultural logic; it also has a significant degree of inventive freedom and it relativizes cultural norms. A mediated carnival, however, does not necessarily have the same social effects that an actual carnival might have. The carnivalesque atmosphere of programs such as *Treasure Hunt* or *Singled Out* will often be contained within the program through various techniques. Nevertheless, Bakhtin emphasizes that the moment of transformation from the actual practice of carnival to the carnivalesque element in art and literature retains some of its power to ignore dominant norms, to relativize cultural forms, to challenge conventions, and to imagine a new order of things.

Similarly, Robert Stam suggests that the anticipatory consciousness in cultural forms can be seen as an indication of their utopian/transgressive potential.[25] Nevertheless, Stam claims that modern carnival moves away from the utopian promise of alternative culture and becomes degraded and co-opted, and he specifically fails to acknowledge Bakhtin's claim that a subversive element still can be present in representational forms of carnival.

Although Stam thus dismisses the transgressive potential of most media texts in Western industrial societies, Stoeltje offers a more balanced view of the ideological role of ritual in industrial society. She points out that rituals in industrial society are often considered an element of entertainment and frequently appear in the form of a festival, incorporating elements of play in their form:

In today's society, secular rituals are frequently situated in larger events that we recognize as festival, or annual celebrations. This context facilitates the business of ritual by declaring the situation to be a form of play or entertainment, thereby making it possible to engage in fantasy.[26]

Ritual in industrial society can be seen as a way to respond to ruptures in dominant discourses and social relations, attempting to reconcile potentially irreconcilable ideological contradictions. It is centrally concerned with addressing these contradictions as they emerge in a culture. "Rituals evolve in parallel with social and political life, providing a formal arena through which issues can be symbolically enacted, contradictions addressed, and resolutions proffered."[27] Ritual is thus shaped through the exertion of power that organizes its production. A ritual is not a representation of universally held beliefs of a culture, but a specifically structured form that is usually articulated to dominant cultural formations. Similar to Rick Altman's[28] claims about the formation of a genre, which requires some stability from both a syntactic and a semantic perspective, Stoeltje points out that the form of ritual not only has to be established over time, but it is always also subject to specific changes:

> Forms do not occur in abstract time. They evolve through repeated performance in specific social contexts. This evolution of form may involve experimentation and conflict before it stabilizes. Significant changes at every stage in the history of a form reveal information about the organization of production.... An examination of the evolution of the form reveals key points in the process of production, the points at which decisions were made affecting the aesthetic organization and access to production, and thus control of meaning.[29]

To paraphrase Stoeltje, one of the important tasks in writing the history of quiz shows is to analyze how broadcast institutions have attempted to influence or change the meaning of the genre and its texts by modifying the genre's form or structure. Such an analysis will also reveal how quiz shows as cultural form relate to their larger cultural context, exposing or hiding cultural contradictions and prohibitions.

To summarize some key theories of genre, ritual, and cultural power, most authors seem to emphasize the ability of ritual forms to address central, often contradictory, ideological positions in a society. Especially in modern industrial societies, the form of a ritual seems open to change, challenges, and playful subversions. Although the institutions encoding ritual genres exert a significant amount of power in this process, I want to emphasize the tentative nature of the control over the structure as well as the meaning of a genre. Thus, quiz shows, especially after the scandals, need to be seen as an unstable form over which broadcasting institutions attempt to exert a significant degree of control in the process of production.

Chapter 1 argues that quiz shows—along with talk shows—are the programming forms most endemic to broadcasting because they do not adopt clearly established genres from other media. Whereas quiz shows do relate to "everyday genres"[30] such as parlor games and interviews, they are not clearly defined through established industry practices or audience expectations. Consequently, film genre theory, which has frequently emphasized the interplay of industry and audiences, does not provide an adequate framework for understanding quiz shows. The radio quiz show *Vox Pop*, arguably the first of its kind, illustrates the instability of various genre definitions and points to the flux of generic form and generic terminology. Starting out as a show focused on the man on the street, *Vox Pop*, according to its creator Parks Johnson, developed into a quiz show, an interview show, and a talk show. Whereas genre theory continues to use a system of fundamentally stable, structural categories to describe the development of genres, the case of early radio quiz shows in the 1930s suggests that genre might be better theorized as a system of fundamental hybridity and arbitrariness.

As Jacques Derrida points out, genres as classificatory systems are ever present, but tend to be invoked in a contradictory manner in everyday practice.[31] The instability of genre definitions in early broadcasting therefore does not just speak to a general sense of confusion in the industry, but to the multiple generic affiliations of any given program.

Although the broadcast industry established a fairly consistent system of industry practices and audience expectations for quiz shows in the 1940s and 1950s, the impact of the quiz show scandals speaks further to the malleability of such classificatory systems. The renaming of *quiz shows* as *game shows* in an effort to rid the genre of its negative connotations not only shows the polysemic character of genre definitions, but also points to the importance of institutional discourse to redefine established categories and audience expectations.

Chapter 2 focuses on a particularly crucial aspect of radio quiz shows: audience participation. Whereas the broadcast industry internally regarded quiz shows as selling tools with a special ability to deliver audiences to sponsors, they also publicly marketed the genre as giving voice to the common man. This chapter argues that the commercial effectiveness of quiz shows does not exhaust their cultural significance. Through a variety of strategies, shows such as *Stop the Music, Strike It Rich,* and *Chance of a Lifetime* attempted to draw the audience into a close relationship with the program. For example, some shows encouraged audience members to mail in quiz questions for expert panelists to answer, whereas other shows used telephone calls to integrate the home audience into the competition. Not only were audience members then involved in the program's contest, but they were also put in a position of limited cultural authority vis-à-vis the "experts" featured on the show. The rhetorical mode that quiz shows adopt in these cases serves the dual purpose of providing new forms of involvement for the audience and of enticing the audience into an ever closer relationship with the text. As Ien Ang points out, many forms of interaction and feedback from the audience can stabilize the operation of broadcasting.[32] For the broadcast industry, audience participation becomes a crude method of "knowing" the mass audience,[33] and a programmatic tool that can be used to explore and (re)define text-audience relationships.

The strategies used in the industry to negotiate the transition from radio to television in the late 1940s and the early 1950s illustrate the fact that audience participation had become a commonplace characteristic assumed of the genre as a whole. Television producers attempted to solve the task of "visualizing" a radio genre through a variety of techniques, such as the host's using direct address, but the simple incorporation of the studio audience replaced the close relationship between home audiences and programs common in radio. The strong integration of the audience was no longer a necessity because television viewing and the audience's relation to programming forms had stabilized in the early 1950s.

Chapter 3 deals with big-money quiz shows such as *The $64,000 Question*, *Twenty-One*, and *The Big Surprise*. These shows adopted a fairly unusual content and style, including high production values, extremely big prizes, and a focus on forms of high cultural distinction. This chapter analyzes the style and ideology of big-money quiz shows, their reception in the popular media, and internal industry documents outlining the incorporation of educational content into broadcast programming. Big-money quiz shows are a particularly interesting site for the production of knowledge because their focus on presumably serious questions put these shows in a position of cultural authority and legitimacy. The specific conditions of the United States in the 1950s, especially national debates over the importance of education in the cold war, and pressures on the networks to incorporate "enlightenment material" created shows that emphasized rigid cultural hierarchies rooted in Anglo-European culture. Big-money quiz shows thus celebrated the ongoing validity of traditional forms of cultural distinction and hierarchies of knowledge. The discovery of the rigging of these shows led to the quiz show scandals, which caused significant changes in the genre and a public relations crisis for the television industry as a whole.

The remodeling of the genre after the quiz show scandals is the focus of chapter 4. Over three years, the broadcast industry restructured the genre by redefining quiz shows as *game shows*, entertainment forms with low cultural prestige. The genre was generally removed from prime time, its stakes significantly reduced, and the required knowledge became less demanding. The industry engaged in a conscious effort to rescue the genre from its scandalous connotations and set the stage for new types of game shows that would emerge in the 1960s and 1970s. These shows increasingly adopted consumerism and gambling as the center of their competition. Their visual style was colorful and flashy, and the shows frequently emphasized studio audience participation in the games. Because the genre had been moved to daytime and redefined as *game shows*, it increasingly incorporated knowledge of trivia and everyday life. Women emerged as the new primary audience for shows such as *Let's Make a Deal, Supermarket Sweep, Shopping Spree, Treasure Hunt*, and *The Price Is Right*. Although these shows relied on a problematic equation of women with consumerism, trivial knowledge, and low culture, they also lacked a clear articulation of cultural authority and hierarchies of knowledge. They constitute a liminal space that responded to the contradictory cultural environment of the 1960s and 1970s.

Since their first appearance on U.S. television in the 1960s, dating shows have been a regular feature in U.S. broadcasting. However, the late 1980s and the 1990s, the focus of chapter 5, is the period in which dating shows are most visible on network and cable television. Dating shows embody the trend to reorganize the politics of knowledge in U.S. culture. They replace "serious" knowledge or forms of high cultural distinction with knowledge of people and relationships. This chapter argues that dating shows and the types of knowledge they represent gain in popularity in response to the renewed debates over the role of families and heterosexual relationships since the 1980s.

On the one hand, shows such as *Studs, Singled Out*, and *Change of Heart* foreground the instability of personal relationships. The breakup of a couple or a failed date with a catastrophic outcome is showcased in these shows as much as a successful date or a continuing relationship between two contestants. On the other hand, a majority of dating shows (for example, *The Dating Game, A Dating Story*, or *The New Newlywed Game*) focuses on the creation and maintenance of stable relationships and traditional family structures. Although dating on television might have become an unstable enterprise, many shows still operate with a narrative blueprint that emphasizes the primacy of healthy heterosexual relationships. Dating shows exhibit the dual drives toward a celebration of mandatory heterosexuality and a radical questioning of this very tendency through the ritual of coupling in the overdetermined context of the dating show format. Dating shows in the 1980s and 1990s exhibit some ambivalence about the validity of categories such as sexuality, family, and relationships. However, whether the genre as a whole manages to question the primacy of heterosexual relationships and patriarchal family structures is doubtful. Surprisingly, the genre becomes a forum in which some of the central elements of the discourse of family values can be negotiated.

Chapter 6 explores the connection between the quiz show genre and a variety of interactive technologies. Game shows have been a part of a variety of interactive television systems. The QUBE experimental cable system in Columbus, Ohio; the ATC-Berks Television system in Reading, Pennsylvania; Interactive Network, and Full Service Network have all incorporated game shows as part of their interactive offerings. Since its start in 1994, the Game Show Network has regularly featured original programs labeled *interactive*. These interactive games seem to offer the possibility for an enhanced interaction with the program and even other viewers. However, interactive games primarily define the audience's engagement with the televisual text in very narrow terms, that is, as participants in the show, and they do not leave opportunities for other forms of involvement with a program. The fantasy of interactivity primarily works as a strategy for networks and advertisers to create a close text-audience relationship.[34] Similar to the audience participation in early quiz shows, interactivity thus serves the industry's interests in controlling or knowing their audiences. Nevertheless, the limited participation that these "reactive systems"[35] offer still constitutes a utopian fantasy for mediated communication.

This book is organized primarily chronologically. However, each chapter also has a distinct theoretical outlook or discusses a specific subgenre of quiz shows. When necessary, additional examples are used even if they seem to step outside of the chronological organization of the book. Although I attempt to cover a large variety of quiz shows and myriad programs, chronicling the entirety of programs that have been broadcast on radio and television over the last seventy years is impossible for one study. For example, the importance of syndicated quiz shows (*Wheel of Fortune*, *Jeopardy!* and others) warrants further study as do celebrity panel programs such as *Hollywood Squares*, *What's My Line?* and *The Match Game*. Another fascinating study might concern the celebrity status of popular quiz show hosts such as Bob Barker, Monty Hall, Richard Dawson, Chuck Barris, Wink Martindale, and others who developed their own distinct star personas and fan base.

Along with the rise of cable television in the 1980s came the rise of signature quiz shows on specialized cable outlets: *Designated Hitter* and *NFL Trivia Game* on ESPN, *The Great Getaway Game* on the Travel Channel, *Clash* and *Whose Line Is It Anyway?* on Comedy Central, and *Remote Control* and *Turn It Up!* on MTV all seem to provide a unique format that connects them to their respective networks. The ways in which these programs are used to express a condensed version of the identity of their originating channel gives us insight into the programming philosophy behind cable television outlets. Cable television of course also brought us the *Game Show Network*, an entire channel devoted exclusively to quiz shows, showing reruns of vintage

programs and popular favorites along with original programming. The strategies employed on the Game Show Network in selecting and presenting parts
of the history of the quiz show genre likewise warrants further scholarly
attention. Finally, more research on the politics of race and ethnicity might
give us additional insight into the cultural significance of this genre and its
relation to the politics of U.S. culture in general.

Other aspects of quiz shows that remain to be studied are virtually end-
less. I hope more scholars will be inspired to fill in the inevitable gaps this
book leaves. Moreover, I also hope that *Rules of the Game* will help to stimulate new research from a multitude of perspectives and give quiz shows a
more prominent place in the field of media studies.

CHAPTER 1

What Is a Genre? Quiz Shows/ Game Shows

More than any other genre on radio or television, the quiz show genre has been notoriously difficult to define. Radio and television genres routinely form hybrids and cross-fertilize each other, as can be seen in various recent popular comedy-drama hybrids such as *Ally McBeal*, *The Wonder Years*, or *Sports Night*, as well as in failed hybrids such as *Cop Rock* or *Medicine Ball*. In the case of quiz shows and game shows, however, the terms hide a myriad programming forms under these seemingly unifying generic labels. Shows as different as *The Price Is Right*, *Who Wants to Be a Millionaire*, *Dr. I.Q.*, *Survivor*, *Family Feud*, *Double Dare*, *Supermarket Sweep*, *Jeopardy!*, *Queen for a Day*, *The Newlywed Game*, *Singled Out*, and *Take It or Leave It* are united through a common generic label, yet their similarities are often difficult to discern.

Although we sometimes see all of these shows referred to as game shows, some of them are also categorized with other generic labels, for example, the term *reality show* for *Survivor*, the term *quiz show* for *Take It or Leave It*, or the term *dating show* for *Singled Out*. The variation of such generic labels partly stems from historical changes in terminology, yet it also points to a fundamental instability of generic categories. In this chapter, the term *quiz/game show genre* indicates that the use of generic labels in everyday discourse, industry practice, and scholarly work has consistently failed to address the complexities and shifts in this genre. Specifically, the example of radio in the 1930s and 1940s is used to illustrate some of the inadequacies of current genre theory.

One of the most common problems in writing about this genre is that the terms *quiz show* and *game show* are often applied interchangeably. However, these terms also correspond to important changes in the history of the genre itself. A differentiation between quiz shows and game shows did not exist prior to the quiz show scandals in 1958. Shows such as *Truth or Consequences* and *People Are Funny*, which rely mainly on physical activity and do not have any significant element of academic or factual knowledge to them were called quiz shows. The same is true for shows such as *The $64,000 Question* that emphasized factual knowledge. The quiz show scandals were an important turning point because the genre formerly known as *quiz shows* was renamed *game shows* in the years following the scandals. The new name, *game shows*, removes the genre from the realm of serious knowledge and cultural centrality and instead creates associations with play and leisure time, which connect it to less sensitive cultural areas.[1] Although the *quiz* versus *game* distinction is indeed an important strategy for the broadcast industry in the wake of the scandals, it does not necessarily imply a clear, long-term shift in the style or content of quiz/game shows. As the recent popularity of *Who Wants to Be a Millionaire* illustrates, quiz shows once again incorporate knowledge-based questions and are featured prominently on prime-time television. In the case of *Who Wants to Be a Millionaire*, even the generic label *quiz show* has been recycled. These shifting generic distinctions are an important site for the analysis of the discursive struggles over program control, cultural hierarchies, and social acceptance in the broadcast industry. Despite the historical conflicts over the use of the terms *quiz* and *game*, the term *quiz shows* is used herein for practical purposes, denoting an overarching, descriptive term for the genre as a whole.

THE CASE OF THE MISSING CORPUS

One of the basic concerns of genre criticism and genre theory has been the identification of a body of texts and the study of its organization according to common characteristics. As Rick Altman points out in *The American Film Musical*, genre theory (for example, Tzvetan Todorov's *The Fantastic*) has often differentiated between historical and theoretical genres.[2] A historical genre describes the cultural practice of encoding and decoding genre texts without any a priori theoretical assumptions about the genre. However, the constitution of a genre requires that certain (theoretical) assumptions about commonalities between texts be made. This observation holds true for media practitioners as well as genre theorists: each group attempts to understand a genre based on an implicitly theoretical understanding of it. Therefore, historical genres are always also theoretical ones. In reverse, the observation of a theoretical genre always relates to the reading practices of the audience or the critic, who is also historically situated and who is also part of an audience. Consequently, the history-theory split ultimately only masks the subjectivity of the researcher and the theoretical basis of all historical genres.

Attempting a synthesis of these two views, Rick Altman suggests that the historical definition of the corpus of a genre can be used as a first step in the critical process of genre studies. This first definition will be fairly broad, based on stock elements such as location, sets, and characters, which Altman refers to as the semantic level:

> The fact that a genre has previously been posited, defined, and delimited by Hollywood is taken only as prima facie evidence that generic levels of meaning are operative within or across a group of texts roughly designated by the Hollywood term and its usage.... The broadest possible corpus implied by the industrial/journalistic term is taken as the critic's preliminary corpus.[3]

On the basis of this broad definition, Altman argues, the critic can proceed to limit and modify the body of the genre according to specific critical standards that reflect the requirements of the study. In this second step, the interests, preoccupations, or goals of the critic take precedence over the "historically existing" structures of a genre. "The critic will identify and describe certain traits and systems present and operative within a large number of the texts constituted by the preliminary corpus."[4] This theoretical framework is based on two beliefs: First, Altman assumes that the critic can find a stable genre structure, and second, he assumes that finding, identifying, and reproducing this structure is desirable for the critic. This notion of genre is not focused on the margins of a genre and it does not specifically look for points of instability, contradiction, and breakdown in the seemingly stable structure of a genre. Instead, the methodology that Altman outlines in *The American Film Musical* and his subsequent work *Film/Genre* emphasizes and reinforces those cases where a genre as a classificatory system works and displays relatively stable genre conventions.[5]

If this book simply were to follow Altman's propositions, it would include all shows designated as quiz shows or game shows in popular and industry discourses in the preliminary corpus of the genre. As comprehensive sources to establish a preliminary corpus, one could use books such as David Schwartz, Steve Ryan, and Fred Wostbrock's *Encyclopedia of TV Game Shows*, John Dunning's *Tune in Yesterday: The Ultimate Encyclopedia of Old-Time Radio 1925–1976*, and Jon Swartz and Robert Reinehr's *Handbook of Old-Time Radio: A Comprehensive Guide to Golden Age Radio Listening and Collecting*.[6] Written by three representatives of the broadcast industry, all of whom were involved in the production of game shows at some point, the *Encyclopedia of TV Game Shows* provides an inclusive collection of game shows or quiz shows that were aired on U.S. television. Similarly, Jon Swartz and Robert Reinehr and Dunning list many radio programs commonly regarded as quiz shows. Although this strategy would neatly identify a preliminary corpus, the analysis

herein is not confined to a limited number of specific traits present throughout the history of television quiz shows. Although these sources might help to
identify a corpus of texts, they are hardly comprehensive and in particular
might fail in view of texts that were considered marginal to or outside of the
generic corpus. In other words, we have to ask what happens to shows that
are outside of standard industry practices or that cannot be clearly placed
within accepted genre designations.

Borrowing Foucault's notion of a genealogy,[7] this chapter is particularly
concerned with identifying the beginnings of a discursive practice, which
imply the emergence of differences and ruptures. This project is positioned in
opposition to traditional historiography, which tends to emphasize linearity
and a search for historical origins. As historian Patricia O'Brien points out:

> the genealogist/historian looks for beginnings, not origins. This
> for Foucault was an essential distinction. Origins imply causes;
> beginnings imply differences. A genealogy, therefore, "will culti-
> vate the details and accidents that accompany every beginning."[8]

Observing the contradictions, struggles, and accidents that accompany all
beginnings can render new insights into the development of a discursive form
such as a genre.

Following these arguments, the observation of shifting traits within the
genre as a whole is more important than the critic's identification of a unified
genre system. My method for studying quiz shows, then, relies on the identification of changes and ruptures in the genre. This history of the quiz show
genre does not exclusively focus on the solidification of a corpus of texts, but
on the changing articulations of quiz shows throughout the history of the
genre. The following section investigates the emergence of early quiz shows
in U.S. broadcasting in the 1930s. Observing the beginnings of the genre will
demonstrate that some of its history is located outside of the consensual
generic corpus.

GENERIC CONFUSIONS

As a new type of show emerged in the mid-1930s and started to spread in
national networks' and regional stations' programming lineups in the following years, trade publications as well as the popular media were trying to make
sense of this new phenomenon by tracing its origins and identifying the first
show of its kind. An article in the *New York World Telegram* lamenting the
proliferation of quiz shows tries to define the genealogy of the genre:

> Who Started It? The oldest quiz on the networks is the Saturday
> evening *Vox Pop*, which was brought up from Texas to take over
> a summer half-hour four years ago. You can't blame the deluge
> on *Vox Pop*, however. The blame should probably go to Major

Bowes, who made the first resounding success of bringing strangers to the microphone and conversing with them in a more or less bantering tone."⁹

Figure 1.1. Major Edward Bowes, host of Major Bowes' Original Amateur Hour. *Courtesy University of Maryland/Broadcast Pioneers Library.*

The article is referring to *Major Bowes' Original Amateur Hour*, a program that originated as a local broadcast in 1934 on WHN in New York City and became a network show in 1935 on NBC.¹⁰ The show was focused on amateurs coming to New York and hoping to perform musical, dramatic, or other talents and embark on a career in show business. Top winners continued to appear on the program up to a yearly championship round. Other than Frank Sinatra, who appeared on the program in 1937 as part of the Hoboken Four, few amateurs seem to have actually broken into show business. Given the setup of *Major Bowes' Original Amateur Hour*, why the article quoted previously singles out this particular program as the originator of quiz shows over a variety of other programs is difficult to imagine.[11]

Instead, one could argue that *Uncle Jim's Question Bee* is the legitimate original quiz show.[12] An NBC press release indicates that it was focused on the straightforward asking of knowledge-related questions and on a competition between several contestants:

> *Uncle Jim's Question Bee* to test fan's knowledge: Whose cow kicked over a lantern and started the famous Chicago fire? What is the distance from New York to San Francisco? How many rolls in a baker's dozen? Attempts to answer these and many other questions will be made by members of the studio audience participating in the broadcasts of a new program, *Uncle Jim's Question Bee*, to be inaugurated Saturday, September 26, from 7:30 to 8:00 p.m., E.D.S.T., over the NBC-Blue Network.... During the broadcasts, McWilliams [the master of ceremonies] will call six members of the studio audience to join him before the microphone. Where he will ask each one, alternately, six questions on a wide variety of subjects. An answer, right or wrong, must be made within ten seconds. [Joseph] Bell, as referee, will rule on accuracy and keep score. Members of the radio audience will be asked to send in sets of questions and answers for use on the programs.[13]

As this quote illustrates, *Uncle Jim's Question Bee* exhibits traits one might consider conventional for a quiz show: a competition for money between candidates, the asking of questions on a variety of subjects, the presence of a master of ceremonies, and the integration of the studio audience in the program. Interestingly, however, the press release itself does not include any clear genre designation, even though it refers to "testing fan's knowledge." Labeling this program the first quiz show would entail the retroactive imposition of today's genre conventions onto this program, proving only that *Uncle Jim's Question Bee* is prototypical of the quiz genre because it fulfils our expectations after the fact.

However, instead of *Uncle Jim's Question Bee*, the previously mentioned *Vox Pop* was cited much more frequently in various media accounts as the grandfather of quiz shows or the original quiz show.[14] Its creator, Parks Johnson, and various staff members working on the program extensively described and promoted *Vox Pop*. David K. Grant, the program director for *Vox Pop* at the McCann-Erickson advertising agency, wrote an article for the June 1946 issue of the advertising industry trade magazine *Advertising and Selling* discussing "The Rise of the Audience Participation Program." Trying to position himself as an expert on the genre, he emphasizes *Vox Pop*'s status as the origination point of the genre:

In Houston, Texas, a little over fourteen years ago, a microphone was lowered out of the windows of KTRH in the Rice Hotel, and in a few minutes, curious bystanders and chance passer[s]by were making radio history. They were taking part in radio's first "Audience Participation" broadcast—*Vox Pop*. Persuaded to participate by a local advertising man, Parks Johnson, they found themselves answering questions that ranged all the way from the personal to the ridiculous.[15]

In a promotional booklet on *Vox Pop*, the narrative of this program is continued and further elaborated:

There were a lot of gag questions and riddles on *Vox Pop* in those days. And at a dollar a question, the participants entered merrily into the program's slightly zany spirit of fun. But *Vox Pop*, without realizing it, was pioneering a new departure for radio programs. Because out of those sidewalk question bees developed the quiz programs and audience-participation shows which play such a prominent part in present day radio programming.[16]

In promotional materials, the producers of *Vox Pop* also emphasize the program's status as being "the first radio quiz show," "radio's original interview program," and "the first program to pay money on the air to participants who answered questions correctly." Articles in newspapers and popular magazines almost verbatim repeat *Vox Pop*'s claim as the original quiz/audience participation show and of Parks Johnson as the pioneer of quiz shows.[17] This illustrates not so much the truth-value of the claims made for *Vox Pop* or any other program, but the effectiveness of program publicity to support such claims to historical precedence. Gregory Lukow and Steven Ricci introduce the term *intertextual relay* to describe the power of publicity materials to advance certain meanings and apply generic labels in the case of cinema.[18] Such an intertextual relay seems to operate similarly in the case of broadcasting, structuring public discourses on media texts and lending credibility to certain historical claims.

However, ultimately we can only note the variety of competing claims regarding the invention of the quiz show genre. Genre history cannot confirm or authenticate the pioneering status of an individual film, radio program, or television show. Identifying one radio program as the originator of quiz shows would reinforce traditional notions of linear history through which we can identify the exact origination point of specific practices or events. We have to resist the drive to identify Uncle Jim, Major Bowes, Parks Johnson, or anyone else for that matter as the individual genius behind an entire genre. Instead, other documents from the history of quiz shows in the 1930s and 1940s offer an alternative explanation for the beginnings of the quiz show genre.

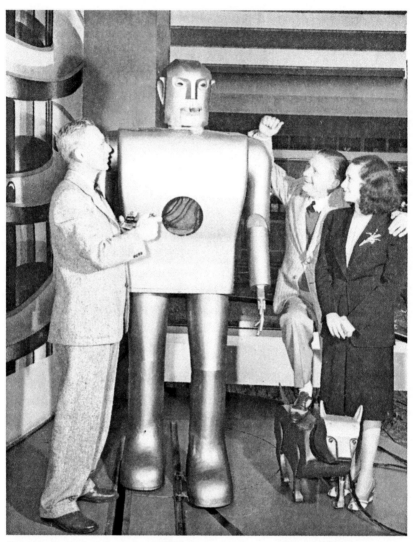

Figure 1.2. Parks Johnson and Wally Butterworth at a publicity shoot for the New York World's Fair. *Courtesy University of Maryland/Broadcast Pioneers Library.*

Whereas the various texts speculating on the origins of quiz shows already displayed a startling multitude of categories and generic labels, this tendency can be observed even more clearly in quotes from magazines targeted to radio listeners in the late 1930s. An article describing *Vox Pop* shortly after its 1935 network debut points to preelection "sidewalk interviews" as the first inspiration for the program and then connects it to amateur hours as an additional possible generic affiliation. The *Radio Mirror*, on the other hand, labels *Vox Pop* a "parlor game," and *All-Wave Radio* magazine chooses "question and answer" as designation for the same program.[19] In a letter to NBC's sales department, Robert P. Myers, an attorney for Procter and Gamble, points out that the programming idea behind *Truth or Consequences* is not original to radio at all, but dates back to a children's game of the same name. He uses this observation to defend *Truth or Consequences* against allegations that it copied significant parts or ideas from a local program entitled *Can You Do It*, broadcast on KFWB in Hollywood, California.[20] However, Myers's remarks point to a much more profound theoretical point: Quiz shows are not necessarily rooted specifically in broadcasting alone, but relate to everyday practices outside media industries. This point invokes Bakhtin's notion of everyday genres. Such genres, Mikhail Bakhtin points out, are conventionalized and serve to facilitate everyday discourse. Whereas everyday genres require a minimum of shared expectations, they do not have the same classificatory power as literary or media genres.[21] A 1939 article in a popular magazine illustrates the connection of quiz shows to everyday genres even further:

> Quizzes in some form have always been popular, because there is not one of us who doesn't like to parade his knowledge, if any. We remember years back the old *Chatterbox*, an English magazine which used to appear in this country in bound form every Christmas. They had a puzzle department of riddles, acrostics and anagrams that would have stumped Minerva.... Then you remember the Ask Me Another craze, and anagrams have been popular from times dim.[22]

The article gives a long list of terms to refer to quiz shows. On the one hand, at least five terms are offered to serve implicitly as genre labels:

- audience participation programs
- sidewalk question bees
- sidewalk interviews
- question and answer
- amateur hours

On the other hand, six additional terms are offered that connect quiz shows back to everyday genres of various kinds:

- parlor games
- children's games
- puzzles
- riddles
- acrostics
- anagrams

The first set of terms reinforces the general sense of instability of these genre designations, offering dramatically different terms for essentially the same shows. Relating quiz shows to a rather diffuse set of everyday genres further underscores this already weakened genre identity. Again we face the impossibility of assigning shows such as *Uncle Jim's Question Bee* or *Vox Pop* to appropriate categories. Instead, the everyday genres listed earlier point to the alternative of theorizing genre as a nonexclusive process of tentative classification. That a quiz show could incorporate elements of parlor games such as puzzles or riddles seems clear. Terms such as these seem to demand none of the classificatory exclusivity that our standard notion of genre demands. Several genre theorists have recently used Jacques Derrida's essay *The Law of Genre* to theorize this point.[23] Derrida argues that a text cannot belong exclusively to one genre, that its affiliations are tentative, multiple, and nonexclusive. He opposes the law of absolute belonging and replaces it with the notion of participation in a genre. We can thus think of texts as productively invoking a genre as a communicative act, but we have to surrender our belief in the absolute rule of the law of genre. Genre cannot be regarded as a universal process that equally or universally speaks to all viewers or listeners. From this perspective, the claim, "even if we cannot provide an essential definition of a genre's core identity, we all still know a sitcom when we see one," is rendered inappropriate. Such a statement does not take the dynamic nature of genre into account and instead only pays lip service to understanding the dynamic nature of genre.[24]

Applying Derrida's theoretical position to the quiz show genre, we can then replace the question, "Is *Vox Pop* an audience participation program, a sidewalk question bee, a sidewalk interview, a question-and-answer program, or an amateur hour?" with the question, "In what genres does *Vox Pop* participate?" Derrida considers the law of participation as a mode of excess where multiplicity is unavoidable and singularity is unattainable, so that a variety of these categories can simultaneously serve as genre designations. In general, indicators of genre participation can be found in multiple sites: the textual structures of the program itself, the often contradictory classificatory attempts of program creators, program publicity, and the reading practices of various audiences, as far as those are accessible.

GENRE AND HISTORY

Numerous media scholars have noted that genre theory tends to privilege synchronic relationships within a genre. For example, genre theorists working from the framework of structuralism argue that a genre is structured like a language.[25] We assume that the overarching language of the genre structures and determines the production of individual texts within the genre. This language analogy regards a genre as a system that distributes and shares its cultural currency more or less evenly in a culture. It is connected to theories of communication as ritual, which I discuss later.[26] In her article on television genre, Jane Feuer points out that the relationship between text and genre is balanced somewhat differently than language analogies imply; that is, individual texts can elicit change, and rupture and innovation in a genre is more crucial than often assumed.[27] For example, programs such as *The $64,000 Question, Let's Make a Deal*, or *Singled Out* introduce an element of innovation that constitutes an important break with existing genre conventions. Approaches based on the language analogy can very easily lead us to privilege the power of genre as a system over individual texts, creators, and the audience. As genre theorists point out, we are running the danger of excluding the history of the genre as well as its relationship to historically specific social and cultural contexts.[28] Genre becomes a stable, transhistorical phenomenon with little room for contradiction or multiplicity.

Altman's semantic/syntactic approach to genre attempts to resolve some of the problems of genre theory's lack of historical consciousness. He claims that a genre comprises semantic elements (for example, stock characters, sets, and standard editing patterns) as well as syntactic elements (the combination of semantic elements into meaningful patterns).[29] Although semantic elements can offer a basis for a genre, a genre does not stabilize until a meaningful syntax develops. Change can then be conceptualized either on the semantic level or on the syntactic level so that a recombination of semantic elements can significantly change the meanings that can be developed out of a genre text: "A genre does not exist fully until a method is found of building its semantics into a stable syntax. In other words—and this notion has rarely been recognized by genre critics—genres are made and not born."[30] Altman provides a theory of genre that opens up the possibility for significant change in a genre and that acknowledges the power of media institutions to create and change the semantic-syntactic structure of genres. However, we still have to consider the role that cultural context and the audience play in the development of a genre. Additionally, Altman also assumes that the strategies of the media industries with regard to a genre represent purposeful behavior and are informed by conscious reflection. However, as the previous section noted, some discourses on genre are far from straightforward or rational.

In the development of the quiz show genre, we can nevertheless notice some efforts toward a consolidation of genre terminology. Going along with the increasing importance of the ratings system and efforts in mass communication research to measure and categorize television programming, several 1950s' publications attempted to speak about the quiz show genre in a more stable terminology.

A study titled "The Television Audience of Today" differentiates between *quiz programs* and *panel-quiz programs* in 1952, but changes these categories to *quiz* and *panel* for its 1956 version without, however, including significantly different programs in each case. In an attempt at genre definition, the 1952 study provides the following classificatory scheme:

> Quiz programs: Basic theme of program is offering prize for performance or answer by contestant. Panel-quiz program: Basic theme of program is reply or solution by panel to problem or question. Contestant participates by providing question or problem.[31]

No similar definition is offered in the 1956 study. The attempt to provide a genre definition solely on the basis of who asks the question and who answers it is, of course, somewhat tedious, but not necessarily less persuasive than any other. One might conclude that the authors of the study assume that the panel-quiz program is actually a subgenre of the quiz program, but they never clearly follow through with any such proposition. A 1953 NBC publicity booklet for *Name that Tune* offers the following appraisal of the show:

> Name that Tune: One of the most popular program types in radio. Audience participation shows are reaching an average of 11% more homes than in the previous season.
>
> Created by Harry Salter, co-producer of *Stop The Music*— one of radio's most successful quiz programs.... A half hour of songs, quiz, and fun . . . with a built-in merchandising hook which guarantees in-store traffic.... An audience participation show created by Harry Salter—one of radio's most successful producers of musical quiz programs.[32]

The main generic markers this booklet establishes for *Name that Tune* are audience participation and quiz programs, while using the terms *musical, songs,* and *fun* as additional qualifiers. A 1956 NBC press release for master of ceremonies Jack Barry, associated with *Tic Tac Dough* and *Twenty-One,* refers to *Tic Tac Dough* both as a "new audience participation show" and a "new quiz show," implying either that these terms are synonymous or that one is a subgenre of the other.[33] The idea that one of these terms might serve as a general designation for the genre and the other as a subgenre is also implicit in Parks Johnson's notes for a 1947 speech at a radio conference. Johnson seems to consider audience participation as a metagenre with categories such as quiz, musical, information, forum, games, and giveaway as subgenres to audience participation.[34] The interesting point here is that most of the elements that Johnson lists as subcategories did not disappear or lose importance in quiz shows of the 1940s or 1950s. The programs listed in *The Television Audience of Today* as quiz programs include an amazing variety:

- *Strike It Rich,* a show where contestants tried to win prizes and gifts through support from the home audience based on the personal hardships they endured.

- *You Bet Your Life*, a program hosted by Groucho Marx which did not take the quiz aspect of the show too seriously and instead often functioned as a vehicle for Groucho's antics.
- *Stop the Music*, a show where contestants had to guess or recognize the name of a tune played on the show.
- *Winner Take All*, a show that pitted two contestants against each other answering general knowledge questions.[35]

These short examples from the listings in *The Television Audience of Today* indicate that the diversity of forms in the quiz show genre did not change or decrease. Instead, an increasing amount of reflexivity seems to have developed in the media industry regarding the use of genre terminology. The previous examples illustrate the attempts of the industry to fit a variety of programs within one or two unifying labels. I would like to evoke Altman's point that genres are made, not born, and argue that these classificatory attempts denote the exertion of institutional power to define and stabilize genre categories.[36] After obvious generic confusion in the early history of the genre in the 1930s and 1940s, we see an attempt to impose classificatory order, or the law of genre.[37] The developing genre categories not only serve as a unifying descriptive terminology, but also as a potential blueprint for future program development. Parks Johnson's speech mentioned previously, commissioned as a short lesson for broadcast executives in how to understand and design an audience participation program, is especially useful as a guide for the development of future products in this genre. These attempts at defining a genre out of the body of texts labeled giveaways, panel shows, quizzes, games, forums, and so forth seem to imply that the perception of similarities among texts is as important as their actual existence. Perhaps producers and industry observers of the quiz show genre increasingly emphasized the seemingly obvious similarities in a body of texts over the now less-obvious differences between them. The development of semantic and syntactic structures in a genre does not necessarily predate our recognition of these structures. Instead, the discursive act of defining these semantic and syntactic structures might be the very act that actually constitutes them as real. Thus, a revised model of genre history suggests itself that considers the theoretical definition and the empirical observation of genre structures as mutually constitutive. Although this notion of genre development refutes the static and ahistoric model of genre implicit in the language analogy, it leaves open questions regarding the material forces underlying the development of a genre.

GENRE, RITUAL, POWER

Based on the previous discussion of definitional shifts surrounding the quiz show genre, we may reasonably assume that the development of a classificatory system is important in the long-term development of a genre. We may assume further that this genre development takes place in an environment where shared cultural meanings are evenly circulated among industry, texts, and audiences. Championed by critics such as Thomas Schatz, John Cawelti, and Will Wright, this ritual model of genre describes a *genre* as a contract that structures the relationships between production and reception.[38] Although this concept explains the cultural function of genre to some extent, it does so in terms similar to James Carey's notion of ritual communication; that is, it excludes the analysis of the operation of power or ideology in this communicative process.[39] The ritual model in genre theory assumes an even distribution of power between industry and audiences. Consequently, Vivian Sobchack and numerous of other critics of the ritual model emphasize the operation of ideology in a genre system.[40] Ideological approaches therefore underscore the power of media industries to create messages that support dominant ideologies. Importantly, however, writing from a cultural studies perspective, genre is not just another system to impose a false consciousness on audiences. We cannot readily assume that a quiz show will position spectators so that they automatically succumb to its ideology. However, we must remember that ideological approaches to genre supply an important critique of the limitations of the ritual model. Cultural studies shows that ritual and ideological models of communication can be combined to some extent within a larger analytical framework that complicates the institution-text-audience relationship. To understand the operation of power in relation to genre, we have to go beyond commonplace statements calling for the analysis of power relations in a genre such as Jason Mittell's claim that "linking genre distinctions to other systems of difference can point to the workings of cultural power."[41] Again, making a connection between genre and power is not a novel idea. Instead, we need to investigate how power is exerted in specific terms in the production of genre texts.

Folklore scholar Beverly Stoeltje proposes a model for the study of ritual that instead of marginalizing the issue of ideology, emphasizes on the interconnection of power and ritual.[42] In her analysis of American rodeo, Stoeltje argues that power in ritual has three interdependent sources: form, production, and discourse. Although the form of ritual provides pleasure through repetition and recognition, discourse provides an interpretive framework for the event that frames its interpretation. The organization of production, however, in many ways is at the center of the exertion of power in rituals. It is the place where the actual performance of a ritual in all its aspects is put together. Stoeltje argues, "in this process power is circulated, claimed, displayed, and exercised, and finally, power enables the performance, which further enables the circulation of power."[43] For radio and television, the organization of production is of course rather complex. On one level, it involves the interaction of individual producers, production staff, and performers such as announcers, emcees, and hosts. On another level it also involves the larger scale interaction of producers with representatives of sponsors and networks, and the oversight of broadcasting in general by regulatory bodies such as the Federal Communications Commission (FCC) or the U.S. Department of Justice.

The production of a long-running radio program such as *Vox Pop* provides an interesting case for understanding how many factors influence the organization of production, leading to a divergence of outcomes over its sixteen-year history. Although Parks Johnson maintained ownership and, in general, control of *Vox Pop* throughout its history, programming decisions on the network level, and, in particular, the constant demands by sponsors to structure the program in a particular way, nonetheless heavily influenced him. The changing form of the program is frequently commented on in promotional literature for the show as well as in Johnson's internal notes. One promotional booklet takes particular pleasure in emphasizing *Vox Pop*'s unique and seemingly extrageneric status:

The question before the house . . .

Q.: Is it a Quiz Program?

A.: Well, it used to be, but isn't now. A lot of questions are asked, but no, it's not a Quiz Program. It isn't a matter of what the participants *know*, but rather of who they *are*, what they *do*.

Q.: Is it a program of opinion?

A.: Not exactly. Although the participants always have their full say.

Q.: Is it a man-in-the-street interview?

A.: No, you couldn't call it that. Although, in the long run, participants on the program have certainly been a cross-section of America, which is supposed to be the mark of man-in-the-street interviews.

Q.: Then what is it?

A.: Why, it's *Vox Pop*—and it's in a class by itself. . . .[44]

Similarly, the program director of *Vox Pop* describes the show as an audience participation program, a quiz program, and an interview program.[45] What can be observed in the history of *Vox Pop* are at least two shifts in the structure or form of the program. When NBC picked up *Vox Pop* as a regular network program in 1935, the Ruthrauff and Ryan advertising agency started to exert pressure on both NBC and Parks Johnson to modify their earlier strategy of asking questions of the audience in a very informal format. Johnson was asked to focus more on questions about general knowledge and trivia.[46] A second shift in the form of the program occurred in 1940 when *Vox Pop* began featuring military personnel in a more interview-oriented setup. Promotional materials for the program explained this shift primarily as a patriotic move on the part of Parks Johnson:

Figure 1.3. Vox Pop at a remote broadcast in Winner, South Dakota. *Courtesy University of Maryland/Broadcast Pioneers Library.*

Parks Johnson felt that the American public should be mobilized at once for the preparedness crusade...From 1940, until the last shot of World War II was fired in 1945, *Vox Pop* dedicated itself to the war effort. For five years it rendered distinguished service, traveling the length and breadth of America to bring its millions of listeners glimpses into the lives of fellow Americans in Army and Navy stations, in hospitals, in war plants, in home front activities of every description....When *Vox Pop* began to direct its inexhaustible energies toward the winning of the war, it ceased to be a quiz program. Its mark, however, had been left indelibly on the numerous quiz programs it had fathered. Now, *Vox Pop* was an interview program—its questions still good-humored, but pointed to a new purpose. That was to introduce the interviewees to the listeners—to tell who they were, what they were doing, what they thought.[47]

Although a review of *Vox Pop* programs over various periods indicates that the amount of interviews and quiz questions was indeed balanced somewhat differently in each period, the program does not go through the radical trans-formations the previous quote implied. As Jason Loviglio points out, "the network version of *Vox Pop* incorporated elements of interview, quiz, and human interest shows." He continues his description of the development of *Vox Pop* by observing that as early as 1937, the quiz format was de-empha-sized and interviews once again moved to the foreground.[48] These shifting traits of the program are also discussed in "What Is *Vox Pop*." In this docu-ment, Parks Johnson outlines the central elements of the program and ulti-mately argues for the malleability of the format rather than its fixity: "*Vox Pop* [was] never STATIC. *Vox Pop* adapts itself to changing times and trends. Its basic technique remains the same, but its applications are quite flexible."[49] Implicitly, Johnson points to the instability of generic labeling and makes *Vox Pop*'s fluctuating form and its unstable genre affiliation a key characteristic and selling point for the program. In one of his notebooks from 1940, Johnson also points out that he "felt the quiz fading...and began to put spot-light on personalities."[50]

The impending military conflict in 1940 was probably only one reason for the switch in *Vox Pop*'s format. The "fading of the quiz" Johnson expected might also be rooted in the FCC's increasing scrutiny and criticism of several "give-away shows," which were accused of constituting illegal lotteries.[51] Among these giveaway shows was *Pot of Gold*, a program that featured phone calls to randomly selected radio listeners and awarded cash prizes primarily for answering the phone. Although no legal action ultimately was taken against any show at that point and quiz shows continued to feature give-away elements, we are beginning to see that a variety of forces often outside the immediate control of its creator overdetermined the production of *Vox Pop*.

As a result, arguments over the appropriate balance of quiz and interview elements for the program continued to plague *Vox Pop*. In a memo on *Vox Pop*, Nate Tufts of the Ruthrauff and Ryan advertising agency argues, "the structure of the program is flexible."[52] Later he specifically acknowledges that he wants to change *Vox Pop*'s genre designation for strategic purposes:

> The important thing is that we want to disassociate the word "interview" from the *Vox Pop* program in line with our agreement that "interviews," as such, are of no interest. "Interview" programs never secure a large audience. Furthermore, *Vox Pop*, strictly speaking, is not an "interview" program. It is a program where we quiz the man-on-the-street.[53]

Further correspondence reveals that the sponsor of *Vox Pop* at that time, the Penn Tobacco Company, manufacturer of Kentucky Club Pipe tobacco, was eager to achieve better ratings than quiz programs competing tobacco manufacturers sponsored, namely Lucky Strike's *Information Please* and Chesterfields' *Professor Quiz*.[54] Similar disputes emerged among Parks Johnson, the Young and Rubicam advertising agency, and *Vox Pop*'s sponsor for 1946, Lipton Tea and Soups.[55]

Interestingly, both Johnson and Tufts argue that the form of *Vox Pop* is flexible to further their own goals. Tufts wants to develop the program similar to other quiz shows and would prefer to categorize it as a quiz show, which he finds most profitable for *Vox Pop* and preferable over categorizing the program as a interview program. On the other hand, Johnson wants to attract new advertisers and uses the flexibility of format as a sales argument for potential sponsors. Assumptions several people controlling different aspects of the production of *Vox Pop* made influenced both the form of the program and the discourses surrounding it substantially. Power is exerted in the debates regarding the genre affiliation and form of *Vox Pop*. Although economic considerations (the maximizing of profit) primarily motivated this exertion of power, it is also of significance on a cultural level because it influences the form and meaning of the program itself. As the previous sections have shown, decisions made in the organization of program production are often fed directly into public outlets such as fan magazines, trade publications, and publicity materials for a program, defining to a large degree the discursive framing of the program as well. The organization of production might be internally disputed, but it is nonetheless the center of power through which both the discourses about a program and the form of a program are at least partially controlled. Of course, many genre conventions preexist an individual program, and therefore the form of a quiz show cannot be determined exclusively in the process of production. The institutional power we can observe in the interplay of form, discourse, and production is nonetheless an important factor to consider in genre theory.

GENRE IN CONTEXT

Although film theory often treats its texts as clearly separate entities, partly because the conditions of production and exhibition encourage this assumption, this tradition also needs to be reassessed for the study of radio and television genres. Radio and television programs should not be isolated in discrete units. As the example of quiz shows demonstrates, each show works as a cumulative text characterized by a high degree of repetitiveness. At the same time, quiz shows are often organized in a sequence that has its own specific meanings. This does not limit analysis to a general notion of "flow."[56] Instead, we need to account for the significance of scheduling practices in radio and television. For example, at the beginning of its network run, *Vox Pop* was scheduled before *Major Bowes' Original Amateur Hour*, coupling two programs focused on "everyday people" that seemed connected by a common generic bond. Some quiz shows are specifically designed to be shown in sequence (for example the *Dating Game–Newlywed Game Hour*), others are arranged in a specific order due to the decisions of individual stations (the *Wheel of Fortune–Jeopardy!* coupling) and occasionally programs are arranged in a meaningful way through a combination of new material and reruns (USA's combination of its dating show, *The Big Date*, with reruns of *Love Connection*).

Additionally, a high degree of intertextuality characterizes television, which complicates the identification of clearly defined generic bodies that are organized synchronically only. Thus, the generic history of quiz shows is always present in reruns as well as in intertextual references to previous texts, complicating a linear genre history and making genre history an active factor in the creation of meaning in an individual show. For example, *Debt*, a now defunct quiz show that aired on the Lifetime cable channel, which quiz show veteran Wink Martindale hosted, mines the history of quiz shows to create a new product that incorporates elements from *Jeopardy!*, *Name that Tune*, *The $20,000 Pyramid*, and *The $64,000 Question* and is therefore in a very close relationship to the history of this genre. *The $64,000 Question* itself is inspired by its radio predecessor *Take It or Leave It*, and it also got its own spin-off in *The $64,000 Challenge*. In the fall 2000 season, NBC tried to capitalize on intertextual references to the quiz show scandals in its short-lived remake of *Twenty-One*, which talk show host Maury Povich emceed. Intertextual connections are thus a constant presence on television and in the quiz show genre in particular. Although their specific meanings can be ascertained only in individual case studies, they certainly complicate the identification of neatly organized genres even further.

As the Maury Povich example demonstrates, a convergence of the style and content of talk shows and quiz shows often can be observed also. *The Richard Bey Show*, a short-lived syndicated talk show, often used small, physical games to humiliate unpopular guests and exhibited strong affinities to action-oriented quiz shows such as *Family Challenge*. Similarly, many talk shows dealing with personal relationships, especially *INPerson*, have recently adopted specific elements from quiz shows focused on dating to create suspense. They use brightly lit, semitransparent screens behind which the silhouette of a surprise guest is visible. This is a technique, *Bzzz!*, a dating show particularly preoccupied with displaying the physical properties of its contestants, recently made popular. In other words, the history of generic confusion and genre mixing that first defined quiz shows to a large degree, is still present in our current media environment and continues to undermine attempts at clear genre classification. The radical intertextuality of radio and television reminds us that the exclusive focus on individual texts in many genre studies is not adequate for radio and television.

Altman proposes that genre should be studied in a model that considers institutions, text, audience, and interpretive community. Meaning does not reside in any one of these sites exclusively, but is determined by the system in its totality.[57] He at least begins to relate genre to a larger cultural system in that he adds the interpretive community as an additional level of inquiry. Nevertheless, his system is curiously imbalanced in that it proposes the study of larger cultural context primarily in relation to the audience/decoding side, leaving the media industry isolated from outside forces. His model falls short of the propositions of many reception theorists and advocates of historical reception studies in that it does not fully grasp the omnipresence of "extratextual determinations" on the communication process.[58]

Tony Bennett's concept of reading formations argues that text and context should not be split but that both text and reception are structured by the specific properties of a reading formation. A genre is thus both a constitutive part of a reading formation and structured by the extratextual properties of a reading formation.[59] Bennett's concept of reading formations essentially seems to extend the range of Stoeltje's model of power into the realm of reception. The unity of text and reception in a reading formation is not unlike the close relationship of form, production, and discourse proposed in Stoeltje's model of ritual and power.[60] However, poststructuralism also informs Bennett's work because his model of reception introduces the possibility of contradiction within a complexly structured or overdetermined reading formation. He opens up the concept of reading formations to Valentin Vološinov's notion of multiaccentuality of discourse,[61] demonstrating that a moment of absolute ideological closure cannot occur, especially in the sphere of popular culture and the mass media.

CONCLUSION

Following the findings in this chapter, my analysis of quiz shows on radio and television will pay particular attention to the following issues:

1. A genre such as quiz shows cannot be categorized in a univocal, unambiguous manner. Instead, quiz shows participate in multiple genres, many of which are derived from everyday life. The multiple genre classifications that attempt to define quiz shows are constantly shifting and contingent.

2. Looking at the margins of a genre to understand how the cultural logic of a genre operates is particularly important. What are the dynamics of exclusion and inclusion in a genre? How do new or emerging forms enter the "law of genre"? At what moments does the law of genre fail? What ruptures in the genre can be exposed through close analysis?

3. In what ways do the institutions of production exercise their power to define the meaning and structure of a genre? The analysis of *Vox Pop* and other radio programs herein has shown that the act of defining a genre in itself can be seen as part of the constitution of a stable genre structure. Discourses about genre are part of the exertion of power in the production of quiz shows as a ritual form. The instability of the form of a genre in practice is reduced through the organization of production and its surrounding discourses.

4. How is a genre articulated to specific cultural formations? Drawing from the concerns of British cultural studies, this book is also particularly concerned about how dominant and subordinate cultural positions can be expressed within the confines of a highly formulaic genre such as quiz shows. Analyzing radio and television texts in regard to the relationship of the apertures and closures they offer for the production of meaning seems most productive from a historical perspective. By virtue of being located in genres and reading formations, popular texts offer varying possibilities for the formation of historically specific popular reading practices. These possibilities can then be related to social and cultural formations in general, so that the specific involvement of a genre or a text in cultural processes becomes clear.

CHAPTER 2

A Heart Line to America

Creating Audience Participation

In the 1940s James Stewart starred in two films revolving around radio quiz shows, *Pot O' Gold* and *The Jackpot*, both attempting to capitalize on the popularity of the quiz show genre at the time.[1] While *Pot O' Gold* only features a newly created quiz show in its happy ending, *The Jackpot* is centrally concerned with the story of an average man who wins the jackpot on a radio quiz show and whose life is subsequently thrown into turmoil. Unlike the common fantasy of instant affluence associated with winning a jackpot, the film shows Stewart as a victim of the quiz show, receiving useless merchandise and getting stuck with a $7,000 tax bill for $24,000 worth of prizes. *The Jackpot* emphasizes the immediacy of the connection between Stewart and the program *Name the Mystery Husband*: He is put on the air on very short notice via the telephone and merchandise starts arriving at his house the day following his success on the program. *The Jackpot* deliberately takes the get-rich-quick fantasy of quiz shows and turns it into a dystopian fantasy, albeit a humorous one. *Name the Mystery Husband* features one of the most frequently used devices for creating audience involvement and listener feedback in radio quiz shows, the telephone call-in. Quiz shows have used such devices since the beginnings of the genre in the 1930s to involve the audience in the programs and to create various forms of audience participation. This chapter traces the ways in which audience participation is produced through industry discourses and how audience participation is fostered in programs. The critical and theoretical implications of ideologically loaded terms such as "the common man" or "audience involvement" is at the center of this analysis. The idea of audience participation has been central to quiz shows since their emergence in the 1930s; hence, this chapter focuses on radio and television programs from the 1930s to the mid-1950s.

THE CONSOLIDATION OF COMMERCIAL BROADCASTING

The development of radio quiz shows in the 1930s coincides with the fundamental solidification of commercial broadcasting. As cultural forms, the sometimes-conflicting demands of sponsors, networks, producers, and performers constantly influenced quiz shows. The status of quiz shows in the United States as vehicles for commercial messages is predetermined at the beginning of the genre because quiz shows never had an existence outside of or preceding commercial broadcasting. At the same time, genres such as talk shows, soap operas, and quiz shows played an important role in the development of commercial broadcasting because they were often used as proving grounds for new and experimental forms. Networks and sponsors often also found increasing the presence of advertising in genres such as quiz shows easier because they did not carry the high cultural prestige of drama, the news, or the arts.

   In the context of the solidification of commercial broadcasting, the role of advertisers and sponsors as the driving forces warrants specific attention. Many advertising agencies had their own radio departments and major sponsors, such as Procter and Gamble, expanded their radio production departments throughout the 1930s. From the perspective of regulatory law, the commercial structure of broadcasting was fully established in the mid-1930s. In 1934 the foundation of the FCC in combination with the 1934 Communications Act provided a solid legislative and regulatory structure for U.S. broadcasting. The Wagner-Hatfield amendment to the 1934 act proposed to revoke all radio licenses and reassign 25 percent of them to nonprofit organizations such as religious and educational broadcasters, but it was defeated in Congress. As J. Fred MacDonald points out, the commercial and network-dominated structure of U.S. broadcasting would not be challenged again.[2] Although the 1934 Communications Act claims that broadcasters have to serve "the public interest, convenience, or necessity," the FCC usually interpreted this to mean "whatever profits the industry profits the public."[3] Thus, Robert McChesney points out, the "consolidation of the status quo was complete. Congress would never again consider fundamental structural questions in its communications deliberations. The legitimacy of network-dominated, advertising-supported broadcasting was now off-limits as a topic of congressional scrutiny."[4] The significance of this development is even greater when we take into consideration that the structure of radio broadcasting also provided an important framework for the debates over the future of television.

However, arguing that "television was a function of broadcasting and the natural outgrowth of radio"[5] seems problematic. Despite the extremely clear development of television toward a commercial structure, the contested character of the debates over the future of television should be highlighted. For example, Lawrence Lichty emphasizes the central importance of radio in the development of television, but fails to acknowledge other influences present in this process.[6] In contrast, Garth Jowett argues that the way in which television was originally presented to the public had a fundamental influence on the development of the medium.[7] The perspectives on television in the 1930s and 1940s reflect the divergent interests of the institutions and individuals involved. David Sarnoff, president of RCA, the parent company of NBC, created a discourse that seemingly naturally connects radio and television as broadcast media.[8] In a 1936 speech Sarnoff argued:

> we now begin the second decade of this new art by dedicating it to the achievement of television, the broadcasting of sight. It is the only prophecy I shall indulge in tonight—that during the next 10 years the millions who now listen in their homes to this celebration will be able to see as well as hear by radio.[9]

Sarnoff's institutional discourse on television as *broadcasting of sight* tended to frame the more popular (and public) discussions of the new medium. The dominant forces in the media industries of the 1930s and 1940s guided the discussions of television technology in their favor and, similarly, predetermined certain elements of its cultural form. As Jowett explains, the presentation of television to the American public exerted specific pressures and set certain limits to the discussion of the form of television in U.S. culture with "the effect of delimiting the area of discussion about television to a perimeter within the industrial, political and cultural control of these industries."[10] The demands of private business and the ideology of free enterprise framed the development of early broadcasting since the early 1920s and the history of radio in particular. Because the FCC was neither willing nor able to change its established regulatory pattern developed in the context of radio for the emerging television medium, the broadcast industry was able to focus discussions of the future of television only on those aspects that were particularly advantageous for its commercial interests. The creation of a seemingly natural connection between radio and television through the metaphor of visual or sight broadcasting serves to articulate television to the existing interests of RCA and the radio industry in general.[11] Trade and popular magazines often drew parallels between the development of advertiser-supported radio and the future of television as an advertising-based medium. An article in *Scribner's Magazine* points:

> when radio was lacking sufficient funds to sustain attractive programs, the national advertisers stepped in with their subsidies. . . .

Radio advertising has naturally been limited because of its inability
to give listeners a "picture of the product." Television, needless to
say, will remedy it."[12]

The general predictions of television becoming an advertiser supported
medium were particularly clear in those instances where the radio industry was
trying to attract advertisers or keep them loyal to radio. Sarnoff's 1936 speech
to the American Federation of Advertisers exemplifies both the clear connections that he constructs between radio and television as well as his strong interest to entice advertisers to support the new medium. Sarnoff sees television as
the most effective advertising medium available for the industry, arguing:

the benefits which have resulted from the industrial sponsorship
of sound broadcasting indicate that our major television programs will come from the same source. It requires little imagination to see the advertising opportunities in television.[13]

Sarnoff thus not only extols the virtues of commercial broadcasting, but he
also predicts that advertisers and sponsors would remain a driving force in
creating broadcast television programming.

As Michele Hilmes's historical studies of early radio show, Sarnoff's
predictions were accurate.[14] By the mid-1930s, networks were primarily seen
as "conduits" for sponsors and agencies. As a result, networks were not the
primary creators of programming in this period. Instead, advertising agencies
and large national sponsors were usually in charge of producing programming
and placing it in specific slots in the network broadcast schedule. Hilmes
observes an increasing dominance of advertising agencies selling commercial
broadcast time between 1933 and 1945, which corresponds to a significant
overall increase in the percentage of commercially sponsored programs:

By 1944, evening hours consisted almost entirely of sponsored
programs. In terms of concentration of advertising and programming power within the agencies themselves, by 1944 three
of the nation's largest advertising agencies between them controlled about one-fourth of total commercial time on the three
major networks.[15]

The dominance of sponsors and advertising agencies in broadcast programming also made the radio networks extremely uneasy. NBC in particular had
little control over its broadcast schedule in the early 1930s. Whereas NBC
charged affiliates for sustaining programming and paid a flat fee to its affiliates for airing sponsored programming, CBS shared 30 percent of its
national advertising revenues and provided free sustaining programming in
exchange for option time during prime time. Thus, CBS had more control
over network operations and better profits than NBC, which adopted this
model in 1935.[16]

These conflicts between advertisers and networks also involved disagreement over the cultural role of radio broadcasting. Advertisers usually had very specific interests in the production of programming, that is, the creation of an effective vehicle for commercial messages, which overruled any other concerns. Thus, the commercial structure of broadcasting frequently generated anxieties among dominant cultural groups.[17] Consequently, Gwenyth Jackaway claims the commercial orientation of broadcasting frequently undermined elite appropriations of broadcasting for spreading elite culture in support of cultural hierarchies. The National Association of Broadcasters, trying to address this tension, resolved to "foster and promote the commonly accepted moral, social and ethical values of American life." The practice of integrating these values into the content of U.S. broadcasting, however, often seemed inadequate. Jackaway argues:

> because market interests clearly lay in programming for the largest audience, the cultural agenda of the elites was incompatible with the economics of advertising-supported mass media. The dilemma facing these tastemakers was that the programming which they considered to be most cultural was also in fact the least profitable.[18]

The mass media are constantly part of the shifting field of cultural distinctions. On the one hand, we see frequent attempts to incorporate elements of high distinction, including elite cultural forms such as opera, classical literature, drama, and fine art into the media to enlighten the mass audience. On the other hand, the popular tastes of this mass audience seems to be siding with cultural forms of low distinction, such as vulgar comedy, sports, and other trivial forms of popular culture. The cultural logic of audience participation serves as one solution to the high/low and elite culture/mass culture dichotomies. As the following sections demonstrate, audience participation emphasizes "the people" and showcases audience members involved in some form of public performance. Audience participation satisfies the networks' public service obligations and provide programming serving the public interest.[19] At the same time, the discourse of audience participation and the way it was put into practice in radio programs reveals a great deal about how the broadcast industry defined itself and its audience as part of the larger mediated public.

THE IDEOLOGY OF THE COMMON MAN

Vox Pop was one of the earliest programs labeled a quiz show. The program itself initially relied on a loose format of interviews with passersby and correctly answered quiz questions were rewarded with small amounts of money. The strategy of using "common people" as source of programming emerged as a cheap solution for producing local programming at a Houston radio station, as the following description of the program's beginnings illustrates:

> [Jerry Belcher and Parks Johnson] had to be alert when they were working at station KTRH in Houston, Texas....KTRH would sell time on the air to some Houston firm. Then the problem—how to give that program the best possible stuff at the lowest possible price—invariably would come up. The *Vox Pop* program was the Belcher-Johnson answer. No paid talent: no cost."[20]

Although the economic possibility of producing cheap programming might have been a contributing factor in the development of *Vox Pop*, it explains neither the appeal the program had for its audience, nor the cultural logic that determined its form. Parks Johnson, *Vox Pop* creator and producer, created numerous documents about the important role everyday people played in his program. In a memorandum regarding the program, he points out, "[*Vox Pop*] started as a program of, for and by the people, and has held to the belief that the average man is just as interesting as any celebrity."[21] Johnson's first cohost, Jerry Belcher, argues along similar lines for the popular appeal of the show: "Sometimes we wonder, ourselves, why the program is so well-liked. It must be because people like to hear and know about other people."[22] Both statements display some of the egalitarian sentiment that characterized New Deal culture. Responding to economic crisis and the public's decreasing belief in the viability of capitalism, the New Deal emphasized the involvement of the public and encouraged various forms of democratic participation. Of course, this included the burgeoning mass media, including populist programs such as *The People's Platform* and *We, the People*, but also the personalized mode of address of Roosevelt's Fireside Chats. Warren Susman argues that the New Deal provided "a set of significant symbols to give more Americans a sense of belonging and role. It was an era in which participation, or at least some sense of participation, became crucial."[23] An information booklet on *Vox Pop* explicitly links the beginnings of the show to the Great Depression era:

> The year is 1932. The place is Houston, Texas. The scene is Station KTRH. A group of staff members is, of all things, listening to the radio. Among them is their good friend, Parks Johnson, a local one-man advertising agency. Parks is very popular with the KTRH folk, and he often passes the time of day with them. Remember, this is 1932, still a depression year, so there's abundance of time-of-day to pass. Everyone is discussing the upcoming election. Will Hoover be reelected? Does what's his name—that newcomer to the presidential sweepstakes—Franklin D. Roosevelt–does he have a chance?[24]

Figure 2.1. Parks Johnson interviewing Frank Bucacek, a "typical policeman," from Cedar Rapids, Iowa. *Courtesy University of Maryland/Broadcast Pioneers Library.*

Similarly, a script for a Houston *Vox Pop* broadcast on January 1, 1934, contains the following lines:

> OPENING ANNOUNCEMENT: ... And now, Jerry and Parks are down on the street in front of the Metropolitan, ready to find out what the man and the woman on the street at the moment thinks [sic] of this, that and the other. What say, we listen in ...

> CLOSING ANNOUNCEMENT: Another Vox Pop period has come and gone.... Another bit of entertainment brought to you each Monday evening by Metzger's Dairy. The first day of New Year is nearly over, and every one of us feels that this is indeed a NEW year, a new opportunity, and that the New Deal has brought us to the threshold of sound development.[25]

At least in its early development, before its premiere on NBC network radio in 1936, *Vox Pop* considered itself grounded in everyday political culture and sees its presumably male public as politically engaged. Jason Loviglio points out that beginning with its network premiere, *Vox Pop* de-emphasized these political levels of audience participation and instead increased the program's question-and-answer or guessing aspects.[26] This strategy speaks to the anxieties of networks and producers over being unable to control the performances of the public appearing on their programs. This issue is addressed repeatedly in production memos discussing quiz shows as well as fan publications. *Radio Stars* repeatedly mentions this as an important problem for *Vox Pop*:

> Before these boys could put their show on a network they had to convince broadcasting officials of just one thing. That they could keep it clean. With an open mike in a catch-as-catch-can crowd, somebody would surely be tempted to spill a swear-word or so. Up to now, just one little damn has got out.
>
> Inasmuch as the program is entirely an ad lib show, considerable care must be taken to avoid controversial subjects, defamation, civil rights, and unfair competition. The selection of the questions to be used on each program should be made with foresight to all possible answers which might be received from the contestants.[27]

Whereas the occasional swear word seems to be a rare and minor problem for quiz shows, these quotes illustrate that the key issue was to control aberrant social or political subjects that might be outside the acceptable mainstream of network broadcasting. As Warren Susman points out, 1930's culture was characterized not only by the valuation of the common man, but also by a significant pressure to conform to certain roles and behavioral norms:

> Success is measured by how well one is liked by others, how well others respond to the roles one is playing. It is a strange kind of individualism for individualistic America. And what it often means is a stress on roles demanded by traditional and primary relationships.[28]

Quiz shows, with their usually strict set of rules and behavioral norms play well in this setup. On the one hand, audience members perform as individuals and participate in a form of mediated public life, yet at the same time specific rules govern their participation and the authority of a host supervises them. One of the few examples available of a quiz show program where this system of implicit social control failed is an episode of *Double or Nothing* (15 October 1948), in which host Walter O'Keefe asks Anna Miles, a single female contestant, a waitress, and former Navy nurse and prisoner of war, to describe her experiences dating and working as a waitress:

> O'Keefe: Okay, Anna. I want to explain how we play this here. We
> play... We have a $2 question, a $4 question, a $6 question

and a $10 question. You know? Any money you win on those you can take away. Sit down.... Take it. Then if you want to go for Double or Nothing you can go for $20, you know, and you want to go on top of that you can go for $40. And we also have a grand slam question and that makes you $80 if you win and we have the sweepstakes. Now, are we all clear for the game, Anna?

[An introductory interview of Ms. Miles follows.]

O'KEEFE: Oh, Anna, tell me ... Have you had any unusual experiences in your work as waitress? ... For instance, anything that we could do with a daytime audience? You know what I mean?

ANNA: Yesterday I ran into ... I'd hate to embarrass a man that's in the audience.... But he asked me a question that I didn't know how to answer. ... He says his friend went to the doctor and he was very sick.... And he says, "They had to send his wife away on a vacation. So, what do you think we should do with him?" Well, me, I didn't know what to answer there so I says: "Well, I don't know. What'd you suggest?" "Well, I think he should get a good looking girl like you and take her home and just have a big screwing party."

O'KEEFE: Well now!

ANNA: I says: What?

O'KEEFE: Anna! Why don't we....

ANNA: I says, "Why not go down to the....

O'KEEFE: Anna! Why don't we....

ANNA: ... to the hardware....

O'KEEFE: Anna, why don't we....

ANNA: ... and get a screw....

O'KEEFE: Anna, why don't we....

ANNA: ... and have your own party.

[The studio audience is silent, only a few embarrassed giggles can be heard.]

O'KEEFE: Why don't we go on with the questions we have here for Campbell's Soup. What is your favorite kind of Campbell's soup?

[Anna's response cannot be heard.]

O'KEEFE: Vegetable. All right. Put Anna down for vegetable soup. What category would you like to take?[29]

After making this plug for the program's sponsor, O'Keefe quickly asks Anna four questions about the stage names of female entertainers and finishes her appearances in a very cold and abrupt manner. Although the entire appearance of Anna Miles on *Double or Nothing* took about three minutes, the actual quiz questions lasted for only thirty-eight seconds. Even though the host was obviously not able to control the contestant completely, despite his reminder that they were addressing a daytime audience, he attempted to control the situation once an inappropriate utterance had been made. He attempted both to silence Anna Miles and to interrupt her story and subsequently tried to get her through the quiz questions in minimum time so that the program could go on to a new segment. Although controlling Miles's unusual performance was impossible for the *Double or Nothing* host, both the studio audience and home listeners recognized the inappropriateness of her story immediately because of the host's response and because the studio audience members communicated their disapproval of the screwing party story. The implicit rules of the game were clearly violated and this form of nonconformity generated an uncomfortable situation for the audience.

Vox Pop, on the other hand, allowed the audience to perform in a more open format, where answers were often not clearly pre-structured. Broadcasting from the Days of Seventy-Six Celebration in Deadwood Gulch, North Dakota (1 August 1940) Parks Johnson and cohost Wally Butterworth interviewed and quizzed several rodeo cowboys and public figures:

WALLY :   What is your name?

COWBOY: Chet McArdy

WALLY: Where you from, Chet?

CHET :   Hotchkiss, Colorado.

WALLY :   And how long have you been taking part in rodeos?

CHET :   Well, I've done the big shows for about four years or five and I made my first rodeo about twelve years ago.

WALLY :   Well, I got a little dope on you. You won the bareback at Calgary and the saddle busting at Chicago Stadium and just a week ago in Cheyenne, didn't you?
           Boy, you really got something on the wall....Now Chet, if you'll distinguish, for a dollar, between these initials, I'll pay all. What is the difference between R.A.A., W.P.A., and C.T.A.?

CHET :   Well, the R.A.A. is the organization that protects cowboys in their....

WALLY :   Well, what's the name of it? What does it stand for?

CHET :   It's the Rodeo Association....

WALLY :   ...of America. Now what's W.P.A.?

CHET :   Well, that's an organization that was born to help people that are out of work.

WALLY :   That's right, the government W.P.A., all right. Now, how about C.T.A.?

CHET :   Now C.T.A. is an organization that was born to help the cowboys.

WALLY :   What's it mean? What's it mean?
CHET :   Well, it's to standardize rodeos....
WALLY :   What's the name of the organization?
CHET :   Why, it's the Cowboys' Turtle Association.
WALLY :   There you go there. Now you get the dollar, my boy....[30]

Although *Vox Pop* uses a seemingly more open format, blending personal interview and quiz questions quite fluently, it did not encourage of any performance that appeared outside the consensus of good taste. In all quiz shows the audience was aware of the fact that they entered a cultural form governed by strict rules and that their performance, while unrehearsed and participatory in principle, had to remain within very strict limits. A single woman talking about a screwing party or any other aspect of her sex life was clearly inappropriate, but a rodeo cowboy talking about his professional achievements was acceptable. Most problems were avoided altogether in quiz shows by focusing on appropriate, safe topics, but as *Radio Stars* magazine points out, the audience also understood that contestants would receive less than hospitable treatment if they overstepped their boundaries: "Religious and political problems are painstakingly avoided. It's much too easy to be cut off the air if a vulgar or not-nice answer is given."[31]

The selection of contestants for quiz shows in itself also followed certain predetermined scripts that emphasized white male contestants. Loviglio illustrates how the *Vox Pop* selection process defined the specific public that the program revolved around:

> Though mysterious, unrehearsed, and urban, the public interviewed by *Vox Pop* was exclusively white, American-born, and, for the most part, male. Women interviewees were asked questions from a different list, one that emphasized private relationships, the differences between the sexes, and domestic chores.[32]

The media coverage of *Vox Pop* and internal documents on the program often emphasized the openness of the program to all sorts of contestants and its inclusiveness in terms of race, gender, or class. For example, a Parks Johnson dossier on *Vox Pop* argues that the program "believes in the rights of all races and creeds to appear before its microphones. It has presented the stories of dock workers and steel magnates, six-year-old children and 100-year-old Civil War veterans."[33] At the same time, however, a description of the contestant selection process in *Radio Stars* sheds a different light on these claims:

> The two *Vox Poppers* wander around the crowd or let the people wander up to them. Usually they know the type of person they want. Parks, for example, will set out to find a married woman of about fifty, a young unmarried college boy, a married man of

about forty. They are all average types and they're not hard to find."[34]

It is striking that all these "average types" are primarily defined through their marital status, establishing family as a key determinant for people's identity. Additionally, a specific version of family relations is established as well. Although being single when one is in college is acceptable (or normal), once one reaches maturity, one should be in a well-established, heterosexual relationship. It is also striking that other factors that could establish the contestants' identity, such as race, ethnicity, occupation, or class, are completely absent.

The specifically gendered character of the discourse of the common man is demonstrated in a 1936 promotional release for *Our Neighbors*, a new program by Jerry Belcher, the first cohost of *Vox Pop*:

> Sans scripts, and with only a little black microphone, Jerry Belcher, radio originator of the famed *Vox Pop* program, strolls nonchalantly into typical American homes, asks Dad for his political views, Ma for her favorite recipes, Sis for her ideas on holding men, Brother for a description of his newest girlfriend.[35]

The normative character of this description of a typical American family is quite obvious: Dad is interested in politics, and Ma stays in the kitchen, tending to household chores. The brother is allowed to display a certain degree of aggressive sexuality, as he seems to frequently change girlfriends, whereas the sister is already positioned to focus on the domestic sphere and develop a passive, subordinate version of female sexuality, which focuses on satisfying men in general and her future husband in particular.

The ideology of the common man emphasized participation and involvement that spoke to some of the ideals of New Deal culture. It addressed the utopian possibility of participation in a public, mass-mediated forum. Although the ideology of the common man created a certain appeal for 1930's radio audiences, it also created a restrictive definition of common men or average people. In this sense, the utopian possibilities of the ideology of the common man are exchanged for a normative and extremely narrow definition of what being average means. In other words, the ideology of the common man produced an interpretation of normalcy that heavily favored dominant cultural formations and discouraged marginality and difference.

Nonetheless, the quiz show format remained one of the most popular forms of radio programming in the 1930s and 1940s. Even in the transition from radio to television, quiz shows continued to be an important programming form. The following sections examine the underlying meanings of audience participation for the broadcast industry and the radio audience respectively.

THE ECONOMICS OF AUDIENCE PARTICIPATION

When looking at the ways in which the ideology of the common man was put into practice in the quiz shows of the 1930s and 1940s, any form of audience participation occurring on these programs obviously was produced with a specific purpose. As the previous chapter made clear, adopting the term *audience participation* as a generally valid generic label might be inappropriate. However, its use in both industry and criticism points to the importance of the idea of participation in itself. J. Fred MacDonald uses the term *audience participation* as a general designation for numerous popular1930s' and 1940s' quiz shows and talk shows. As a defining characteristic of these shows he notes that they "utilized people in the studio or listening audience to provide the substance of the programs."[36] The listing of audience-participation programs in Jon Swartz and Robert Reinehr's *Handbook of Old-Time Radio*[37] reveals that more than 90 percent of audience-participation programs could also be labeled quiz shows because they were involved in playful tests of various types of knowledge and skills, included different forms of competition, and awarded different prizes to contestants. MacDonald observes that one of the main appeals of radio quiz shows seems to be their close connection to the audience, both in terms of the interaction of home or studio audience with the program and in terms of the identification of the audience with contestants who seemed to be just like them: "Amateurism was a democratic form of radio amusement. It was the average citizen entertaining his colleagues. It was as close as an audience came to controlling directly the content of its own programming."[38] Although arguing that the radio audience actually ever had a significant degree of control over the creation of quiz programs seems problematic, observing that a unique relationship exists between quiz shows and their audience is still paramount.

The close participatory relationship that seems to exist between quiz shows and the home and studio audiences comprising "common people" is closely related to some other strategies networks and their sponsors used to involve the audience in their broadcasts. In *Speaking of Soap Operas*, Robert C. Allen shows how soap opera producers dealt with this problem in the early 1930s.[39] Irna Phillips, creator of some of the earliest soap operas, introduced a strategy called *mailhooks*, offers for free publicity photos or merchandise samples that were placed within the soap opera narratives. Phillips wanted to encourage the audience to write postcards requesting the free products, thereby gaining an understanding of audience size and composition, as well as its involvement in the program. An overarching goal for Phillips was also to attract economically attractive sponsors for *Painted Dreams*, the first soap opera she created. Mailhooks were the broadcast industry's first attempt to elicit audience feedback. The desire to understand and control the audience led Procter and Gamble, the largest producer of soap operas, to "institute an unparalleled program of market research to assure that its advertising budget was spent as efficiently as possible."[40] Through numerous strategies, advertisers and sponsors also attempted to elicit audience feedback on quiz shows. They encouraged audience members to participate in the live broadcasts, to call in to radio quiz shows and participate via the telephone, and generally emphasized the participatory character of the shows.

An article in *All-Wave Radio* uses the feedback *Vox Pop* received as an implicit measure of its success:

> Mail alone keeps them busy most of the time. It averages about three thousand letters a week, most of which have to be answered. They expect it to increase by leaps and bounds very soon, as their sponsor is giving away wristwatches for the best questions sent in by the public.[41]

Beyond the need to simply prove the success of a program, *Information Please*, a quiz show known for its popular host and its challenging questions, also faced problems attracting regular commercial support because potential sponsors assumed that it would appeal only to a small, elite audience. To overcome its presumably highbrow orientation, *Information Please* used listener feedback to demonstrate the program's effectiveness at attracting a broad, but slightly upscale, audience. The program's first major sponsor, Canada Dry Ginger Ale, soon employed a mailhook campaign offering an *Information Please* home game—in exchange for two proofs of purchase—to stimulate audience response further. An article in *Printer's Ink* describes the motivations for such a campaign to elicit audience feedback:

> Since the company has taken over the program it has had an opportunity to check the type of audience listening—to find out generally if it represents a true cross-section of the Canada Dry beverage consuming public. Both the offer of the game and the audience mail by which questions are submitted to the board of experts, provide a clue.... On the basis of this survey [of listener mail] it is convinced that the indictment leveled at the program as reaching only a highbrow audience is untenable.[42]

The feedback the sponsor of *Information Please* elicited is used for much more intricate audience research than a simple demonstration of its popularity. It has the potential to provide many additional clues regarding the demographics of its audience at a point in the development of the broadcast industry when ratings systems barely existed and were unable to provide detailed information beyond the basic listening data. However, such a program of research connected to audience feedback via mailhooks was fairly exceptional. Generally, quiz shows used audience participation in a more routine and naïve fashion.

Vox Pop is one of the earliest attempts of the broadcast industry to develop regular programming centered on audience participation. In a lecture script, Parks Johnson claims that "a show succeeds in proportion to the degree to which the home audience participates. The home listener loves to imagine himself in the participant's spot and feels that he would answer the question quicker, etc."[43] Although Johnson points to a form of listener identification as one reason for the popular appeal of programs such as *Vox Pop*, this quote does not address a second crucial dimension of audience participation: Similar to the mailhooks soap operas used, audience participation can serve as a device for advertisers to ensure audience presence and attention. A promotional text Johnson wrote to attract new sponsors for *Vox Pop* emphasizes the program's effectiveness as an advertising tool:

> *Vox Pop* has pioneered more than its share of new and effective things in radio, and can be counted on to come up with a format to fit the "selling" job of the sponsor. The program has consistently been able to anticipate listener trends, and to adjust itself to changing conditions.[44]

Vox Pop was publicly marketed as a show that gives voice to the common man, but internally it was clearly defined as a selling tool with a special capability to deliver audiences to advertisers. Although the previous quote does not go far beyond the commonplace industry strategy of emphasizing a show's ability to attract audiences for a sponsor, other industry documents focus more specifically on the unique character of audience participation on quiz shows. In his article for the trade magazine *Advertising and Selling*, David K. Grant, the program director in charge of *Vox Pop* at the McCann-Erickson advertising agency, explains how audience involvement in a program can be extremely beneficial to its sponsors:

> [The listener of an audience participation show] finds himself listening avidly to each and every contestant and mentally adding up the money that he, the listener, would have accumulated had he been on the program himself.
>
> A good audience participation program is a decidedly good bet for almost any sponsor. It will get him plenty of listeners, and attentive ones, too, because you can't listen to this type of show and read a book at the same time. It will attain a respectable rating and it will sell his product first and his talent second.[45]

Implicitly, Grant describes audience participation as a feedback mechanism that provides a solution to one of the central questions governing broadcasting, that of institutional reproduction. Ien Ang asks, "How does television as an institution succeed in making people buy TV sets and in making the idea of watching television seem attractive? Which strategies has it developed to persuade people to become members of the TV audience?" As a key theoretical insight, Ang points out that audience-participation programs become a tool to create "complicity of viewing."[46] Producers and sponsors expect that listeners will interface with quiz shows very closely, engaging with the program and becoming particularly susceptible to its commercial messages as well. Consequently, Grant imagines that the instability of the broadcast audience will be reduced and its institutional predictability will be increased.

Figure 2.2. Parks Johnson and Wally Butterworth entertaining the crowd. *Courtesy University of Maryland/Broadcast Pioneers Library.*

The process of listeners interfacing with radio programs receives a significant amount of attention in industry discourse because many articles and memos try to define text-audience interaction. The description of a proposed NBC quiz show, *America Spells*, illustrates what kind of relationship between text and audience the program producers assume:

> The entire country listening to the broadcast, whether they are participants or not, will be tied in a personal way in endeavoring to spell the words which the contestants are trying to do at the same time—and a little more quickly than the contestant is able to do. This silent participation in a radio program, and the achieving the task of making the listener feel that he is a potential part of the program instead of just a silent recipient of entertainment, has been proved to be of tremendous importance in the success of a broadcast.[47]

The notion of active participation laid out in this memo contrasts with the common notion of passive reception of radio programming. The active, participatory relationship theorized here is discussed in detail in a promotional booklet for NBC sales personnel for *Name that Tune:*

A program with proved appeal...plus new features to win and hold listeners....

In the studio –

Each week contestants try to guess the titles of five songs. Such headliners as *Hit Parade* star June Valli, and other guest vocalists, sing the lyrics in English, but song titles are given in a foreign tongue. A contestant's first correct answer is worth a $5 prize, the second answer, $10, building up to an $80 prize for the last song. The contestant with the most prize money wins a chance at the jackpot—the giant music box worth $500.

Throughout the country –

Listeners also play *Name that Tune*. They are invited to submit a list of five songs. To each sender whose selections are used goes a prize equal to the amount won by the contestant who guesses the titles of his songs.

And listeners like it too...230,000 have written in.

As of February 20th, 230,000 listeners had submitted song titles to *Name that Tune*. Representing an increase from 8,338 letters for the first week to a current average of 40,000!

Each week this mass audience tunes in to learn whether its list of songs will prove a winner...an unmatched incentive for regular week-in, week-out listening.

Name that Tune has built-in sales impact....

Name that Tune, by its very nature, is tailor-made for integrated selling effectiveness.

- Sponsor identification throughout the program, as the emcee speaks of ...
  - "the '*your brand*' quiz"
  - "the '*your brand*' jackpot"
  - "the '*your brand*' prize winner"
- Give-away samples to each contestant with suitable product mentions.[48]

This booklet emphasizes numerous key characteristics of *Name that Tune*. The issue of close brand identification and heavy sponsor presence within the program is a relatively obvious feature on *Name that Tune* and other quiz shows, serving as a primary attraction for new advertisers. The relationship the program builds with its audiences is a more fundamental and significant issue, given the emphasis evidenced in the booklet. The direct possibility for studio contestants to participate in the broadcast and win prizes forms one of the features this booklet deems crucial to "win and hold listeners." The intricate system of linking home listeners to winning contestants forms another level of winning and holding listeners. Home listeners are encouraged to participate by sending in songs for the contestants to guess, a feature very similar to other quiz shows asking home viewers to mail in questions. Additionally, listeners should also identify with the on-air contestants because they potentially stand to benefit from the success of one of the contestants. The program claims to create a whole network of interactive relationships among engaged home listeners, studio contestants, the program, and its sponsors. Furthermore, the documents describing *Name that Tune* and *America Spells* both hint at the ability of these programs to link the entire country through an interactive, participatory experience. Although these texts speak to the fantasies of nationwide participation and involvement rooted in the New Deal, they also start to address the idea of national community on another level.

Irene Beasley, the host of *Grand Slam*, a program in which contestants solve riddles with the help of musical clues, also reflects on the way in which her program speaks to a larger community. In an article in *Radio and Television Mirror*, she connects the issue of home participation on quiz shows specifically to the notion of linking an entire nation together:

> Our CBS show is an at-home game played on a nation-wide basis, using questions sent in by you listeners everywhere.... We talked about a game that could be played at home, a game that would give everyone a chance to participate on a national basis.

After a long description of the way in which the usually female home listeners are involved with the program, Beasley goes on to describe *Grand Slam's* potential prizes:

> I enjoy the preparation and planning we do in an effort to make the game a service to our listeners. There's the prize table, for instance—with prizes we have deliberately, carefully collected with the idea of their usefulness uppermost in our minds. And the listener-prizes, which go out to those of you who've succeeded in stumping studio contestants—they're loaded on trucks, by three o'clock of the afternoon of the day they've been won.[49]

Aside from experiencing a nationwide communal experience through participation in the program, the *Grand Slam* audience is also linked to the program through its common appreciation of consumer goods. In other words, the national community addressed in *Grand Slam* and many other quiz shows is predicated on the centrality of consumption. Even though *Grand Slam* as well as *Vox Pop* emphasize the tasteful and useful character of the consumer goods they make available to the contestants and home listeners, they nonetheless insist on the importance of consumption as a key component of U.S. culture.

The creators and producers of many quiz shows actively encouraged the listener's engagement with quiz shows that David Grant and other writers described as a key trait of the genre. The presumed susceptibility of the audience to commercial messages ideally complements the increased focus on consumption in quiz shows in the 1940s.[50] Importantly however, the close text-audience relationship discussed here is meant as a selling point for quiz shows and is supported only by anecdotal evidence of the involvement of the audience with a program. The texts discussing audience participation speak to the inability of various media institutions to know the audience empirically. Audience participation becomes an animation of institutional fantasies of gaining control over the mass audience, which is often thought of as a black box[51] or black hole. Jean Baudrillard specifically points at the inability of various institutions to know the masses empirically and, by extension, the mass audience:

> The mass, an *in vacuo* aggregation of individual particles, refuse of the social and of media impulses: an opaque nebula whose growing density absorbs all the surrounding energy and light rays, to collapse finally under its own weight. A black hole which engulfs the social. . . .
>
> All reserves are exhausted in maintaining this mass in controlled emulsion and in preventing it from falling back into its panic-inducing inertia and its silence. No longer under the will of reign or representation, it falls under the province of diagnosis, or divination pure and simple—whence the universal reign of information and statistics: we must ausculate it, sound it out, unearth some oracle from within it.[52]

The silence and inertia of the masses that Baudrillard describes is one of the governing problems for broadcasters and administrative mass communication researchers alike. It also provides a key motivation to entice the audience to interface with radio and television programs in new ways. However, as the following section discusses, the way in which audience participation is imagined in industry discourse does not exhaust the complexities of audience readings of such programs.

THE PRACTICE OF AUDIENCE PARTICIPATION

A proliferation of social science research, led by pivotal figures such as Paul Lazarsfeld and Edward K. Merton, characterized the developing field of mass communications research in the 1940s. Located at the margins of the dominant quantitative research major media corporations commissioned, the work of Herta Herzog on soap opera and quiz show audiences provides a more subtle account of the audience's uses of such programs. Applying qualitative research methods, Herzog tried to understand the meanings audiences derive from listening to radio. In particular, she points to the existence of multiple

reading positions that can be taken up in the consumption of radio programming. Her 1940 article, "Professor Quiz—A Gratification Study" focuses on
one of the most popular quiz shows at the time.[53] On *Professor Quiz*, five
members of the studio audience competed against each other through several
rounds of question-and-answer periods for a final cash award. In addition, the
home audience could also submit questions for the candidates, for which they
were awarded cash prizes. Public discussion of this show frequently focused
on its educational appeal, assuming that this program could function to
enlighten its listeners significantly. Herzog hints both at the program's popularity and at its presumed educational appeal:

> The program *Professor Quiz* was analyzed because it is a type of
> highly successful quiz broadcast regarded by many of the radio
> public as "educational."...*Professor Quiz* has a very large audi-
> ence, and, in a general way, one can easily account for his suc-
> cess. Such programs have a multiple appeal: different aspects of
> them appeal to different people.[54]

Herzog finds that quiz show listeners are highly involved with the shows,
citing (1) the competitive appeal, (2) the educational appeal, (3) the self-
rating appeal, and (4) the sporting appeal as the main lines of identification
with the program. However, her overall analysis indicates that the educational appeal seems to be of much lower importance for the audience than
the various forms of interaction that she observes, so that education often
serves as a culturally desirable pretense for the audience to listen to the program. Listeners thus prefer the competition and identification with people
such as themselves in quiz shows:

> It turns out that all of our respondents prefer the contestants to
> be average people. They say: "It is expected of college people that
> they know everything. I would not want to compete with them."
> "I prefer the people on the program to be people like myself.
> Now, you take a lawyer—I would not try to compete with him."
> The respondents stress emphatically, then, that the quiz contest
> is a contest between average people, and they would not be at all
> interested in competition with people that are not average.[55]

Listeners seem to be much more interested in a cultural product that reflects
some of their own values and their own identity. They most likely would
resist an emphasis on explicit elite values and cultural content in quiz shows.
Part of the reason radio quiz shows are attractive to their listeners is their
ability to address the common practices and experiences of the audience.
Following John Fiske's definition of popular culture texts as products that
audiences can appropriate for antihegemonic uses, radio quiz shows seem to
have a highly popular appeal for their primarily subordinate listeners.[56]

Herzog's interviews demonstrate that the contests in the show are often conceived in terms such as "people like myself" or "average people" competing against "them," the "college people," or other representatives of official knowledge and formal education (for example, teachers). Thus, Herzog claims that "questions of a 'specific,' 'academic,' or 'foreign' nature would be less stimulating than those on 'daily life information.'"[57] This indicates that the *Professor Quiz* listeners described in Herzog's study are actually attempting to negotiate a more advantageous position for themselves within the hegemonic system of cultural/educational distinction.[58] They are not necessarily interested in overthrowing the system of cultural hierarchies as such, but they are trying to increase the relative value of their own knowledge and educational capital. This seems to be the reason why the knowledge required for the *Professor Quiz* program is particularly attractive:

> The questions are not very academic or technical; they deal with things taught in school or known from daily life. The listeners state quite frankly that they would neither be interested in any other type of questions nor be able to answer them. "The questions are not necessarily on an academic subject. That is what I like about it. Of course, if they would be highly specialized, I would not know them; but they are things you pick up in daily life."[59]

Whereas *Professor Quiz* listeners clearly prefer questions related to everyday life, the program still manages to integrate more difficult or specialized questions that relate to high cultural capital. Accordingly, the program is also sometimes called *Professor Quiz and His Brainbusters* and billed a "battle of wits."[60] This implicit element of hierarchical knowledge is often represented even in the titles of radio quiz shows, using the high cultural capital of doctors and professors. Many radio quiz shows seem to be structured by and representative of the dual desires for cultural prestige and popularity.

Dr. I. Q., also known as *Dr. I. Q., the Mental Banker*,[61] attempts to integrate categories referring to traditional educational capital, such as history, geography, and geometry as well as numerous categories relating to common or everyday knowledge, such as popular songs, comic strips, current events, tongue twisters, and riddles. Although home listeners submit a few questions, home audience participation is not very prominent in this program. *Dr. I.Q.* is particularly interesting because it does not use a panel of experts. Instead, the entire show is structured around the host, that is, Dr. I. Q., asking questions of studio audience members. To achieve strong studio audience participation in *Dr. I. Q.*, assistants to the "Doctor" are spread throughout the theater to locate contestants in a seemingly random manner and reward correct answers with silver dollars. *Dr. I. Q.* thus creates an impression of the studio audience as average people representative of the larger home audience. It also makes a strong effort to present questions that relate to the audience's experience of everyday life without sacrificing an appeal to the educational character of quiz shows.

Although the actual integration of the home audience is not particularly effective in *Dr. I. Q.*, many other shows, particularly *Information Please*, make great efforts at integrating the home audience. All of the questions on *Information Please*[62] are taken from listener mail. For every question used on the show a listener received $10, the *Information Please Quiz Book* and, if the question "stumped the experts," the listener was awarded another $25 and a complete twenty-four volume set of the *Encyclopedia Britannica*. Although the audience is in some way involved in the construction of this program, the process of selecting and assembling the questions still seems to be informed by the need to create a program that is popular, yet educational, so that the questions on *Information Please* are not fundamentally different from questions on *Dr. I. Q.* or *Professor Quiz*. Nevertheless, part of the appeal of *Information Please* seems to be the opportunity for audience members to influence show content.

Another pleasurable aspect of *Information Please* is implied in the format of the show, that is, its reversal of the logic of dominant cultural and educational hierarchies. In *Information Please*, the audience at least symbolically plays an important role in the definition of desirable cultural knowledge and achieves a superior position toward the expert panel. The opening announcement states, "It's time to wake up America and stump the experts." To some extent, *Information Please* symbolically makes the home audience the primary source of knowledge and puts it in a limited position of authority in relation to the studio panelists.

The reversal structure present in *Information Please* speaks to the contradictory reception of quiz shows that Herzog describes. On the one hand, listeners seem uneasy having to answer questions of a "highly academic" nature, yet they clearly want to interact with quiz shows in a meaningful way while lacking the educational capital to do so. One 1939 article on quiz shows humorously portrays the public as a victim of quiz show excess with the incessant questioning of the audience as a key feature:

> "Well, now, Sir. I wonder if you can tell me what number added to itself or multiplied by itself gives the same result?" There will be considerable mumbling by the victim and pleasant urging by the questioner, and finally the quizzee gives up. "Why, it's two. Isn't that right? Very simple, isn't it?" The victim steps down shamefacedly and slinks into the ground.[63]

The sense of unease over the hierarchical structure of the question-and-answer format of a quiz show easily translates into a revised format where challenging or stumping an expert is possible. Promotional material from CBS for *What's My Line?* speaks to the appeal of the role reversal taking place in quiz shows involving an expert panel: "While we in the audience are in the know, the panel must grope around guessing. Their wrong guesses keep the nation laughing but their record for right answers is amazing!"[64] Similar to the logic behind this description of *What's My Line?*, an NBC memorandum on *Information Please* also emphasizes the pleasures of the reversal of hierarchies.

> Program: A new type question and answer contest in which the much quizzed public will quiz the experts.
>
> Appeal of Program: Everyone has often tried to pull a surprise question on the teacher hoping to catch him. Some succeed, some did not. And most people are still hankering for an opportunity to stump an expert. This program provides a grand opportunity to satisfy such desire.[65]

What is interesting about these statements is that they play with the pleasures of reversing hierarchies or surprising the teacher with a question, but they still display a significant degree of reverence for the same authorities that they claim to undermine. After all, the reversal of educational hierarchies is only pleasurable as long as we can assume that these hierarchies are still intact—at least in principle. Consequently, an article in *Reader's Digest* juxtaposes the elite status of the *Information Please* panelists with the reversal structure of the game:

> When he first organized the program [producer] Golenpaul's first task was to line up specimens of the superintelligentsia who would be willing to expose themselves to the humiliation of failing ingloriously on a national hookup.... Two never-failing surprises to the devotees of *Information Please* are the breadth of the experts' knowledge and the occasional depth of their ignorance.[66]

Information Please along with other panel-based quiz shows provides an ambivalent pleasure through its reversal of hierarchies. On the one hand, it relies on educational hierarchies to demonstrate the difficulty level of its questions; on the other hand, it allows its listeners to challenge the hierarchical status of its panel of experts. Similar to *Professor Quiz* listeners Herzog observed, *Information Please* listeners might derive pleasure from improving their imagined position within the system of cultural/educational distinction. The following quote from *Host: The Magazine of Home Entertainment* implies that such a negotiation process might be present:

> *Information Please* ... radically changed the quiz idea by having substantially the same experts every week, depending on a display of brilliant memory for their listener appeal. The same program, of course, widens the audience participation angle by paying listeners for questions sent in and used.... When a question is put to the experts and they hesitate, the listener may be able to

dredge up the answer first, and if he gets it before the expert, he feels very smart and tells everybody about it.[67]

Whereas the required forms of knowledge in this quiz and the existence of a designated panel of experts indicate that traditional cultural hierarchies have not been dissolved and still structure the program to some extent, we can see that *Information Please* creates a discursive space in which a temporary reversal of cultural hierarchies is possible and in which the listening audience is at least symbolically involved in the program production.

Audience participation in radio quiz shows serves as a discursive strategy that creates a particularly close relationship between audience and text. It is driven by the advertisers' desire to control and understand the radio broadcast audience. The instability of the radio audience in the 1930s induced advertisers and sponsors to encourage audience activity and participation. Although this close relationship between audiences and texts might serve the advertisers' commercial interests, the combined evidence from several quiz shows, industry documents, and Herzog's study of quiz show listeners indicates that the primary pleasures of the audience seem to lie in the possibility to renegotiate their position within the system of cultural distinction.

THE TRANSFER TO TELEVISION

Although radio quiz shows continued to play an important role on radio up to the early 1950s, much of the history of the genre overlaps with the introduction of television in the 1940s. RCA and its subsidiary NBC originally initiated regular public television service in 1939, but the FCC did not allow commercial sponsors at that point, especially because no unified technical standard for television transmissions and reception existed.[68] After this initial phase, the FCC allowed limited commercial broadcasting in 1940, and in 1941 the National Television System Committee (NTSC) accepted RCA's technical standards for broadcast television. In 1942, World War II prevented further expansion of television. When television was starting to expand into national service, after World War II and in the early 1950s, both its technical standards and its economic base were well established. Whereas RCA was extremely successful in making its technical standards generally accepted and was able to give substantial financial assistance to NBC, CBS as NBC's main competitor was not able to establish a profitable television receiver production unit and ultimately lost out to RCA in the struggles over the technical standards for television. Instead, the production of programming and the sale of advertising time on radio and television became the main source of income for CBS. One of the ways in which CBS tried to improve its position in the broadcast industry was through recruiting some of NBC's top radio talent in the late 1940s with attractive financial deals, a strategy often referred to as the "talent raids."[69] The talent raids were not only intended to enhance CBS's position in radio, but also to provide CBS with an attractive group of performers for television. The CBS 1949 annual report states:

> The major new CBS programs...such as Amos 'n' Andy, Jack Benny, Bergen and McCarthy, Ozzie and Harriet, Bing Crosby, Red Skelton...not only have established value as radio entertainment, but are also particularly well suited to the requirements of television.[70]

Hosts of radio quiz shows were generally not part of the talent raids, mainly because advertising agencies (rather than networks) were in control of their contracts and most radio quiz shows were not centered around the host's personality; consequently the issue of the rise of television and its potential to replace radio as a central entertainment medium in the United States certainly concerned many radio personalities. As guest star on *Information Please* in November 1940, the radio comedian and future television quiz show host Fred Allen engaged in the following dialogue with the show's host, Clifton Fadiman:

> FADIMAN : You know, the radio audience can't see what you're doing with your hands, Mr. Allen.
>
> ALLEN: I'm rehearsing for television; I'm looking ahead....I'm prepared if it comes.
>
> FADIMAN: What a perspective opens up before you, Mr. Allen....
>
> ALLEN: Quite a joke we're gonna have with this cast when television comes.[71]

The dialogue shows the potential of television as a visual medium to make the quiz show genre more attractive, but it also hints at some of the problems associated with the transfer of individual shows—or personalities—from radio to television. Elaborating on these transfer problems, Jowett even claims that many of the aesthetic problems television faced in the late 1950s and early 1960s stem from the uncritical transfer of radio broadcast content into a new cultural form. He argues that many of the early programming formats on television did not take the specific aesthetic requirements of television sufficiently into account.[72]

Although numerous books from the 1930s and 1940s discuss the future of television, especially its technology and economics, few consider the aesthetic aspects of television or specific genres. Judy Dupuy's book *Television Show Business* comments on difficulties in producing quiz shows:

> Quizzes and games can be visual fun when they are planned and staged for the television camera....Quizzes and games which seem so simple to present on television are a challenge to the producer. Some day, however, an ingenious producer will find a visual format that is effective.[73]

Dupuy fails to give any indication of what quiz shows in a visually oriented medium might look like; another book, however, Thomas Hutchinson's *Here Is Television*, stresses two points in his suggestions for quiz shows. First, he reiterates the general importance of visualizing a program; second, he emphasizes the distinct element of audience involvement necessary for a successful quiz show:

> It is difficult to include the audience in contests of this kind [quiz shows], and yet a way to accomplish this must be found. Aside from either knowing or not knowing the answer, if the viewer at home has no way of entering into the game he really is merely an observer. It is true that this same situation exists in radio, but television being visual should offer more.[74]

For Hutchinson, audience participation becomes a central part of the aesthetics of the quiz show genre, so that he sees the visual structure of quiz shows as centered on intense audience involvement. Yet Hutchinson has very few concrete suggestions how to encourage audience involvement, which are mainly by creating sympathies for contestants and by withholding the answer to a riddle, so that the audience is "in the same position as the people in the studio."[75]

In general, producers of television quiz shows in the late 1940s and early 1950s seem to have structured their shows similar to Hutchinson's suggestions. Virtually all of the shows from this period attempt to integrate the studio audience and home audience in some way. Two of the oldest television quiz shows available in archives, *Americana* and *Quiz Kids*, both rely entirely on viewer mail for their questions. Although the technical problems of live broadcasting probably prevented these shows from using and integrating a studio audience, *Americana* in particular makes an effort to integrate the home audience through some verbal cues:

> ANNOUNCER: Your program about your country. Now it's time to take you once again to our little red schoolhouse, where we meet professor and schoolmaster, NBC's Ben Grauer.
>
> HOST: This classroom session of Americana is devoted to questions which you, the members of our television audience, have sent in. Questions about our great country, its history, its people, its tradition.[76]

The use of the appellative form or direct address in this instance serves to create an imagined national community[77] of television viewers across the United States, but it also serves to emphasize the interactive relationship between *Americana* and its home audience.

Stop the Music, Strike It Rich, and *Chance of a Lifetime* all use the telephone to increase the integration of the home audience.[78] *Stop the Music* consists mainly of contestants guessing the titles of musical numbers played live during the show and it telephones home viewers to integrate them into the ongoing competition. It increases the suspense during the program by cutting to close-ups of a telephone while the band plays a musical number, expecting it to ring and to make a connection to the home audience. This use of a telephone on television is an attempt to visualize the explicit link between *Stop the Music* and its audience. However, it also serves to illustrate the larger, implicit assumptions that are made in this show about the relationship between quiz shows and television audiences. The connection between television and its audience implied here is direct and immediate, without any indication of an uneven power relationship separating institution and audience.

Strike It Rich and *Chance of a Lifetime* attempt to involve their audiences in a more active role. *Chance of a Lifetime* integrates its commercial message and the home audience into the program in a particularly tight manner. The home audience is invited to write to the show and pick one of the letters B-E-N-D-I-X, which spell the sponsor's name (Bendix, an appliance manufacturer). The host then picks one of the postcards with the right letter and calls the audience member, asks a quiz question, and rewards a correct answer with a prize. During the phone call in one specific episode the host points to himself and says, "I'm John Reed King and you're Mrs. Benson," and then points at the camera.[79] Through these elements of direct address, the relationship among audience and host is cast in a particularly close fashion and contributes to the tight relationship among program, sponsor, host, and audience.

Strike It Rich integrated the home audience with different devices and on a different level. This program had particularly needy contestants appear on stage and compete for an amount of money that would help them out, whereas audience members were encouraged to donate money for the contestants over the phone:

> *Strike It Rich* was known as "The Quiz Show with a Heart" and the contestants who appeared on the show were people in need of money or down on their luck.... If unable to answer the questions correctly, the contestant could turn to the "heart line" where viewers would call in and donate money or merchandise.[80]

In one *Strike It Rich* episode a blind women's choir in need of new robes, a starving farmer without a ticket home, and a war veteran who wants to start a flower business appear on stage either to win a sufficient cash prize or to receive donations. Donations are called in continuously and the host announces them toward the end of the show. Another on-screen telephone, this time placed on a shelf below a huge picture of a heart is used to symbolize the close emotional relationship with the home audience, or, as the program touts, the "Heart Line to America."

Although these shows all advance the interest of producers and sponsors in maintaining a close, interactive relationship between text and audience, they articulate relationships to authority and cultural hierarchy much
less clearly. Even though shows such as *Americana* and *Quiz Kids* adopt a
schoolroom setting in which a wide variety of students from elementary
school through college are quizzed on largely hierarchical knowledge, the
quiz show genre as a whole does not seem to adhere to these kinds of standard educational capital in this early phase of network television. For example, *Chance of a Lifetime* emphasizes physical games and everyday knowledge
as does *Strike It Rich* and a variety of other shows. However, between 1952
and 1955 some other significant changes in the genre can be observed: quiz
shows began to move away from actively integrating contributions of the
home audience in the production of the program, for example, through
phone calls or the mailing in of quiz questions. Some shows allow the home
audience to participate by mailing in answers to a specific question for home
viewers, for example, on *The Price Is Right*, where home viewers can mail in
their guess for the correct value (without going over) of a showcase with merchandise, such as a variety of mink coats and accessories. Otherwise, incorporating a studio audience often replaced the close text-audience
relationship common on radio and early television quiz shows.

Although quiz shows in the late 1940s and early 1950s either did not
have an audience present in the studio or did not present a studio audience
on screen, shows such as *Break the Bank* or *Name that Tune* frequently use
close-ups of individual audience members or long shots of the studio audience as a whole.[81] Additionally, contestants for some of the shows are chosen
from the studio audience, a strategy for which *The Price Is Right* has become
famous throughout its forty-year history in broadcasting. A representation of
common people from the studio audience replaces the almost utopian element of integrating home audiences into a program, which seemed central to
many early quiz shows. Thus, integrating a visual representation of the audience in quiz shows in the mid-1950s seems to serve as a surrogate for the
close text-audience relationship from the earlier history of the genre.

CONCLUSION

The analysis of radio and television quiz shows and industry documents relating to these shows suggests that the genre occupied a special role in invoking
a strong audience involvement with the programs. Robert C. Allen describes
television's direct appeals to viewers and its encouragement of interaction
between audience and program as a "rhetorical mode."[82] He claims that the
rhetorical mode of television entices us to "enter into a contractual relationship that simulates what we experience in face-to-face situations."[83]
Although the rhetorical mode of television—or radio—involves the viewer in

a close relationship with the program, audience participation on quiz shows is often a programmatic tool that the broadcast industry uses to explore and define text-audience relationships. A sense of experimentation and lack of stability of the shape of the audience and the form of the genre characterizes the period in the history of quiz shows covered in this chapter. The rhetorical mode of quiz shows thus seems to function as a method to stabilize the complex relationship among industry, genre, and audience.

Many of the early television quiz shows discussed so far were produced during the FCC's suspension of the station application process from September 1948 until April 1952, a period known as "the freeze." Because the FCC refused to issue licenses for the construction of new television stations, the rapid expansion of television in the United States slowed considerably. During this period the broadcast industry was able to consolidate both technical and economic elements of television and again to solidify the role of networks as the driving force in broadcasting. Jowett explains:

> the introduction of television had been anything but smooth, and the four-year freeze had a great deal of political maneuvering as the "pre-freeze" stations, including those owned by the radio (and now television) networks tried to maximize their positions and hold-off the competition.... Television's expansion was much faster than radio's; radio had taken more than a decade to reach beyond 33% penetration of U.S. households; television did it in only seven years (1946–1952) despite the freeze on expansion.[84]

By 1956 television had entered 64.5 percent of all U.S. households, and the competition between networks over the limited resource of audiences rapidly increased. Thus, the creation of attractive programming for a large audience became of central importance. The tendency of quiz shows to move away from a close connection between audience and text, which was often actively enacted during a live broadcast, and toward a visual representation of "the audience" within a program coincides with the changing economic needs of the individual networks.

Audience participation on quiz shows is closely related to industry efforts to control the audience and transform the fleeting character of radio listening and television viewing into a more fixed relationship. Although the industry's need to know the audience in empirical terms, as both Baudrillard and Ang discuss,[85] cannot be fully satisfied through various forms of increased text-audience interaction, the symbolic representation of listeners and viewers on quiz shows still leaves a "sense of participation"[86] that highlights the unique text-audience relationship found in the majority of quiz shows from the 1930s, 1940s and early 1950s.

CHAPTER 3

Big Money

The Scandal and Quiz Shows in the 1950s

THE DEVELOPMENT OF BIG-MONEY QUIZ SHOWS, 1954–1959

By most standards, the 1950 film *Champagne for Caesar*[1] is an insignificant part of film history. However, if this film is related to the history of quiz shows in the United States, it becomes a remarkable historical document. In this film the protagonist, Beauregard Bottomley, appears as a contestant on a grotesque and banal quiz show named *Masquerade for Money* and single-handedly transforms it into a showcase for intellectualism and academic knowledge. Because he refuses to quit after winning the customary maximum of $160, the jackpot continues to grow to $20 million, at which point he decides to sacrifice this amount in the interest of the love life of both his sister and himself. As a final irony, the morally upstanding protagonist has agreed to a secret deal with the sponsor of *Masquerade for Money*, the Milady Soap Company, which gives him a significant amount of money, stock, and merchandise in return for not answering the $40 million question. In a surprising series of historical parallels, the film presages many elements of the big-money quiz shows that became popular five years after the premiere of *Champagne for Caesar*. Not only does the film voice common concerns over the possible rigging of quiz shows, but it also makes academic knowledge the topic of a quiz show and transforms a bookwormish, out-of-work, arrogant intellectual into a popular hero at the center of media attention.

Champagne for Caesar's vision of a jackpot quiz show with spectacular amounts of prize money centered around a highly popular intellectual contestant did not become reality for several years. In 1954, however, a U.S. Supreme Court ruling gave the impetus for the development of a new type of quiz show. This decision settled an ongoing dispute over the legality of jackpot quizzes and ruled that they are not a form of gambling and are therefore legal. Thus, using jackpot quizzes as a form of television entertainment became possible. Producer Louis Cowan, in cooperation with CBS and the sponsor Revlon, developed the idea for a new jackpot quiz show based on the radio quiz show *Take It or Leave It*. The result was *The $64,000 Question*, which premiered on June 7, 1955, and raised the prize money to a new spectacular level and changed the style and format of quiz shows significantly.

The *$64,000 Question*, its spin-off *The $64,000 Challenge*, and other imitations following between 1955 and 1958 (for example, *Twenty-One*, *The Big Surprise*) focused on high culture and factual, often academic, knowledge.[2] They were part of television's attempts in the 1950s to gain respectability and a wider audience. They introduced a much more elaborate set design and visual style and generally created a serious and ceremonious atmosphere that corresponded well with the placement of these shows in the most lucrative part of the network television schedule, that is, prime time. During high-stakes questions ($30,000 and more), *The Big Surprise* would darken the set and put only a spotlight on the contestant. Additionally, a rotating spiral of light could be seen in the background, providing an additional indicator of the intensity and seriousness of the competition. Extreme close-ups of audience members squirming while a contestant attempted to come up with the correct answer were often inserted as well. To emphasize its seriousness, *The $64,000 Question* similarly introduced an IBM sorting machine, bank guards, an isolation booth, and neon signs; other shows used similar features to create similar effects. To keep big-money quiz shows attractive, the prize money was constantly increased and became unlimited on several shows. *Twenty-One* and *The $64,000 Challenge* also created competition among contestants to heighten audience identification with individual contestants.[3] Big-money quiz shows transformed people who were not celebrities or recognized experts in their field into superstars and created an audience appeal significantly different from the previous quiz shows. However, their reliance on returning popular contestants also motivated producers and sponsors to manipulate the outcome of the quizzes. Quiz show sponsors in particular required and advocated rigging quiz shows to create the desired audience identification with popular contestants. The quiz show scandals consequently undermined the popular appeal of big-money quiz shows and, together with lower ratings, led to the cancellation of all these shows in 1958–1959.[4] Following the scandals, the networks used sponsor involvement in the rigging of the shows to advocate for the complete elimination of sponsor-controlled programming in prime-time television.

Figure 3.1. Hal March, host of *The $64,000 Question*, welcomes special celebrity guest Ed Sullivan to the show. *Courtesy Wisconsin Center for Film and Theater Research.*

THE FIELD OF KNOWLEDGE AND EDUCATION

Previous research on big-money quiz shows[5] has emphasized the importance of discourses of knowledge on big-money quiz shows so much that it has become commonplace. However, this particular form of production of knowledge is usually treated as a highly decontextualized phenomenon and is not related to industry practices or larger cultural formations in a satisfactory manner. This chapter analyzes the specific formations in U.S. culture in general and within the broadcast industry in particular, which might explain the distinct form and ideology of big-money quiz shows. For this purpose, I use

Pierre Bourdieu and Loic Wacquant's notion of the field as an organizing entity that informs a variety of seemingly unconnected practices. Bourdieu and Wacquant describe the operation of a field as follows:

> The field as a structure of objective relations between positions of force undergirds and guides the strategies whereby the occupants of these positions seek, individually or collectively, to safeguard or improve their own position and to impose the principle of hierarchization most favorable to their own product. . . . In a field, agents and institutions constantly struggle, according to the regularities and the rules constitutive of this space of play, with various degrees of strength and therefore diverse probabilities of success, to appropriate the specific products at stake in the game.[6]

We can assume that the field of knowledge and education informs and structures a variety of institutions, individuals, and forms of cultural expression without, however, determining these entities in any sort of reductive manner. The field of knowledge and education would therefore structure a quiz show because all individuals in charge of such a show are familiar with and influenced by this field. Although Bourdieu and Wacquant observe a significant degree of coherence within a given field, they also insist on the contingency of its determinations and on the existence of struggle over the meanings and logics of the field.

This chapter focuses on three sites related to big-money quiz shows in which issues of knowledge and education emerge in particularly interesting ways. First, I assess the public debates about education in the United States in the 1950s, especially in connection to the 1957 Sputnik crisis to illustrate the ideological stakes in the debates over the role of knowledge and education in postwar United States. Second, the chapter discusses 1950s' broadcast network programming policies and their relation to the field of knowledge and education. NBC's operation frontal lobes, a programming policy specifically designed to address concerns over education in cold war culture, is of particular importance for this purpose. Finally, the chapter analyzes several big-money quiz shows and their popular reception to understand how the logic of the field of knowledge and education is connected to the production and reception of quiz shows as a specific form of cultural expression. The chapter emphasizes the ways in which big-money quiz shows naturalize class-based cultural distinctions,[7] while they also produce a hegemonic form of white, upper-class cultural identity under which all other class and ethnic identities are submerged.

EDUCATION AND KNOWLEDGE IN COLD WAR CULTURE

In his book *The Culture of the Cold War*, Stephen Whitfield argues that 1950s television was largely complicit with the mainstream political climate of the time and with McCarthyism in particular. He claims that a general cold war consensus that characterizes 1950s' culture can be traced in genres such as game shows:

> The commitment of television to the Cold War consensus can also be found in the popular, apolitical [sic] genres of entertainment.... Shows that on the surface had nothing to do with foreign or domestic policy nevertheless reinforced the faith in "the American way of life" that Communism seemed to threaten. Game shows demonstrated that ordinary people could seize the fabulous economic opportunities that capitalism promised....[8]

Whitfield also claims that big-money quiz shows were important in reinforcing the ideology of consumption, but does not acknowledge that consumerism was clearly subordinate to the issue of knowledge in big-money quiz shows. Similarly, Elaine Tyler May also emphasizes the issue of consumption. She argues that the construction of domesticity and the suburban family as the most desirable form of social organization in 1950s' culture provided an element of social and ideological stability that was seen as an important weapon in the cold war. "Although they may have been unwitting soldiers, women who marched off to the nation's shopping centers to equip their new homes joined the ranks of American cold warriors."[9]

Importantly, however, consumption is not a monolithic ideology at the center of 1950s' culture that informs all cultural products. As big-money quiz shows illustrate, knowledge and education provided an important counterbalance to consumerism and also informed popular culture to a significant degree.

Despite the centrality that these historical accounts give to consumption in 1950s' culture, consumption was not necessarily approved of in U.S. public discourse. The threat of the cold war and the need to compete with the U.S.S.R. in myriad fields prompted many cultural critics to call for a national renewal. The conservative Senator Styles Bridges alluded to the relation between consumption and the cold war:

> The time has clearly come to be less concerned with the depth of pile on the new broadloom rug or the height of the tailfin on the new car and to be more prepared to shed blood, sweat and tears if this country and the Free World are to survive.[10]

Robert Divine shows that other 1950s' intellectuals also voiced their concern over the prevalence of consumption in U.S. culture, claiming that "pundits such as Walter Lippmann and Norman Cousins joined in the chorus advising Americans to give up their love affair with material goods and strive instead to improve education, science, and the quality of national life."[11]

As these examples demonstrate, the criticism of America's obsession with consumerism is often articulated to an emphasis on education. National survival in the cold war is difficult to reconcile with a culture focused on leisure and consumption. Thus, education was frequently considered a key to cold war survival. Barbara Clowse argues that "the cold war rivalry seemed to dictate that the nation mobilize her brainpower, including schoolchildren and undergraduate and graduate students, on an emergency basis."[12]

These calls for an increased national effort in education were present throughout the 1950s, but clearly escalated in urgency when the U.S.S.R. launched its first Sputnik satellite on October 4, 1957. Although the immediate reactions to the Sputnik launching emphasized the national need for more scientists and engineers to support the defense industry, the public debates in general incorporated the humanities and social sciences in the call for educational and moral renewal as well. The specific engineering demands identified in the Sputnik crisis were translated into a general demand for educational reform. The intense competition with the U.S.S.R. in military technology was extended into the realm of culture and values, that is, into the realm of ideology.

At the center of debates over education in the early to mid-1950s was the tradition of progressive education, which originally encouraged critical, independent thinking in students, but was gradually replaced by "life-adjustment education," which focused on job preparation and practical training. Conservative critics claimed, however, that life-adjustment education neglected to instill moral values in students and did not lead to the formation of a new intellectual elite of students in the service of the nation. The unspoken subtext of these criticisms is the demand that education return to traditional—supposedly American—values to educate a generation of students who are morally and intellectually prepared to fight the Communist threat. Peter Dow, for example, points out:

> many Americans believed that the challenge posed by the expanding scientific and military power of the U.S.S.R. could only be met in the long run through the development of more effective scientific training. Mental flabbiness had become equated in the public mind with moral weakness.[13]

Whereas the 1957 Sputnik launching intensified the debates over education and ultimately led to legislation, it did not initiate these debates. Although most accounts of the 1950s school reform movement focus on the response to Sputnik, Clowse in particular points out that the issue of educational reform has been present in debates throughout the 1950s.[14] A second issue present in these debates was a conservative criticism of the lack of ideological commitment in the practices of progressive education. Critics of the U.S. educational system frequently demanded an emphasis on moral as well as intellectual education. In the context of the cold war, even before the Sputnik crisis, it was an almost universally held belief that improving the quality of education was one of the keys to winning the cold war.

This new emphasis on excellence in education was also connected to specific forms of social organization. Especially in response to the egalitarian thrust of progressive education, the idea of equality in education was redefined. In 1956 the Federal Educational Policies Commission stated, "naïve egalitarianism which urged in the name of democracy the same amount and kind of education for all individuals is giving way to a more genuine democracy which calls on education to lift every individual to the highest of his capacities."[15]

Whereas this critique of egalitarianism and encouragement of individualism in education seemingly advocated a meritocracy, the educational policies implied here translated into very specific educational and cultural values, namely an emphasis on the creation of educational elites, a focus on dominant cultural values, and an increasing sense that education needs to serve the interests of the nation-state. The types of knowledge desirable under these policies would be utilitarian, that is, easily put to use in the cold war, based in a positivist belief in the value of seemingly neutral facts, and again, concurrent with dominant cultural distinctions. Big-money quiz shows, with their emphasis on fact-based questions and a frequent reliance on topics that belong to areas of high cultural distinction, were clearly structured by the field of knowledge and education and were in close connection to the highly contentious debates over educational policy in the United States.

NETWORK PROGRAMMING POLICY AND
OPERATION FRONTAL LOBES

One of the important characteristics of a field is that it has the power to extend its logic over a variety of institutions and agents, government and nongovernment.[16] Thus, the reproduction of cultural distinctions becomes a crucial, if unacknowledged, part of the policy of public and private institutions. Bourdieu and Wacquant emphasize the fact that the state as an assembly of various fields of culture has "the power to constitute and to impose as *universal* and *universally applicable* within a given 'nation,' a common set of...norms."[17] Despite the inherent contradictions in state policy and discourse, we can witness in educational policy a relatively stable network of discursive positions that articulate dominant interests in the public as well as the private sphere. The operation of some of these processes is witnessed through the efforts of representatives of higher education and government of bringing high culture back to the center of U.S. public discourse.

Whitfield makes explicit the relationship between big-money quiz shows and the debates over education that surrounded the Sputnik crisis arguing that "the sense that intellect itself had to be drafted into the Cold War, which was one general consequence of Sputnik, may explain why the [quiz show] scandal was so reverberant."[18] The increasing focus on education after Sputnik grew out of the existing notion that education and the production of knowledge would be of central importance for the survival of the United States in the cold war. Whitfield's quote illustrates that the debates over education, the nation, and big-money quiz shows as a cultural form are clearly informed by the logic of the overall field of knowledge and education, displaying the same ideological orientation while retaining a degree of autonomy from each other. In Raymond Williams's terms, this relationship can be referred to as a homology, that is, specific social or cultural forms that have common forms of origin.[19]

The power of a field becomes most obvious where it succeeds at influencing policy decisions in a seemingly independent institution such as a broadcast network. One of the most pronounced cases in which this power manifests itself is NBC's operation frontal lobes. Operation frontal lobes was a policy NBC's chief executive Sylvester Weaver designed with the intention of integrating culturally desirable, educational, or enlightenment material into a variety of programming forms on television. Vance Kepley sees operation frontal lobes primarily as a tool for NBC to demonstrate the network's efficiency in providing public service programming, which can be differentiated from commercially oriented entertainment fare.[20] He claims that operation frontal lobes was primarily "pro bono broadcasting"[21] and ignores the influence of Weaver's frontal lobes policy on entertainment programming. Kepley argues that the main significance of frontal lobes lies in its character as a symbol for NBC's efforts to create quality programming in the public interest. However, Pamela Wilson demonstrates that the reach of frontal lobes extended well beyond the area of public service programming. The areas on which operation frontal lobes touched regularly included the area of high culture, art, opera, and theater; intellectual debate about current social and scientific issues; and issues relating to politics or democratic processes in general.[22]

The increasing demands for a return to classical educational values in 1950s culture clearly also provided a framework for the articulation of these discourses on network television. The enlightenment ideology of frontal lobes was closely connected to the U.S. national agenda in the cold war and "television as 'a democratic arm of national enlightenment' was seen as a way to develop the intellectual levels of America's citizenry, to build up the intellectual forces against the Communist threat."[23]

NBC executive Davidson Taylor illustrates the integration of operation frontal lobes into the ideological formation of cold war anticommunism:

> The self-interest of American industry demands that the American idea shall grow and spread. It will continue to grow and spread if the American people learn how to live up to their position of world leadership. How pleased would the Communists be if television, with its great power to command attention, spent

all its time amusing the American people and never brought them information or made them think.[24]

As these statements evidence, recruiting the media as a central tool in the construction of national unity is fairly common in the 1950s, as it was in previous decades.[25] Similarly, Michael Curtin's discussion of public debates over the role of broadcast media in U.S. culture in the early 1960s shows significant parallels to the debates over television's role in the 1950s' cold war. In both cases, the media are regarded as an important tool in the fight against communism. Curtin argues that criticism of television, "when articulated with debates over citizenship and the 'national interest,' led in turn to the suggestion that television, with its privileged access to the suburban family home, had an important role to play in the global struggle against Communism."[26]

The television spectacular as an important programming form in the 1950s makes it clear that the networks were particularly interested in creating a television viewing experience that would incorporate a large part of the nation. The spectaculars were specially scheduled programs outside of the regular broadcast routine that were meant to command nationwide public attention and increase viewership. As Chris Anderson explains, the television spectacular "represented a potential strategy in the networks' early efforts to constitute the experience of television viewing, in this case as an extraordinary national event delivered to the American home."[27]

Many of the highly successful big-money quiz shows certainly shared one central trait with media events or spectaculars, that is, their ability to unite large portions of the nation in a shared televisual experience. Consequently, frontal lobes is closely related to creating an ideologically unified and enlightened nation.

Although NBC is usually credited with attempting to integrate high culture into its programming, primarily through operation frontal lobes, CBS had a reputation for focusing on producing widely popular programming. Accordingly, William Boddy points out, "CBS maintained its reputation for popular, less elevated fare."[28] However, both CBS and NBC were obviously subject to debates over educational reform and the function of television in the nation during the cold war. Consequently, CBS's efforts at prestige programming reflecting the sensibilities of elite culture and a traditional system of cultural distinction also need to be taken into consideration. Although CBS gained a reputation in the area of high cultural distinction primarily for its news division under the leadership of Edward R. Murrow and Fred Friendly, the calls for cultural uplift and national renewal also influenced other types of CBS programming. CBS's programming strategies needed to negotiate between the network's desire to gain cultural acceptability and its economic need to retain a large popular audience. As a result of these contradictory forces, CBS initiated the wave of big-money quiz shows in 1955 with the premiere of *The $64,000 Question*. Despite the prominence of big-money quiz shows and their well-known focus on intellectuals, knowledge, and education, the specific strategies for integrating "enlightenment material" into regular television programming has not been adequately addressed.

According to NBC policies, operation frontal lobes was to be implemented in programming on three levels:

1. "Single programs—enlightenment": Special programs exclusively geared toward enlightening the audience;
2. "Regularly scheduled informational, educational, and cultural programs": News, current affair, and educational programming; and
3. "Integrated enlightenment material—on regularly scheduled programs": Enlightening elements integrated in regular shows that are usually regarded as entertainment.[29]

The first and second were comparatively easy to accomplish because they dealt with programs that were often specifically created to enlighten the audience, but according to most historical accounts operation frontal lobes failed crucially at implementing its third level.[30] The 1954 Responsibility Report lists seven programs in category 1, and eighty-three programs in category 2, but only eleven in category 3, indicating NBC's difficulties at accomplishing the integration of enlightenment materials into regularly scheduled programs. The network attempted to incorporate some lessons into children's programs (for example, *Kukla, Fran, and Ollie*), to address social issues in sitcoms (for example, *The Goldbergs*), and to showcase high art in programs such as *Texaco Star Theatre*, but NBC's responsibility reports on the success of operation frontal lobes included long lists of programs that had failed to integrate content of high cultural distinction or enlightenment material. In general, NBC regarded frontal lobes as most successful when it provided specific high-culture programming or documentary programming on a variety of social and cultural issues.[31] Thus, most historians assume that operation frontal lobes influenced entertainment programming only to an insignificant extent. Wilson in particular claims that operation frontal lobes' "most notable failure seems to have been its attempts to integrate 'enlightenment material' into existing entertainment series" and even points to the fact that according to NBC's own assessment in 1952, "a few sitcoms, several game shows, and many comedy and musical variety shows" did not live up to frontal lobes' standards.[32] Whereas NBC's own negative assessment of its enlightenment project indicates the amount of public pressure on the network, the extent to which operation frontal lobes actually did shape entertainment programming and quiz shows in particular is not clear.

Beginning with the premiere of *The $64,000 Question* on CBS and *Twenty-One* on NBC, big-money quiz shows were closely linked to the enlightenment project operation frontal lobes proposed. As part of this enlightenment project, big-money quiz shows are notable for the strong presence of educators as contestants:

> Educators were especially popular as contestants; a Brooklyn school teacher appeared on *The $64,000 Challenge* in 1958 and told the host that his salary was $400 a month. The host responded incredulously: "After eighteen years of study, they pay you only $400 a month?" "That's correct," the teacher replied. The host: "It may be correct, but see me after the show and we'll campaign together."[33]

The frequent appearances of educators or highly educated contestants on big-money quiz shows and the centrality that these shows gave to high culture and academic knowledge is one of the articulations of operation frontal lobes. Another articulation of this enlightenment project is the reproduction of specific forms of cultural capital such as classical music, literature, European history, and culture, which were at the center of operation frontal lobes. As Wilson points out, operation frontal lobes "reinforced the dominance of patriarchal, Anglo-European social formation which reflected the supposed culmination of cultural evolution through Western civilization."[34]

If one compares the cultural forms preferred in operation frontal lobes to the content of any big-money quiz show, an astonishing correspondence can be found. An overview of the subjects covered on several episodes of big-money quiz shows currently available in several archives demonstrates this:

- *Tic Tac Dough*: Geography, history, comic strips, kings, politics.
- *The $64,000 Question*: current events, the history of the Wild West, opera.
- *Twenty-One*: film, English literature, poetry, current events.
- *The Big Surprise*: the roaring twenties, big band music, ships and the sea.[35]

Margo Rieman, the big band expert on *The Big Surprise*, had to name four members of the Benny Goodman Orchestra for $1,000, then had to identify a recording by two members of the Bob Crosby Band for $2,000, and finally, for $3,000, had to answer questions about the Original Dixieland Jazz Band and the New Orleans Rhythm Kings. As a special celebrity contestant on the same show, Errol Flynn had to define four nautical terms and then, for $30,000, had to answer a question about the nautical insurance Lloyd's of London, name several ships which were lost at sea, their country of origin, and identify the oceans in which they were last seen. As we would expect from Wilson's description of operation frontal lobes, most of these questions are closely related to Anglo-European culture and represent relatively high forms of cultural capital.

Operation frontal lobes is a pronounced version of the cultural preferences and ideologies circulating in the broadcast industry and to some extent
in U.S. culture in general in the early to mid-1950s. Although operation
frontal lobes was closely identified with NBC executive Sylvester Weaver,
who held various network positions from 1949 to 1956, it articulates the
broadcast industry's widely held   programming philosophies. The way in
which frontal lobes is caught between the ideal of audience enlightenment
and the need to produce popular entertainment is indicative of the way the
broadcast industry as a whole was positioned in U.S. culture. In this instance,
the field of knowledge and education and the economic requirements of the
broadcast industry created a cultural form that bears some of the contradictions in which broadcasting itself was caught. The cultural tensions that
inform operation frontal lobes also clearly informed the structure and ideology of big-money quiz shows.

BIG-MONEY QUIZ SHOWS AND THEIR POPULAR RECEPTION

Many historical accounts of the 1950s as well as many contemporary debates
emphasize the high degree of uniformity in U.S. culture, stemming from the
dominance of consumption as a unifying discourse as well as from the rise of
broadcast television as a homogenizing force. Jackson Lears concludes that
the emphasis on homogeneity in debates of the 1950s implies an unwilling-
ness on the part of intellectuals to investigate class structures or power relations.[36] In contrast, Lynn Spigel and George Lipsitz describe the process
through which 1950s' television facilitated a smooth transition from an
urban-based lifestyle encompassing a variety of ethnic identities to a suburban lifestyle that erased differences in class and ethnic identity.[37] However,
Roland Marchand claims that the popular media in the 1950s largely portrayed the United States as a classless society in which consumption is an
egalitarian activity uniting all citizens and consumers. He sees big-money quiz
shows as inserted in this system of classlessness because their emphasis on
"common people" as contestants also tends to erase social difference:

> Producers of the big money TV quiz shows nurtured popular
> enthusiasm for illusions of equality by creating such folk heroes as
> the "cop who knew Shakespeare." The sponsor of *The $64,000
> Question* explained: "We're trying to show the country that the
> little people are really very intelligent."[38]

What Marchand does not acknowledge is that the appeal of the "cop who
knew Shakespeare" or "the cobbler who knew opera"[39] to a significant degree
stems from acknowledging the contradiction between their class and the cultural capital with which they deal. These working-class contestants become
interesting precisely because they are willing to accept the superiority of a

cultural capital identified with the ruling class, but certainly not with the working class. These candidates are instrumental in constructing a cultural consensus under the leadership of a white, Anglo-European upper class. The process of giving upper-class cultural capital a character of universal validity works specifically by rewarding the adoption of a particular cultural capital with financial capital. Hence, elite cultural capital becomes desirable for the common people (television viewers) who might not desire educational capital, but who certainly desire and appreciate financial capital.

This emphasis on the outstanding financial rewards of education is, for example, also present in an episode of *The $64,000 Question,* in which host Hal March constantly emphasizes a contestant's low family income, which is dwarfed by the comparatively high winnings on the show. The contestant's field of expertise is opera, and her husband is a medical resident at Mount Sinai Hospital.

MARCH: What do medical residents get these days?

MARILYN SOUTHERN (contestant): Seventy-five dollars.

MARCH: Seventy-five dollars a week?

SOUTHERN: A month.

MARCH: Seventy-five dollars is what your husband makes? Well, you can live on that if you cut [out] break-fast, lunch, and dinner!"

After finding out that Marilyn Southern also has two children, the host gets even more upset and continues to refer to the financial rewards of *The $64,000 Question* in the following rounds of competition.

MARCH: Want to try for $2,000? We're getting wealthy so fast....

MARCH: Want to go for $4,000? Seventy-five dollars a month... (whistles).[40]

This episode demonstrates the articulation of various forms of high cultural capital (the husband's profession) and the wife's interests in elite culture, (opera), and rewards these forms of distinction with financial capital, which previously had been missing from the equation. Again, this episode of *The $64,000 Question* performs a hegemonic cultural function by naturalizing class-based cultural distinctions and rewarding them financially, thus fulfilling the 1950s version of the American Dream.

The egalitarianism that is seemingly displayed in big-money quiz shows is also an important focal point of the popular media coverage of quiz shows before the scandals. The popular reactions to big-money quiz shows are organized in what Tony Bennett calls a *reading formation.* Bennett explains that a reading formation activates a given body of texts and the relations between them in a specific way. Reading formations organize extratextual relations within and around texts and often create a unity between text and context. However, these relations are not structured evenly, but are subject to the power relations already present in a culture.[41] One can assume that the reading formation of big-money quiz shows that can be observed in the popular media will to some extent be structured by the field of education and knowledge as well.

The premiere of *The $64,000 Question* was anticipated and commented on regularly from March until June 1955. Previews of *The $64,000 Question* refer to the sensational amount of prize money on this show and to the similarity to the radio quiz show *Take It or Leave It*. After the premiere these first reports were gradually replaced with detailed descriptions of the show and behind-the-scenes stories on the show in popular magazines such as *TV Guide*. All these reports were entirely uncritical and generally detailed the rules of the game, the money that could be won, and how the questions were selected. At the same time, several magazines (*Newsweek, Cosmopolitan, TV Guide, Life,* and *Look*) began to treat host Hal March as well as some of the successful contestants as stars. March was characterized as a dedicated show-business professional, whereas the contestants were usually portrayed as regular people within the context of their families. However, the emphasis on the quiz shows' hosts was increasingly superseded in the following two years by articles focusing on the contestants as stars, Charles Van Doren in particular. Van Doren appeared on *Twenty-One*, an NBC imitation of *The $64,000 Question*, between November 1956 and March 1957 and won the then-record amount of $129,000. His job as instructor at Columbia University is regarded as one reason for his success and he even published an article in *Life*[42] explaining his position on education and quiz shows.

The reasons given for the success of big-money quiz shows implicitly explain the treatment of contestants as stars in the popular media. Experts contend that audiences identify more easily with "normal" people as contestants. An article in *TV Guide* for example observes, "plain people—not big names—provide the world's best entertainment. It's 'real folk,' like Gino and Gloria and Myrt, who register best with the viewers.... The amateur on television is apparently here to stay."[43] Similarly, television critic Jack Gould argues that "there's no people like non-show people. The TV that deals with actuality, with real unglamourized people behaving as themselves, is still the most fascinating TV of all."[44] This emphasis on "plain people" as stars ultimately led to an egalitarian rhetoric that the producers of these shows adopted as well. Charles Revson (sponsor of *The $64,000 Question*) exemplifies this position saying, "we're trying to show the country that the little people are really very intelligent and knowledgeable. That's why the show has caught on—because of the little people."[45] The creator of *The $64,000 Question*, Louis Cowan, agrees with this position in a *Newsweek* interview:

> I've never subscribed to the belief that the average American radio and TV listener has a 12-year-old intelligence. The average American has a brain and an integrity that's really wonderful. You just have to look for it. Everybody's smart at something.[46]

This egalitarian rhetoric that aggressively tried to claim cultural respectability for quiz shows, television, and its viewers remained fairly common until the rigging of the quiz shows became publicly known.

Overall, this popular reading formation is highly uncritical of the genre. Most of the texts dealing with the big-money quiz shows focus on the star contestants of the shows and the egalitarian potential they represent. This discourse of egalitarianism erases the social differences implicit in the class-based, elite cultural knowledge of quiz shows. The reading formation of big-money quiz shows that emerges in the popular media naturalizes class-specific forms of acquired (educational) cultural capital by articulating these shows to the discourse of the common man.

One of the most famous moments from the history of quiz shows, the competition between Charles Van Doren and Herb Stempel on *Twenty-One*, brings the preferred cultural heritage and the dominant ideology of big-money quiz shows well into focus. The competition between these two contestants is seen as a staged event that expresses specific cultural predispositions in a particularly interesting way. Michael Real contrasts the two contestants-as-cultural-symbols in relation to the cultural capital they carry:

> Stempel is the common man, a self-taught working-class New York Jew with phenomenal recall, doggedly accurate, but lacking charm and charisma . . . with his unflattering haircut and ill-fitting clothes. At the opposite extreme, Van Doren is superman and the boy next door, an intellectual's hero, an Ivy Leaguer with graduate study in astrophysics, mathematics, and literature at Cambridge, the Sorbonne, and Columbia, but also a charming and self-effacing nice guy.[47]

The confrontation between Stempel and Van Doren captures the dynamics of cultural politics in the genre, the medium, and U.S. culture rather well. In particular, big-money quiz shows provide a highly reified form of ethnic identity that overrides a diversity of other experiences and identities. For example, the Italian-born Gino Prato becomes acceptable within the discursive realm of *The $64,000 Question* only because as an expert on opera he is willing and able to subsume his Italian-American cultural identity under the larger issue of Eurocentric cultural literacy through his unexpected connection to high cultural capital. In contrast, Charles Van Doren is a combination of two types of cultural capital that Bourdieu differentiates: On the one hand, as an instructor at Columbia University he possesses high acquired capital, that is, an Ivy-League education; On the other hand, he possesses high inherited capital

Figure 3.2. Famous quiz show contestant Herb Stempel in the isolation booth of *Twenty-One. Courtesy Wisconsin Center for Film and Theater Research.*

because he belongs to the well-known and highly regarded Van Doren family, which also includes Pulitzer prize winners, professors, and magazine editors.[48] As a result, Van Doren demonstrates his mastery of *both* high culture and trivial knowledge. Michele Hilmes observes in relation to radio in the 1930s that many programs created a compound white identity that included a wide variety of European ethnicities, but specifically excluded African Americans from the imaginary American mainstream.[49] A similar process of creating a "unifying and nationalizing discourse"[50] is at work in quiz shows, even though its character seems to be less all-encompassing. Big-money quiz shows as part of 1950s' television relied on an extremely rigid model of cultural distinctions rooted culturally in European high culture and ethnically in the East Coast white elite, which Charles Van Doren exemplified. They demonstrate that the field of knowledge and education does not simply produce specific, preferred forms of knowledge, but articulates forms of knowledge closely connected with dominant groups to specific cultural practices.

CONCLUSION

The proliferation of big-money quiz shows between 1954 and 1959 represents a unique instance in the development of the genre and in the history of broadcasting. These shows represent knowledge as "the accumulation of discrete facts, atomized and offered unproblematically within a priori categories and levels of difficulty."[51] Independent thought, reflection, or any sort of critical thinking were clearly precluded on these shows. Instead, they tended to celebrate the centrality of accepted authority figures, such as college professors or bank presidents. Both in terms of the knowledge required on quiz shows and in terms of the people appearing on these shows, traditional versions of cultural authority were maintained. The highly coherent ideological structure of the shows, as well as their spectacular visual style, reminds us of the power a variety of forces exerted in the process of cultural production.

Whereas Bourdieu and Wacquant rightfully emphasize the contradiction in and between given fields,[52] the case of big-money quiz shows demonstrates that often we can also observe the existence of cultural products that are heavily (over)determined by dominant cultural formations. The specific conditions in the United States in the 1950s, especially the debates surrounding education and the diverse pressures on broadcast networks, created television programs that, for a short period, presented a highly reductive model of national values and norms. This interpretation of big-money quiz shows contrasts sharply with most historical accounts that simply cast quiz shows and the scandal in terms of a conflict between attractive and disagreeable contestants. The motivations for rigging quiz shows are exclusively located in excessive corporate greed and in the quest for higher ratings.[53] What is usually absent from such accounts is the extent to which big-money quiz shows were connected to the production of knowledge in 1950s' culture.

The image of Charles Van Doren sums up one of the crucial hidden contradictions in the ideological operation of big-money quiz shows. On the one hand, the discourse of the common man was evoked to demonstrate the universal validity of the knowledge and values quiz shows represented. On the other hand, Van Doren, a representative of a small elite culture, stood at the center of the egalitarian discourses in *Twenty-One*. A naturalization of this contradiction is a central part of the ideological work of big-money quiz shows.

CHAPTER 4

Dealing with Change

The Evolution of Quiz Shows in the 1960s

The movie *Quiz Show* shows how the quiz show scandals heavily influenced the history of the genre.[1] In its conclusion, *Quiz Show* implies that several big-money quiz show producers took exclusive blame for rigging these shows. Neither network executives nor sponsors were found guilty of rigging their programs. The networks thus deflected some of the public hostility toward the burgeoning medium. Nevertheless, public criticism of television was significant and resentment of quiz shows was high. In the years following the scandals, the networks struggled to keep quiz shows alive which entailed remodeling the genre. The broadcast industry attempted to distance quiz shows from connotations with the scandals by renaming the genre and by emphasizing the differences between 1960s' quiz shows and 1950s' big-money quiz shows.

In the process of remodeling the genre, the form of quiz shows changed as well. Quiz shows started to focus primarily on gambling and consumerism and were moved to daytime programming slots. In the process of creating programming that appealed to the growing youth market, networks incorporated some of the elements of the 1960s' counterculture in quiz shows. The genre increasingly relied on everyday knowledge and the integration of home and studio audiences, challenging traditional forms of cultural authority that previously had been at the center of the big-money quiz shows.

This chapter first analyzes the discursive strategies the broadcast industry used in the remodeling of the genre during the early 1960s. Second, Iit relates the changes in the form of the genre to the cultural context of the

1960s, particularly the youth culture and counterculture. Finally, the chapter shows how notions of everyday culture were again transformed in 1970s' quiz shows.

REDEFINING A GENRE

Following the detection of the rigging of the big-money quiz shows, NBC canceled all quiz shows in any way associated with the scandals, and CBS removed the whole genre from its daytime and prime-time lineup for the 1959–1960 season. The third network, ABC, was fortunate in that it did not rely on quiz shows in its prime-time schedule and its daytime shows did not use large prizes. Although the genre was culturally discredited, it retained much of its economic attractiveness, namely its simple production values, low production costs, especially low talent costs, and a solid popularity with the audience. Accordingly, the broadcasting industry made several attempts to rescue the genre and keep quiz shows on the air. In November 1959, before Charles Van Doren confessed to his involvement in the rigging of *Twenty-One* in congressional hearings, *Broadcasting* magazine claimed that the scandals had hardly left an impression on television audiences: "Only a few (10.2 percent) of those who know about the investigation say it has affected their enjoyment of television and only a slightly larger number (18.9 percent) say it has affected their attitude toward television."[2] Broadcasting industry representatives continually argued that quiz shows should remain on the air. They asserted that programs that do not rely on substantial prizes are not truly implicated in the scandals and are therefore not inherently dishonest. An NBC press release states:

> We do not believe that amputation of one of the oldest and best-liked program forms is the answer to television's current difficulties. NBC's answer to this serious and perplexing problem is to accept the challenge of devising and implementing every conceivable safeguard that our resources and our abilities can fashion.[3]

Forrest F. Owen, a former quiz show producer and advertising executive, attempted to rescue quiz shows as an outlet for advertisers by pointing out that the rigging of some shows was an exception that should not reflect on the genre as a whole: "The important point is that for every bad apple there are hundreds of good solid apples. Must we dump out the whole barrelful to get rid of the few rotten ones?"[4] The public image of quiz shows and television in general became even more tarnished when congressional hearings in 1960 showed the extent to which quiz shows were rigged and the extent to which highly popular contestants, namely Charles Van Doren, whose testimony before a congressional subcommittee was a climax of the scandals, were also implicated in the rigging. As a result, the networks continually had to defend one of their financially most attractive genres.

Not all of the quiz shows were canceled due to the scandals. Several shows that did not rely on extremely high-value prizes remained on the air in the late 1950s and early 1960s, and the networks emphasized this fact in an effort to show the vitality of the genre. Quiz shows remaining on the air after the scandals include *Who Do You Trust* (ABC, 1957–1963); *Music Bingo* (NBC, ABC, 1958–1960); *Top Dollar* (CBS, 1958–1960); *The Big Payoff* (NBC, CBS, 1951–1960); *Name that Tune* (NBC, CBS, 1953–1959); *Tic Tac Dough* (NBC, 1956–1959); *Dough Re Me* (NBC, 1958–1960); *Treasure Hunt* (ABC, NBC, 1956–1959); *What's My Line?* (CBS, 1950–1967); and *I've Got a Secret* (CBS, 1952–1967).[5] These programs usually had low production values and small prizes. Most of them used different types of everyday genres, such as parlor games, or used a celebrity panel as the center of the show.

Generally, quiz shows were removed from prime time, their stakes were significantly reduced, and the knowledge contestants needed became less demanding. The postscandal era is marked by a move away from expert knowledge and toward a stronger reliance on everyday knowledge. Only *G. E. College Bowl* and *Alumni Fun* still focused on "academic" knowledge, but their prize money was greatly reduced and, in contrast to big-money quiz shows, their production values were very simple.

Beginning in the 1961–1962 season, all networks started to introduce new quiz shows. In response to the success of NBC daytime quiz shows in the previous season, CBS in particular decided to bring quiz shows back on the air. Although industry statements during and immediately following the scandals emphasized that not all quiz shows were rigged and therefore did not deserve to be tainted by the scandal, the broadcast industry's discursive strategies changed significantly in this period. The broadcast industry's ultimate goal was to remove the genre from its connection to the scandals and redefine it as a genre category separate from big-money quiz shows. The phrase *game shows* was ultimately adopted as a way to redefine the genre.

The appearance of new quiz shows was referred to as a "resurgence of the genre"[6] and was accompanied by numerous attempts to redefine the genre in major industry publications such as *Broadcasting*, *Sponsor*, and *Advertising Age*. As early as July 1959, the industry attempted to separate certain quiz shows, particularly *What's My Line?* and *I've Got a Secret*, from the big-money quiz shows. An article in *Sponsor* emphasizes that Nielsen identified a new category of "quiz panel programs," which is viewed as different from both "quiz-giveaways" and "audience participations."[7] In comparison, another article in *Sponsor* collapses some of these categories and lists a variety of shows all under the "audience participation" label. An article in *Advertising Age*, discussing the return of quiz shows on CBS, lists four categories for the

Figure 4.1. *Robert Earle hosting G. E. College Bowl. Courtesy University of Maryland/Broadcast Pioneers Library.*

genre formerly known as quiz shows: "Games, quizzes, audience participation telecasts, and giveaways."[8] The general confusion that these statements exhibit was not consolidated until 1961 when publications increasingly started to use the term *game shows* to describe the genre as a whole, incorporating all previously mentioned terms under this label. An article in *Broadcasting* summarizes the strategies to redefine the genre best: "'Game shows' are being scheduled primarily in daytime, and precautions are being taken by the networks to police the programs and keep merchandise and money prizes comparatively modest."[9] Identifying game shows (albeit incorrectly) with a different time slot and emphasizing structural differences between games and quizzes separates them from quiz shows. Game shows are also set apart from one of the defining features of big-money quiz shows, their large merchandise and money prizes, which are assumed to have played an important role in the scandals. Thus, the networks attempted to contain and control the cumulative and scandalous meaning of the quiz show genre.

Emphasizing the changes made in individual quiz shows after the scandals was a first attempt to redefine the genre, although the success of this strategy is doubtful. Henry Jenkins describes the inevitable effects that the history of a term—or an event such as the scandals—will have on future connotations:

> Writer's mastery over appropriated terms does not come easily; old meanings are not striped [sic] away without a struggle; writers can never erase the history of their previous use or the complex grid of association each term sparks in the reader's mind. At most, writers can hope to activate certain pre-existing meanings while suppressing, albeit imperfectly, others.[10]

The strategies of the industry in redefining the genre seem to be informed by their desire to control the history of the genre and de-activate its scandalous meanings. The broadcast industry's intent to suppress the specific unwanted meanings of the quiz show genre are made explicit in another passage, in which *Broadcasting* quite overtly adopts the networks' redefinition of the genre, "Network officials stressed . . . that game programs never were tainted in any way, but that CBS-TV and ABC-TV became reluctant to schedule them because of the climate of opinion which evolved from the quiz scandals."[11] The redefinition of the genre is obviously connected to the networks' desire to control the historical reception of the genre. The industry statements indicate that the networks would only maintain quiz shows or game shows as a standard broadcast genre if its history could be rewritten and removed from the scandals. A final passage indicates the discursive strategies the networks used to redefine the genre:

> There is a distinct difference between a game show (which offers merchandise or money to a contestant who participates in a game), a quiz program (which usually offers large sums of money for the right answers), and a panel show (which spotlights the panel, rather than the contestants).[12]

By providing this new definition of the genre, the newly named game shows were efficiently set apart from quiz shows, which were exclusively identified with the scandal. Although the term *game show* was not used prior to the scandals, network officials here claim that game shows historically were always separate from quiz shows. As Foucault points out, the power of discourse lies to a significant degree in the masking of its operations.[13] The exertion of discursive power is therefore most effective when it is invisible. The construction of categories of genre that seem to be part of a long-term, common usage and are accordingly natural or part of common sense is an exertion of discursive power in the broadcast industry.

The new definition for a game show focuses on smaller monetary prizes, merchandise, and the centrality of audience participation. The emphasis on the new term *game* also indicates a move away from the serious, high-culture connotations of the term *quiz*, which granted the genre a significant degree of cultural centrality. The networks' specific use of language is clearly an attempt to exert their power in restructuring the preferred meaning of these terms. The industry's redefinition of the genre indicates that game shows were now seen as an entertainment form or leisure activity that had little connection to serious culture. This change is also reflected in the removal of the genre from prime time, where it occupied a prominent place during the successful years of the big-money quiz shows. The *Encyclopedia of Television Quiz Shows* effectively illustrates this shift: Between January 1946 and December 1959, 316 new quiz shows premiered, 261 of which were nighttime shows (aired between 6 P.M. and 11 P.M.). In comparison, from January 1960 until October 1987, only 367 more shows premiered and only 48 of these were nighttime shows.[14] Similarly, Julie D'Acci suggests that the expansion of public affairs programming under the pressure of FCC chairman Newton Minnow and the new frontier ideology in the early 1960s necessitated that unrespectable programming genres—such as the quiz show—be removed from prime time and be left in daytime.[15] By removing quiz shows from prime time, by renaming them, and by emphasizing the formal differences between (big-money) quiz shows and game shows, the broadcast industry accomplished its goal of remodeling the genre and removing it as much as possible from connotations with the scandals.

Merv Griffin's introduction of *Jeopardy!* in 1964 runs counter to the quiz show overhaul. Similar to shows such as *Twenty-One* and *The $64,000 Question*, it reintroduces a serious atmosphere, fairly elaborate sets, and returning contestants. Although *Jeopardy!* focuses on factual knowledge as the main source of questions, it emphasized sports and entertainment trivia over forms of higher cultural distinction such as the arts, literature and science. Seemingly reversing the logic of the 1950s' big-money quiz shows, contestants on *Jeopardy!* have to phrase their response in the form of a question after the host reveals the answer. Besides the playful denial of its quiz show heritage, *Jeopardy!* puts more emphasis on gambling because wagering is a regular feature on the program.[16] Even though the host regularly emphasizes

Figure 4.2. Art Fleming, host of the original version of *Jeopardy!* with assistant Nancy Pensey. *Courtesy Wisconsin Center for Film and Theater Research.*

contestants' intellectual abilities, the questions are structured to enable contestants to guess correct answers. The program combined multiple clues to the correct answer in a question, so that most questions did not require in-depth knowledge of a subject. This contrasts sharply with the nature of questions on big-money quiz shows, where contestants often had to answer multipart questions that required detailed knowledge of a given subject. Additionally, the prize money on the 1960s' version of *Jeopardy!* was also greatly reduced, with prizes for correct responses ranging from $10 to a maximum of $100. According to *The Encyclopedia of TV Game Shows*, the first contestant on *Jeopardy!* won a rather modest $345, an amount dwarfed by the prize money contestants on *Twenty-One* or *The $64,000 Question* regularly won.[17] Although *Jeopardy!* does not necessarily follow the development of 1960s' quiz shows toward low cultural distinction, it still avoided any close replication of many of the main characteristics of big-money quiz shows. Considering its low prize money and its location in NBC's daytime schedule, *Jeopardy!* conformed to the strategy of remodeling of the quiz show genre in most of its key aspects.

Beverly Stoeltje points out that a ritual is controlled through its form, the production process, and the discursive framing of the meaning of the ritual.[18] The broadcast industry publications on quiz shows in the early 1960s worked to control the meaning of the genre and were clearly intended to provide this discursive framework. However, in the case of the industry discourse on quiz shows in the early 1960s, one of the most interesting things to observe is that the power of the broadcast industry is not so much manifest in the maintenance of a stable definition of the genre, but in the ability of the industry to redefine the genre and its relation to the history of the scandals.

1960s' TELEVISION AND ITS CULTURAL CONTEXTS

How the broadcast industry produced the discourses necessary to redefine the meaning of the quiz show genre has become clear, but investigating the ways in which the redefinition of the genre also impacted the form of the genre and individual programs is still necessary. Quiz shows can be seen as a form of ritual in industrial society. The works of Victor Turner and Beverly Stoeltje on ritual in modern culture emphasize that such ritual forms do not necessarily express a unified ideological position, but attempt to address some of the contradictions underlying a given culture.[19] In other words, we can define quiz shows as forms that address contradictions in their social and cultural environment and often serve as a site of conflict. Looking at the shifts in the form of quiz shows might illustrate the changing cultural background of television in the 1960s.

The rapid changes in the cultural environment of the 1960s forced the television industry to adjust its programming and marketing. Teenagers and the growing youth culture of the 1960s were seen as a growing market the television industry targeted.[20] By the late 1960s, viewers between ages 18 and 49 formed the majority of the television audience; teenagers were considered the most constant television viewers. Additionally, the networks were particularly interested in attracting a middle-class, college-educated audience with a high disposable income.[21] The baby boomer generation, which the networks considered so attractive, was the first generation in the United States to grow up with television. Baby boomers were considered more open to television, but at the same time a large percentage of the youth audience aligned itself with a political ideology highly critical of the consumer culture that network television endorsed. Thomas Frank explains the attractiveness of the youth audience in two ways: One the one hand, the size of the youth market is regularly mentioned as a strong motivation for advertisers and networks alike to pursue new forms of advertising and television programming geared for these audiences. On the other hand, advertisers also associated the youth culture with radical change, an emphasis on style, and an increased hedonism:

> The counterculture seemed to have it all: the unconnectedness which would allow consumers to indulge transitory whims; the irreverence that would allow them to defy moral puritanism; and the contempt for established social rules that would free them from the slow-moving, buttoned-down conformity of their abstemious ancestors.[22]

Advertisers welcomed the rapid change youth symbolized and hoped to capitalize on it by offering a new consumerist ethic that transgressed any restrictive moral codes related to traditional U.S. culture. Although most accounts of the 1960s' claim that counterculture elements only appeared on television in a highly co-opted form,[23] Jackson Lears mentions that "the broader ferment of the counterculture" reemerged in many forms of popular culture, for example, in the overturning of "conventional hierarchies of authority."[24] Lears argues that commercial interests did not completely co-opt the countercultural style featured in advertising and popular culture. More specifically, the growing youth culture and counterculture fundamentally challenged the dominance of patriarchal, capitalist ideologies (often referred to as Protestantism) that had been at the center of many televisual forms, the big-money quiz shows in particular.

Historians of gambling have also traced the challenges posed to dominant culture in the 1960s. Gambling in the United States had been repressed from the late nineteenth century until the 1960s due to the strength of the Protestant work ethic.[25] According to Jan McMillen, Protestantism leads to the notion that gambling as an attempt to make "easy money" evades the Protestant work ethic and constitutes a threat to production.[26] Similarly Wendy Selby points out, "those in power maintained that the values of thrift and prudence were major components of 'what made America great,' and successfully outlawed popular gambling practices, such as lotteries."[27] The conflicts over the legality of jackpot quizzes in the early 1950s are an example of these struggles over the legitimacy of gambling in U.S. culture.

The first legal lotteries in the United States in the twentieth century were organized in New Hampshire in 1964 and New York in 1967. Both of them were unsuccessful, primarily because they were subject to severe state regulations. The New Jersey lottery, founded in 1970 and subject to fewer restrictions than the previous efforts, was significantly more successful and led to a proliferation of lotteries in the United States for the next twenty years.

While the big-money quiz shows clearly had the ideology of Protestantism at their center, the challenge to Protestantism that both Lears and McMillen describe seems to inform quiz shows in the 1960s.[28] Many shows incorporated elements of gambling into their competitions, providing a fundamental change in the structure of the genre. In a show such as *The $64,000 Question* if a contestant knew the answers to all questions losing was impossible. However, in shows in which rolling a dice (or other forms of gambling involving luck) is central to the outcome of the contest, the intellectual competence of contestants no longer drives the program.

One of the earliest quiz shows to emphasize gambling was *Video Village*.[29] The show resembled a board game on which two contestants moved as pieces competing for merchandise. A throw of the dice determined their progress on the board. *Video Village* exhibits some of the central features that governed quiz shows in the 1960s, namely gambling and an emphasis on playful games. In contrast to the serene, rule-governed competitions in shows such as *The $64,000 Question* or *Twenty-One*, it emphasizes individual pleasure and performance. Quiz show producer Jerry Hammer describes the changed mood of quiz shows after their "comeback" in 1961 as relying on "visual appeal, fun and entertainment, rather than big prizes, which were more common two years ago."[30] The visual style of 1950s' quiz shows is distinctly different from those of the 1960s, as Jefferson Graham also observes in his popular account of game shows, *Come on Down!!!*

> [On 1950s' quiz shows] sets were very simple; there were no flashing lights, categories in boxes were turned mechanically, and there were no wild colors, mainly because everything was in black and white. [On 1960s' and 1970s' quiz shows] the carnival, the circus, the downtown strip—they are the game show set, with the game show host as barker. The colors are loud, the sounds are louder, and the people step right up, or come on down, to take part in the action.[31]

Most of the new quiz shows that appeared in the 1960s and early 1970s reflect these developments, the most prominent examples being *Let's Make a Deal* and *The Price Is Right*. Most of these shows are, of course, broadcast in color and have extremely bright and flashy sets with strong, primary colors and a myriad aural and visual elements. Consumerism starts to play an important role in quiz shows, especially where knowledge of prizes and products becomes the focus of a show. The centrality of both gambling and consumption on 1960s' quiz shows connects these programs to the demise of the Protestant work ethic. The late 1950s and early 1960s are often identified as a key period where a shift from a productive ethic—which is at the core of Protestantism—to an ethic of consumption occurred. Consumption is seen as an unproductive practice outside of traditional social control, which emphasizes self-indulgence over the subjection of the individual to social rules. Similarly, gambling does not reward traditional forms of (hard) work and instead awards money purely on the basis of luck.

As Graham points out, in the 1960s and 1970s quiz shows had to adapt to a new cultural environment that included flourishing youth culture and countercultures.[32] Similarly, Lynn Spigel and Michael Curtin explain that television had to respond to the "cracks in the traditional structures of authority," which emerged in the course of the 1960s.[33] The remodeling of the quiz show genre in the postscandal years opened up the possibility for a presentation of some of these cracks in the structure of authority. Gambling and consumption are some of the ways in which values such as thrift and restraint are undermined and replaced by "formerly forbidden pleasures such as unrestricted spending and leisure."[34]

CONSUMING THE FEMALE AUDIENCE

The larger project of remodeling the quiz show genre entailed removing of these shows from prime time and rescheduling them in the less prestigious daytime period. Although big-money quiz shows in the 1950s were primarily articulated to the "patriarchal, Anglo-European social formation," the 1960s' quiz shows were clearly geared toward daytime's main implied audience, women.[35] Thomas Frank provides some striking examples of how the media industries in the 1960s were operating with a very reductive notion of gender:

> The symbol for the 1966 Art Directors' show is a color photograph of a woman nude and supine for the camera, her body painted from head to toe with elaborate dayglo [sic] flowers and rainbows and the words, "46th Annual NY Art Directors' Show."[36]

This example illustrates how the desires of the advertising industry were literally written on the female body. Certain assumptions about the gendered character of media audiences were at the core of the operation of the media industry. The switch in the ideal audience for the genre in combination with the shift to the devalued areas of everyday life and common knowledge in these daytime quiz shows recalls Andreas Huyssen's argument about the construction of mass culture as woman. Huyssen analyzes how women have always been constructed as the consumers of "inferior" cultural products.

Along with this quality judgment, crowds or the masses are also ascribed feminine characteristics:

> It is indeed striking to observe how the political, psychological, and aesthetic discourse... consistently and obsessively genders mass culture and the masses as feminine, while high culture, whether traditional or modern, clearly remains the privileged realm of male activities.[37]

Big-money quiz shows were not articulated to images of mindless masses or weak, feminized viewers because they represented dominant (male) culture and forms of high cultural distinction. In contrast, daytime quiz shows are described precisely in relation to a weak, susceptible, even defenseless, female audience.

An NBC advertisement for its daytime quiz show lineup in *Broadcasting* magazine demonstrates this strategy. The two-page advertisement features text on the left side occupying approximately one-third of the space and an image of a woman occupying the rest of the space. The woman is slim, average looking, and wears a skirt and a blouse. In her right hand, she holds a feather duster. She smiles slightly as she looks into the camera. This image of the woman is then duplicated and repeated twelve times so that we see the same woman standing next to herself thirteen times. Superimposed over the multiple images of the woman are the names of the hosts of the quiz shows, the names of the shows, their audience shares, and the average number of homes per minute. Intended to extol the attractiveness of NBC's daytime quiz show lineup to advertisers, this advertisement resorts to an image of the female daytime audience as extremely uniform, faceless, and commodified. The text of the advertisement elaborates on this impression of the audience even more. Its title reads, "Seven men capture the most responsive audience in daytime television," and the text describes the powers of the NBC quiz show hosts over housewives:

> These men are alive—alert, spontaneous—seven top salesmen who operate in broad daylight. They attract the ladies; entertain them; and lead them gently but firmly into a sales story woven deftly into their plot.[38]

This advertisement clearly represents women as easy prey for advertisers, as weak and unable to resist the lure of consumption, which the dominant quiz show hosts presented. The sales act is itself seen as an implicitly sexual act of seduction and treats women as victims both sexually and in the sphere of consumption. The discourse of consumption is similarly framed in sexual terms in an article in *Sponsor*, which discusses the activities of the Television Bureau of Advertising and refers to the sales act as "a daytime rendezvous."[39] In the struggle to attract and know the female daytime audience, male quiz show hosts have become a tool to ensure faithful and continued viewing behavior.

Although both of these advertisements conceive of women primarily as targets or victims of advertisers, women are also granted a certain degree of agency in each of these cases. The rhetoric of seduction and female suscepti- bility seems to be geared at NBC's clients, that is, advertisers who operate on the belief that their ads have a high degree of sales effectiveness. However, the first advertisement to some extent also allows women to desire not only consumer goods, but also the NBC quiz show hosts as agents of consumption. Despite the imagery of control and seduction, sexuality and consumption cannot be fully controlled in this context. The repressed subtext of women's agency that had been of great importance for the feminist movement in the early 1960s thus reemerged. One of the main strategies in industry publica- tions is to collapse the terms *woman* and *consumer* and treat them synony- mously.[40] Consequently, women's role as preeminent consumers is featured prominently in industry discourse as well as on quiz shows.

A variety of daytime quiz shows premiered in the early to mid-1960s, all of which focused on consumption and also generally constructed con- sumption/shopping as a female activity. On *Shopping Spree*,[41] contestants first compete to win time for play in the second round, in which the winner then plays for prizes such as a mink coat, a cabin cruiser, or a car. On *Seven Keys*,[42] contestants competed for one or several keys that would allow the winner to access different prizes, such as a Hawaiian vacation, a Polaroid camera, a television set, a home movie projector, perfume, a wrist watch, or an air puri- fier. Although both these show are clearly focused on consumption as a women's practice, *Supermarket Sweep*[43] makes these connections even more explicit. The 1960s' version of *Supermarket Sweep* was set in actual supermar- kets on the East Coast, whereas the 1990s' version on the Lifetime Channel uses a set closely resembling a supermarket, including aisles filled with super- sized packages of groceries and daily specials that reward the shopper with bonus points. Not only does *Supermarket Sweep* use consumer products as rewards, but it also makes knowledge of consumer products and knowledge of the layout of a supermarket the subject of its competition.

Feminist criticism has emphasized the positioning of women as both a perfect consumer of commodities and as a commodity.[44] Lynne Joyrich observes that female subjectivity necessitates a multiplicity of identifications, which also makes "the female subject susceptible to the lure of consumerism which plays on her fluctuating position."[45] Joyrich makes an observation other feminist scholars echo, for example Susan Douglas, who also mentions the multidimensional reading positions that women assume:

> Whether studying women's responses to romance novels, film, or
> music, [feminist] scholars have argued forcefully that women
> have been socialized to become proficient at multiple, sometimes

conflicting, readings of media texts in which they empathize and identify simultaneously with several characters.[46]

Although media studies has convincingly argued that all media texts offer multiple identifications, one may assume that 1960s' quiz shows, as media texts primarily targeted at women, will be particularly likely to offer multiple reading positions.

COUNTERCULTURE AND IMMEDIACY

Outside of the larger political project of the left in the 1960s, the "structure of feeling"[47] of the counterculture and youth culture had a clear impact on the quiz show genre. Writers such as George Lipsitz, Aniko Bodroghkozy, and Elaine May see issues such as agency, participation, and immediacy of experience as central for the countercultural project.[48] May shows that the women's movement, which was one of the most important political movements of the 1960s, was originally aimed at reclaiming women's individuality, identity, and agency outside of the confines of suburban homes.[49] The centrality of the issue of agency for individuals is also a driving force for the 1960s' music subculture. Lipsitz connects the desire for immediate experience and participation to the growth of the 1960s' amateur music. "The participatory democracy of the New Left that encouraged people to take control of the decisions that affected their lives found a cultural concomitant in a music subculture that asserted that everyone could be a star."[50] Wayne Munson observes that 1960s' radio talk shows attempted to encourage audience call-ins to create an element of "involvement and participation" and address some of the sensibilities of the counterculture.[51] Such an element of participation and immediate involvement is one of several important elements that emerge in 1960s' quiz shows.

This sense of immediacy is often connected to the impression of liveness on television. Feuer points out, "due to its electronic nature, television is far more capable of affirming its own mode as one of absolute presence than is film, even though the vast majority of television programs are not broadcast 'live.'"[52] Quiz shows use three strategies that are particularly helpful in creating an impression of liveness and immediacy: using a proscenium stage, using direct address, and creating presence in time.

Although most filmed or taped television programs use a single camera production style, a significant number of talk, variety, and quiz shows still use a multiple camera proscenium technique. They use a space resembling a theater stage with multiple cameras in positions usually facing the onstage action. Some sitcoms (following the example of *I Love Lucy*) and soap operas similarly employ proscenium style, thereby preserving production techniques that have their origins in the live performances of early television. Nevertheless, as

David Barker explains, television attempted to adopt the already-established patterns of continuity editing (or "classic realism") from film:

> Television attempted to approximate continuity editing as a way to construct screen space coherently. "Approximate" is a key term here. Since the execution of virtually any element of continuity editing in live television requires multiple cameras running simultaneously, consistently maintaining a fourth wall is almost impossible. Thus, television could approximate, as opposed to duplicate, some elements of continuity editing.[53]

Although a multiple camera proscenium style can replicate a continuous editing style that avoids any violation of established visual codes (for example, jump cuts), it cannot fully incorporate all elements of the classic realist style. The proscenium style indeed engages viewers differently than other programs that use the "classic realism" derived from film: Classic realism (1) tries to construct a linear plot development, (2) tries to mask or naturalize its formal characteristics, and (3) encourages the spectator to identify with the points of view of the characters in the narrative. Laura Mulvey suggests how cinematic realism structures the look of its spectator:

> There are three different looks associated with the cinema: that of the camera as it records the pro-filmic event, that of the audience as it watches the final product, and that of the characters at each other within the screen illusion. The conventions of narrative film deny the first two and subordinate them to the third, the conscious aim being always to eliminate intrusive camera presence and prevent a distancing awareness in the audience.[54]

The representational techniques used in quiz shows, of course, to a large degree still construct a linear plot line, but they do not readily allow identification with the characters or an adoption of their look because the proscenium format usually places the viewer in an observer's position apart from the space of the stage and, consequently, apart from the characters/protagonists, preventing strong identification with a character and creating some awareness of the viewing situation.

Closely related to the proscenium setup in its aesthetic effect is the use of direct address. Direct address is used in commercials and in the program itself. It can be seen, for example, when a narrator verbally addresses the (implied) viewer as "you" or when the host is pointing at the camera and implicitly at the viewer (which is usually combined with a direct verbal address), or it can be seen in instances where the narrator/host talks directly into the camera, but without any pointing or direct verbal address. Michele Hilmes explains:

direct address on television occurs when the presence of the camera/viewer is directly recognized by the actors on the screen, by variety and talk shows which openly acknowledge the presence of an audience both in the studio and "at home."[55]

This open acknowledgment of the audience of course also occurs in quiz shows. As Margaret Morse points out, direct address tends to break down the well-established barrier in cinematic realism between the spectator/voyeur and the screen space/pro-filmic event:

> The tube or lens is no longer a fixed boundary between the planes of the story and discourse; that boundary shifts forward and backward from us into the illusory depths of the tube—but always includes us in the implied discourse space.[56]

In a big-money quiz show such as *The $64,000 Question*, direct address is mostly used as a lead-in to commercials, which are very smoothly integrated into the flow of the program. An eyeline match at the beginning of commercials links Hal March's look with the products in the commercial. The commercials are also the place where direct verbal address is used most consistently, so that direct address here is used to elicit the viewer's position as a consumer. Direct address is a process that works to make a program more attractive for the audience and thus more profitable for its producer. Television producer/director Tony Verna describes the attractiveness of quiz shows:

> But why do game shows succeed? Like sports, they usually provide a winner—and a loser. They give viewers someone and something to root for and to empathize with. A good game show involves the home audience as well as the studio audience. How many contestants on *The Price is Right* have told Bob Barker how much better they do guessing prices at home?[57]

The commercial reasons for a higher degree of audience involvement notwithstanding, the specific way in which the audience is addressed in live television necessitates a reduction in the control that a television text can exert over its audience.

Although direct address is frequently only used as a cueing device for commercials, its potential is not limited to that. A simple attempt to increase viewer involvement with the text—and especially with the commercial—can easily break down the traditional event-text-viewer relationship that classic realism proposes.

Witnessing an actual event live implies that a copresence exists between spectator and event in time and space.[58] Although live television cannot recreate its presence in space, it does create the impression that time of event and time of broadcast can be equated. Even when parts of a program might have been edited, the diegetic time of the broadcast appears to be identical to the elapsed time of the original event. The use of real time also implies that the action taking place in front of the camera is less controlled and more spontaneous than a heavily edited fictional program. Robert Vianello argues, there "is an objective 'uncontrolled,' unscripted element in the sports program that is missing in live drama or talk-entertainment programs and which the quiz show seeks to incorporate."[59] This presumably unscripted element offers, however, only limited space for spontaneous developments of the diegesis. The structured setup of a talk show or the rigid rules of a quiz show provide a preexisting formula for the development of the diegesis that makes the general outcome of the program more predictable and controllable. Thus, a framework for the partially uncontrolled forms of live television is in place that can limit any transgressions to the realm of specific "rules of the game."

DECENTERING THE AUDIENCE ON *LET'S MAKE A DEAL* AND *THE PRICE IS RIGHT*

Let's Make a Deal was one of the most popular quiz shows of the 1960s.[60] Although it was on prime time for a short time, it enjoyed its highest popularity while it was on NBC daytime (December 30, 1963–December 27, 1968) and ABC daytime (December 30, 1968–July 9, 1976). The 1963 pilot for *Let's Make a Deal*, which Monty Hall hosted, provides some interesting insights into the way in which its producers conceptualized the show. Hall makes the connection between women and consumerism, but he emphasizes the element of agency, which was rather suppressed in previous industry discourses, much more. He talks about women as being in control of finances, and he also hints at the fact that women's activities—trading, swapping, and so forth—will be at the center of the program.

Before the show itself starts, the pilot begins with Hall sitting in the audience section of an empty studio, the set for the pilot. While the camera zooms in on him from a wide shot to a medium shot, he gives an introduction to the program:

> This is television's only trading floor, where every day the individuals who control the finances of America, the women of course, come to make deals. And what's more exciting to a woman than trading or swapping or looking for a bargain! It's suspense every second as men and women bring in their old white elephants and try to deal me out of big cash or big gifts.
>
> Well, do you have a leaky umbrella you'd like to get rid of? You know, I might pay $500 for it. Or, if you're a clever trader and know when to stop, you could drive home in a brand new automobile.

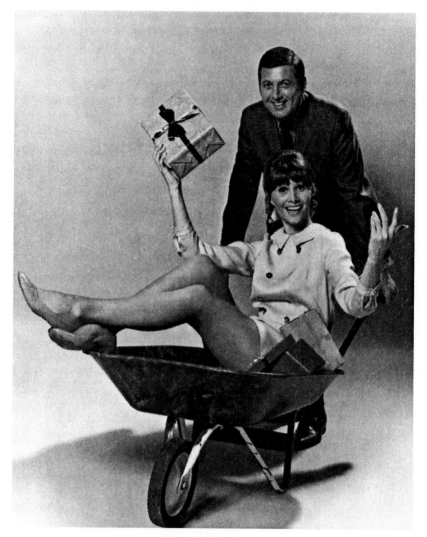

Figure 4.3. Monty Hall and assistant Carol Merrill. *Courtesy Wisconsin Center for Film and Theater Research.*

> On this trading floor, we'll buy, sell, or trade everything and anything, from the aardvarks to scissors. There are millions of deals to be made and we'll make them every day on Let's Make a Deal. Watch, we'll show you how it works.[61]

The Let's Make a Deal set design is also an interesting departure from the mise-en-scène and visual style that dominated quiz shows in the 1950s. Since the mid-1950s quiz shows focused on the host or an expert panel and did not incorporate the home or studio audience as they had done in the late 1940s and early 1950s. The camera position was usually focused on the proscenium stage, where host and contestants were interacting. The audience was only present in occasional reaction shots featuring the family and relatives of contestants. Big-money quiz shows in particular managed to create a strong separation of spectators and participants.

In comparison, *Let's Make a Deal* changes the spatial organization of its set significantly. The center of events in the show is the dealing area, which is in the middle of the audience section. The actual stage of the studio is used only for the display of larger prizes, which are hidden behind curtains. The camera continuously moves in and out of the audience section, alternately being a part of it and facing it. Camera positions in front of the audience or the stage are used primarily to provide cover shots; otherwise the camera (sometimes handheld) enters the audience to focus on the host making deals with audience members. By making the audience section the real stage, which is accomplished mainly through set design and camera style, *Let's Make a Deal* achieves a formal style that almost perfectly replicates Mikhail Bakhtin's description of the collapse of the separation of spectators and participants in carnival.[62]

Similar to my observations on the mise-en-scène of *Let's Make a Deal*, Bodroghkozy also observes specific elements in the visual style of the *Smothers Brothers Comedy Hour* and connects them to attempts to create a stronger impression of participation in the show.[63] Bodroghkozy's analysis of the visual style of the *Smothers Brothers Comedy Hour* indicates that some of the cultural sensibilities of 1960s' counterculture were taken up in individual television programs and incorporated in the form of a show. The element of participation and egalitarianism that seems to inform 1960s' youth/alternative culture structures the development of the form of shows such as *Let's Make a Deal* or the *Smothers Brothers Comedy Hour*:

> The Smothers experimented with a number of concert-in-the-round programs that broke the proscenium arch performance environment and thus brought the audience into the scene. The kind of performance space suggested the folk music/coffee house roots of the Smothers and the non-hierarchical, participatory ideals of that entertainment form.[64]

The aesthetics of the youth culture and counterculture represented a strong contrast to the institutionalization of culture and the cult of the expert that seemed to be prevalent in 1950s' social life.[65] *Let's Make a Deal* seems to have adopted the ideal of participation put forth in youth cultures and countercultures to some extent, even though control of the production process in this instance still primarily lies on the side of cultural institutions such as networks and television production houses.

At the end of the *Let's Make a Deal* pilot, Monty Hall again addresses the camera directly:

> No matter who you are or where you live, you make deals every day of your lives, now we're gonna make more deals in the marketplace tomorrow at the same time, and who knows, somebody may wind up with a stuffed moosehead, a thousand live sardines, $1,000 in cash, or that brand new Pontiac Tempest automobile...caveat emptor.

The host defines making deals or participating in the marketplace as an important element in the practice of everyday life, a strategy that corresponds to the program's focus on common audience members. Although the organization of production might have been able to determine the outer form of *Let's Make a Deal*, fully controlling the performance of the audience members seemed impossible. In 1964, during the first season of *Let's Make a Deal*, audience members, whose active participation in the show had been encouraged, started to wear costumes to attract the host's attention and, "before long, everyone was wearing outlandish costumes."[66] Encouraging studio audience members' participation led to a festival atmosphere, which was not fully controllable by encoding institutions:

> *Deal* began as a simple audience participation show; Hall and the audience were dressed quite conventionally. As the show evolved, it became a circus, with Hall still decked out in suit and tie in front of a crowd of folks in pizza and chicken suits. People had gotten excited on game shows before—but never to the extent that they did on *Deal*.[67]

Monty Hall gives a detailed account:

> About a month into the show, a woman came to the show and brought a sign that said: "Roses are red / Violets are blue / I came here / To deal with you," and I picked her. Well, for the next couple of weeks we had signs flourishing like crazy, and then somebody started wearing a crazy hat to attract my attention. Then it went crazy. They all started wearing all sorts of things."[68]

Overall, *Let's Make a Deal* appears to be a show that in many ways is decentered. The way in which it addresses women as its main audience on the one hand defines them in terms of traditional female roles, but on the other hand also recognizes their agency to some extent. Similarly, the program not only exhibits a dual focus that has the host as the focal point of the show, but that also gives the studio audience a central function that does not fully remain under the host's authority. The resulting form of *Let's Make a Deal* encompasses multiple viewpoints that address the instability of the cultural context from which they emerge.

The Price Is Right was a popular quiz show between 1956 and 1963. Although it already focused on consumer goods at this point, its visual style was fairly similar to other quiz shows of the time. In particular, it did not seriously integrate the studio audience in the show, but relied on a preselected panel of contestants. Its return to network television on CBS daytime in 1972[69] brought a variety of significant changes:

> The Price Is Right, after a hiatus of several years, was altered and revived. The "panel" set was gone, and in its place contestants were chosen from the studio audience and exhorted by announcer Johnny Olsen to "come on down!" to the stage, making the show look a bit more like Monty Hall's Let's Make a Deal.[70]

One of the important new elements on The Price Is Right is its strong integration of the studio audience into the show. As one of its trademarks, the program foregrounds the transition of contestants from the audience section to contestants' row by showing it on camera while the studio audience is wildly cheering. Besides the element of audience involvement, Graham hints at another major change in the look of The Price Is Right, its expressive use of color:

> The original went off the air in 1964 but came back in 1972 when CBS executive Bud Grant asked Goodson for a revival. Goodson said the old show wouldn't work in the '70s—so he revamped Price, making it a high-tech series of pricing games presented in a colorful, noisy carnival atmosphere.[71]

An article in Sponsor, for example, articulates the hope that the proliferation of color television might attract more advertisers to television because color seems to stimulate consumption.[72] An advertisement for The Price Is Right also claims that "the magic of the modern super-market" can be communicated to homemakers through color television.[73] Although individual articles speculate that colorful sets might stimulate consumption, Victoria Johnson also sees the use of color as connected to counterculture style. Johnson emphasizes the importance of bright colors in an episode of the Lawrence Welk Show dealing with rock dances and implies a connection to the visual style of shows more closely connected to the 1960s' counterculture.

> Aesthetically, this segment is very different from the black-and-white period of shows and remains distinct from the syndicated series. Not only are the colors splashy, with clashing contrasts, but the television technology is revved up in floor camera transitions that simulate rapidly animated movement—a departure for

Welk, but characteristic of shows marked by counter-culture appeal such as The Smothers Brothers Comedy Hour or Laugh-in.[74]

Through its reliance on audience-centered games, its emphasis on noisy, excessive audio, and its bright, flashing sets, *The Price Is Right* became a cultural form closely connected to the carnivalesque.

The Price Is Right also develops a decentered viewing position through its proscenium stage setup and its camera style. The camera constantly switches from confronting the audience to entering it and almost becomes part of the studio audience. In a similar fashion, the camera first faces host Bob Barker when he enters the stage, but then reverses its angle to take a position behind Barker, looking at the audience with Barker's back in the frame, approximating an over-the-shoulder shot. *The Price Is Right* repeatedly changes the viewer's position within the screen space and almost completely collapses home viewer, host, studio audience, and contestants. The use of direct address is also particularly pronounced on *The Price Is Right*. For example, Barker talks directly at the camera and additionally points at it while saying, "I welcome you to *The Price Is Right*." In this gesture, he combines four forms of direct address: verbal direct address as well as looking, pointing, and talking at the camera. Through these techniques, the viewers are invited to leave their traditional voyeuristic or detached positions and enter into a quasi-participatory position instead.

The carnival atmosphere of *The Price Is Right* is similar to the one on *Let's Make a Deal* and creates similar connections to stylistic elements of the 1960s' counterculture. The presence of the studio audience in the program, as well as the transition of the contestants to the stage, creates a strong element of participation and immediacy of experience. However, incorporating the sensibilities of the youth culture is accomplished only at the level of style. The audience participation and carnival atmosphere of *The Price Is Right* are not directly connected to the political projects of the counterculture and "promote the form and not the substance of the counterculture's ideals."[75] Importantly games on both *The Price Is Right* and *Let's Make a Deal* are centered around consumption. Both shows regularly provide merchandise such as refrigerators, living room sets, boats, and cars as their top prizes and much of the excessive visual appeal of these shows revolves around the colorful display of such consumer items. Additionally, basic consumer knowledge is also rewarded in many games, for example, when contestants are asked to price merchandise as accurately as possible to win yet another piece of merchandise. On *The Price Is Right*, a contestant might have to identify the correct prices for a can of beans, hair shampoo, pain medicine, a waffle iron, an alarm clock, and a cordless phone to win a $15,000 truck. *Let's Make a Deal* relies on chance to a greater degree, but it also features similar pricing games that emphasize the importance of consumption and address the audience primarily in its role as consumers.

Dismissing shows such as *Let's Make a Deal* and *The Price Is Right* for lacking any cultural significance or for promoting blatant consumerism would be easy, yet they nevertheless represent a departure from the dominant values of the Protestant work ethic. Carnival elements such as the collapse of performers and spectators and the overturning of hierarchies of taste contain a challenge to the "managerial values"[76] of dominant culture. Although these shows effectively decenter the viewing experience and create an excessive and carnivalesque atmosphere, they also naturalize an excess of consumption and normalize consumerism as a central part of U.S. cultural identity.

CONCLUSION

The changes in the quiz show genre in the 1960s and 1970s were driven by both the need to distance quiz shows from their scandalous history and the need to adapt to the changing cultural environment of the times. The quiz show genre was remodeled by redefining the terms *quiz* and *game* and by changing the form of quiz shows correspondingly. Through broadcast industry publications as well as through the evolution of form, quiz shows were redefined as a part of leisure, everyday life, and women's culture. These strategies remove the genre from the respectable and culturally central sphere of elite culture, and they also create a liminal space in which addressing some of the contradictions of dominant culture became possible. The advertisers' demand for new programming that catered to the demographically crucial youth audience gave an additional impetus to create new contents and a new visual style for the quiz show genre. Consequently, quiz shows were able to redefine the traditionally subordinate position of women to some extent. Whereas participation and immediacy enabled new forms of audience identification to appear on quiz shows, the genre continued to rely on excessive consumerism.

The remodeling of the genre demonstrates the ability of production institutions to exert power in shaping the genre according to industry needs. As part of the process of keeping quiz shows an economically productive genre, the industry also revised some of its assumptions as to how quiz shows appeal to their viewers. Through the use of various techniques to create forms of personal address, quiz shows found new ways of appealing to their new target audience, the female consumer. This process implies a turn toward a consumption ethic and a turn toward lower forms of cultural distinction.

Everyday knowledge and knowledge of people became the predominant forms of knowledge used on quiz shows following the scandals. Up to this day, the use of serious or elite forms of knowledge has been the exception on quiz shows, the success of *Who Wants to Be a Millionaire* notwithstanding. However, as the following chapter shows, the instability of identification and the visual excess of programs such as *Let's Make a Deal* or *The Price Is Right* easily gave way to new programs that were invested in a much more stable version of ostensibly normal American values and ideas.

CHAPTER 5

Dating Games

Playing Relationships in 1980s and 1990s Television

Confessions of a Dangerous Mind features a television producer who leads a double life as a trained hit man for the Central Intelligence Agency (CIA).[1] Despite considerable turmoil in his private life, he creates numerous new television programs that draw network attention and that subsequently become highly popular with television audiences in the 1960s, 1970s, and 1980s. The film implies that due to his own corrupt character, this producer is able to tap into some of the base instincts of television viewers and create programs that appeal to the lowest possible taste. *Confessions of a Dangerous Mind* is, of course, based on Chuck Barris's tongue-in-cheek, fictional, and unauthorized autobiography of the same title. Whether Chuck Barris actually ever was an agent and hit man for the CIA remains unclear, but he certainly created several highly popular television shows, including *The Dating Game, The Newlywed Game, Three's a Crowd, Treasure Hunt, The $1.98 Beauty Show,* and *The Gong Show*.[2] Barris's programs were frequently criticized for their crudeness and sexual innuendo. Yet, *Confessions of a Dangerous Mind* argues that Barris's ability to cater to the tastes of the "average American" ensured his ratings successes.

Programs such as those Barris created constitute a significant departure from 1960s and 1970s programs such as *The Price Is Right* and *Let's Make a Deal*, which rewarded skill in gambling and bartering as well as knowledge of consumer products. The ironic character of Barris's shows, which often parody other programs and tend to poke fun at their own contestants, is an even greater departure from the serene and serious atmosphere of programs such as *Twenty-One* or *Jeopardy!*, where so-called serious knowledge forms the basis of competition. Instead, Barris's shows display amazing similarities with a variety of current television programs such as *Blind Date, Joe Millionaire, American Idol,* and *Cupid.* However, the label *reality television* applied to a lot of current television is misleading because it only masks the fact that we are in most cases still dealing with quiz shows. This seeming departure from what is often considered quiz shows or game shows is primarily a shift to new categories of knowledge within the genre.

John Fiske points out that knowledge on quiz shows can be located on a large, hierarchically organized spectrum.[3] His major differentiation is between factual knowledge and human knowledge. The majority of programs Barris created and the majority of programs discussed in this chapter rely on human knowledge. Fiske divides human knowledge further into knowledge of people in general and knowledge of specific individuals. *The Newlywed Game, Joe Millionaire,* and *Blind Date* rely on the interaction among a limited number of individuals in direct contact with each other and therefore require knowledge of specific individuals. *Family Feud,* on the other hand, relies on the more abstract knowledge of a large body of people.

What can be observed in 1980s' and 1990s' television programs is that the use of human knowledge as a basis of competition, which Barris popularized so efficiently, becomes increasingly dominant in the quiz show genre. Whenever *Family Feud* host Richard Dawson shouts "survey says," he evokes a powerful discourse of what it means to be an "average American." As discussed previously, terms such as *common man* or *average man* are ideologically charged and require further scrutiny.

This chapter discusses how notions of "the average man" are connected to a naturalization of dominant values in U.S. culture. One major site for this normalization is the debates over family values that informed much of U.S. political culture in the 1980s and 1990s. The second half of this chapter discusses how issues of gender and sexuality are negotiated in the new wave of dating shows that has populated U.S. television since the mid-1990s.

FINDING THE AVERAGE

The 1970s' and 1980s' television culture saw significant changes, both relating to programming forms and relating to new technologies and regulations. Syndication and independent producers were becoming more common in the television industry and videocassette recorders, pay television, and cable television were all entering U.S. culture.[4] As far as the quiz show genre is concerned, *Let's Make a Deal* continued to run in syndication into the early 1980s and *The Price Is Right* continues to run up to this date. However, new quiz shows that emerged in the late 1970s and early 1980s also provided new forms of competition and new forms of identification. Gambling became an increasingly important element in many quiz shows. *High Rollers*, for example, used a casino setting and featured rolling dice as the main form of competition between contestants. Although trivia were used in toss-up questions to determine which contestant would control the dice, the outcome of the game was primarily decided through luck and gambling strategy.[5] *Card Sharks* is another program that focuses heavily on gambling. Two contestants compete by unveiling a sequence of five playing cards, guessing whether the next card to be turned would be higher or lower than the previous one.[6] After completing two sequences, the winning contestant goes on to play a bonus round in which a sequence of seven cards had to be turned. Starting out with $200, the contestant has to wager part or all of their money on each card. For the final card, the contestant has to wager at least half his or her winnings. Aside from the reliance on gambling that is particularly pronounced on *Card Sharks*, the program also used short questions to determine which player controlled the board. The questions were polls that asked the first contestant to estimate how many people in a poll (usually consisting of 100) answered the poll in a certain way. The second player would then guess whether the actual poll result was higher or lower than the estimate of the first contestant. In contrast to consumption-oriented shows such as *The Price Is Right* and *Let's Make a Deal*, this show did not require knowledge of consumer goods, but instead rewarded those contestants able to predict the responses of average Americans particularly well.

In *Family Feud* the use of the idea of "average" is powerfully combined with the technology of polling.[7] Teams of contestants are required to guess top answers to a survey. At the start of the show, one contestant from each team answers a survey question to win control of the game. The contestant with the most popular answer earns the right for his or her team to continue guessing answers to the survey. If one family gives three wrong answers, the opponent family has a chance to "steal" that round of the game by giving one correct answer. The points that a winning team scored on each survey corresponded to the number of people who responded to the survey. In a bonus round, two members of the winning family guess the most popular responses to five questions. If they attain 200 points, they win $5,000 or, in later versions of the program, $10,000.

Following is a typical survey question on *Family Feud*: Richard Dawson (host): "One hundred people surveyed, top seven on the board. Find the most popular answer. Find something you might do that would require you to undress." The top seven answers were: (1) take a bath/shower, (2) see doctor/physical, (3) model, (4) make love, (5) go to bed, (6) skinny dip, and (7) try new clothes on. The three incorrect answers contestants gave were (1) sunbathe, (2) change clothes, and (3) getting ready for work. Examples of other survey questions include, which magazine is most often bought by U.S.

Figure 5.1. Scenes from *Family Feud*, hosted by Richard Dawson. *Courtesy Wisconsin Center for Film and Theater Research.*

Congressmen (it is *Penthouse*); name the most important possession you have; name a food that tastes so bad, you can't believe it's good for you.

The extensive use of (primitive) survey data suggests that the key skill for the contestants is their ability to understand average Americans. As Warren Susman points out, since their emergence as a scientific method, surveys have been used to provide a seemingly objective way of defining an American average:

> The concept of average was born, a kind of statistical accounting of the people seen as a unit. For a culture that originally had enshrined individualism as its key virtue, interest in the average was now overwhelming. The Average American and the Average American Family became central to the new vision of a future culture....Increasingly, this statistical creature—the average American—became central to cultural thinking and planning.[8]

The discourse of the "average American" Susman observed as early as the mid-1930s takes on an important role in shows such as *Card Sharks* and *Family Feud*. Both programs provide strong incentives for the contestants to conform to notions of normalcy. Audience members derive pleasure from their ability to conform to the definition of average Americans provided through the surveys. Conversely, a failure to understand or reproduce such normalcy demonstrates a lack of common sense. Aside from the fact that the logic of the game encourages contestants and audiences to emulate "normality," *Family Feud* also negates the existence of the "abnormal," that is, the existence of significant difference.

Family Feud reinforces the ideology underlying the discourse of the "average American" on the level of visual and sound design as well. As the title sequence of the show starts, country music is playing and we see both families standing in living room sets. The furniture in both sets is traditional and the families seem to be posing for a family portrait. Once they are introduced, the families leave the living room sets and assume their position behind the game consoles. Their family names appear to be embroidered on oversized pieces of cloth which cover the majority of the background. The overall production design of *Family Feud* evokes traditional, rural, middle-America culture and prefigures the discourse of "old-fashioned" family values that would enter U.S. public life on a large scale in the following years. A variety of elements connect the program to traditional notions of family, not the least of which is the idea that families as a whole actually feud with each other. The discourse of average proposes a model of normalized U.S. culture that reinforces traditional notions of family and conformity. The original *Family Feud*, hosted by Richard Dawson, continued to present its definition of normal Americans until 1985.

CONSERVATISM AND THE DISCOURSE OF DIVERSITY

Several scholars have noted that the 1980s' conservative culture often specifically identified the moral excesses of the 1960s as a source for the presumably sad state of U.S. culture. Aniko Brodroghkozy argues:

> the main impulse galvanizing much New Right activism was a reactionary disgust at "sixties-inspired" reconceptualizations of family, gender, sexuality, patriotism, racism, and other social institutions and values that came under such attack from the young during that decade.[9]

Although the New Right was heavily invested in making the counterculture a scapegoat for a vast array of social evils, the media policies during the Republican administrations of Ronald Reagan (1980–1988) and George H. W. Bush (1988–1992) were considerably more complex. Reagan and Bush championed a conservative ideology of diversity that at least paid lip service to the idea that multiple voices should exist in U.S. media culture. Industry analyst Ken Auletta indicates his concern over the increasing fragmentation of audiences and markets and the breakdown of a national consensus'[10] yet

Reaganite ideology defined this development in economic terms, that is, as a desirable increase in competition and an enhancement of pluralism in the U.S. marketplace. However, the decrease of the power of media conglomerates, which has been an important feature of FCC policy-making for the last twenty years is not necessarily equivalent to a decrease of the political power of these industries.[11] The cable deregulation policies of Mark Fowler and Dennis Patrick, the FCC chairmen appointed during the Reagan administration, relied largely on the belief that the marketplace rather than the FCC should regulate cable television. Fowler theorized that only the marketplace can generate a sufficient degree of diversity.

Fowler and Patrick rejected the classic liberal belief that broadcasters, as lessees of the public airwaves, had a special responsibility to serve that public. Fowler enunciated his ideas in 1984 before an audience of radio and television executives: "It was time to move away from thinking about broadcasters as trustees," he declared. "It was time to treat them the way almost everyone else in society does—that is, as businesses."[12] Although Fowler's agenda was to remove all major structural regulations governing broadcasting, the FCC continuously exerted pressure on the networks to limit the amount of obscenity and violence on television.[13] Whereas Reagan's main political endeavors focused on economics and the military, conservative politics were not limited to these issues.

Lawrence Grossberg identifies three factions within the conservative movement in the Reagan years: cold war conservatives, advocating a strong state with strong military forces; big business capitalists, gearing their policies toward deregulation and the creation of business-friendly policies; and moral traditionalist, focusing on conservative Christian values and the moral renewal of the nation in general.[14] The last of these factions, often referred to as the New Right or the New Conservatism,[15] has had a significant influence on U.S. culture in the 1980s and 1990s. Nevertheless, the power of Reaganism was rooted in its ability to unify the disparate ideological commitments of the various movements within the right into one political unit, often with the help of a common enemy such as Arabs, Communists, or South American drug dealers.

Many critics point out that the political climate of the 1980s and 1990s is characterized by indifference toward politics in general and the lack of alternatives to the dominant political environment of Washington in particular.[16] Traditional politics and the operation of a traditional public sphere have become irrelevant to the lives of many Americans. Alan Wolfe observes, "the attitude of the great majority of Americans to traditional political subjects is an unstable combination of boredom, resentment, and sporadic attention."[17] Larry Grossberg as well as James Hunter agree that in this seemingly apolitical environment, cultural rather than political strategies are the tools with which ideological debates are carried out in the United States.[18] Although this retreat from traditional politics appears to be a withdrawal from politics altogether, it actually represents a shift in the terrain of politics. Increasingly, the most hotly debated issues in U.S. culture revolve around practices that are usually characterized as private rather than public. Whereas political and social consideration have always had an impact on private practices, the New Right deliberately focused political debate on issues such as sexual permissiveness, self-indulgence, and the American family.[19]

THE ORIGINS OF FAMILY VALUES

The definition of *family* as well as the preservation of the family has been an ongoing concern in U.S. culture. From at least the late nineteenth century onward, religious organizations have complained about threats to the family, such as modern life, the Great Depression, or the 1960s' counterculture.[20] However, from the 1960s onward, definitions of the term that did not conform to the religious ideal of a nuclear, patriarchal, and self-sustaining family entered public culture and provided competing discourses on the family. These alternative definitions incorporate mixed-race marriages, homosexual relationships, divorces, single-parent families, and so forth. Many conservative politicians claim that a reversal of the values of the 1960s counterculture is a central part of their agenda.

Even though the Carter administration in particular made attempts to "strengthen U.S. families,"[21] these efforts did not take the more fundamental conflicts over the definition of the term into account and did not produce significant results. The concern over the family was intended to be an inclusive term providing common ground for all participants, yet the struggle over the changing character of the family was at the core of controversy. The 1980 White House Conference on Families created a high degree of controversy:

> During the first three hours of the conference's forums, divorce, homosexuality, violence on television, sex education in public schools, welfare and prayer came up, rose to debate, then fell into the boiling pot of controversy.[22]

The intensity of the debates over these issues, and the role of the family in particular, indicate their ideological centrality, but it also points to the fundamental instability of categories such as gender, sexuality, and the family in contemporary culture.

Shifting away from issues such as economics and national security, private issues became the focus of the political efforts of the New Right. Nostalgia for the traditional family and resentment toward independent women were at the center of this effort.[23] The disarticulation of everyday practices from political argument is part of the larger project of the New Right to redefine private practices through its own moral discourses rather than rational public debate. According to Hunter, the New Right derives its moral authority to regulate the private sphere from basic religious values or "non-negotiable moral 'truths,'" which are beyond debate.[24]

Importantly the FCC's deregulation policies and the New Right's discourses of morality and family are interrelated. The FCC's deregulation of the cable industry and cable's subsequent growth in the 1980s allowed many previously peripheral voices to enter television. The conservative discourse of family values often reemerges in the "trauma-dramas" of the 1980s, movies-of-the-week geared toward a female audience and focused on families in distress. Jane Feuer concludes that these dramas usually advocated "the restoration of the old-fashioned American family" and "reinforce a conservative agenda."[25]

Religious broadcasters in particular were able to enter broadcasting in the 1980s because they usually had strong financial support. Evangelists such as Jimmy Swaggart, James Robinson, Pat Robertson, and Jerry Falwell used cable television to reach a national audience.[26] Programs such as *The PTL Club*, *The 700 Club*, and *The Old-Time Gospel Hour*, all of which were (or are) aligned with the political right, were able to exert political influence and solicit donations through television. J. Fred MacDonald points to the political influence of televangelism:

> The potent New Christian Right melded biblical authority and partisan politics to create a compelling mandate for supporting the Reagan presidency. Many televangelists regularly addressed current political topics. On domestic issues they spoke out strongly against abortion, the Equal Rights Amendment, sex education in schools, girlie magazines, and homosexual rights.[27]

One of the most important new cable channels associated with the New Right was The Family Channel. It was a vehicle for Pat Robertson's *The 700 Club* and offered other religious shows along with reruns of westerns and sitcoms that are considered "family oriented."[28] Additionally, The Family Channel also considers quiz shows particularly family friendly and continually offered them in the 1980s as well as the 1990s.

Although cable deregulation in the Reagan era effectively increased the number of outlets for conservative broadcasters, many critics emphasize that the ideology of the traditional family was never unequivocally embraced in television. Douglas Kellner as well as ElizabethTraube point out that the New Right managed to make issues such as sexuality, morality, and family the center of debate, but that it was not able to impose its moral vision on U.S. culture as a whole.[29] Whereas The Family Channel, for example, was able to put religion and pro-family values at the center of its programming, these values were not necessarily part of other cable services.

THE FAMILY AT PLAY

Quiz shows such as *Family Challenge* (The Family Channel, 1995–1997) reflect the conservative, pro-family orientation of the New Right, but at the same time, several quiz shows in the 1980s focused on gambling, shopping, and consumption. *Card Sharks* (CBS, 1986–1989), *The Joker's Wild* (syndicated, 1977–1986), and *High Rollers* (syndicated 1987–1988) have gambling and luck at the center of their competitions. *The Price Is Right* (CBS, syndicated, 1971–present) and *Wheel of Fortune* (NBC, CBS, syndicated 1975–present), both highly successful in the 1980s, primarily serve as contests for consumer goods. *Sale of the Century* (NBC, 1983–1989) and *Tic, Tac, Dough* (syndicated, 1978–1986) are also primarily competitions for merchandise, which is treated as the center of these shows and is often given star status. *Supermarket Sweep* (Lifetime, 1990–present), *Shop 'Til You Drop* (*Lifetime*, 1991-present), and *Shopping Spree* (Family Channel, 1996–present) are all set in supermarkets or malls and use effective shopping behavior as the basis of their competition.

Quiz shows on cable television in the 1980s and 1990s seem to occupy a fairly limited range of expression. A variety of interactive board games on The Family Channel and shopping and dating shows on a variety of other cable channels represented the full scope of quiz shows on cable television in the 1980s and early 1990s. The media industry regarded cable television as a marketing device to target the home audience and amplify its consumption habits. Under Reaganism, cable was thus seen as way to enhance marketplace pluralism. The range of cable quiz shows offered by the late 1980s efficiently increased the menu of consumer choices, but did not offer an actual increase in the diversity of programming. Nevertheless, one of the central elements of the ideology of the New Right, the centrality of the family, figured prominently in quiz shows of the 1980s and 1990s.

As historians such as Ella Taylor and Elizabeth Traube have shown, the family and personal relationships were frequently at the center of films and television programs in the 1980s.[30] Feuer argues that each narrative form and each genre has specific expressive limitations.[31] For example, she claims that the ideological contradictions of the 1980s needed to be expressed in the open-ended and often contradictory form of the melodramatic prime-time serial. Similarly, quiz shows offer certain advantages in representing personal relationships and the family. Quiz shows focused on human knowledge can be structured so that families, couples, or singles looking for a date are at the center of a program, thereby making centering a game around issues involving personal relationships or the family easier. Because contestants are usually drafted from home or studio audiences, they can be presented as normal, everyday couples or everyday families, a strategy that legitimizes the importance of human knowledge in the genre.

Given the centrality of debates over family values and given the possibilities for representing the family and personal relationships on quiz shows, the proliferation of human-knowledge shows since the mid-1990s is not surprising. Conservative ideologies of family and sexuality clearly informed many of the quiz shows offered on the now defunct Family Channel. Even shows that do not have the creation or maintenance of personal relationships as their premise, such as *Shop 'Til You Drop* and *Family Challenge*, usually have families or couples as contestants. *Shop 'Til You Drop* has two married couples compete against each other in various shopping games and emphasizes teamwork and communication between partners. Interestingly, women usually make decisions regarding the selection of merchandise on this show, implying that women as the center of domestic life "naturally" have a superior knowledge of shopping and merchandise. *Family Challenge* is a show that incorporates both parents and children, who go through a series of guessing games and physical competitions together. Similarly, Nickelodeon's *Family Double Dare* also uses teams of parents and children in its competitions. Both of these shows present happy, functioning, conflict-free families and can be regarded as ideologically charged only in that they repress alternative versions of the concept of family. They create an attractive version of some of the central ideological tenets of the New Right with regard to the family. Hunter describes exactly the moral vision that informs these shows:

> The natural and divinely mandated sexual relationship among humans is between male and female and this relationship is legitimate only under one social arrangement, marriage between one male and one female. Homosexuality, therefore, is a perversion of the natural or created order. Building on this is the conviction that the nuclear family is the natural form of family structure and should remain inviolable from outside (state) interference.[32]

The ideology of the sanctity of the family and the legitimacy of patriarchal authority also informs another human-knowledge show on The Family Channel, *Wait 'Til You Have Kids*.[33] Even in its title this show reiterates the New Right's belief in the primacy of the nuclear family. The show itself has three married couples, some with children, some not yet with children, compete in answering questions about proper parenting. An authority on child-rearing provides the correct answers, which are explained after each round. In the final round, the couple with the most points has to answer seven questions in less than a minute. For each question answered correctly a window in a model house is lit up; when all windows are lit, the couple has won a vacation and some merchandise. The house clearly serves as a symbol of the ideology of domesticity and the family, which the show attempts to perpetuate. During the final round, the host describes numerous unusual behaviors of children at various ages and the contestants take turns at determining whether "that's okay" or whether "that's not okay." After the time is up, the program cuts to a licensed psychologist sitting in an armchair on the side of the set. She gives the correct responses to all the scenarios presented and occasionally elaborates on them. Although *Wait 'Til You Have Kids* does not appeal to biblical/religious authority to present its views on parenting, it uses another—secular—authority figure to lay out the proper functioning of a family. Thus, the moral authority of the discourse of family is reaffirmed and the primacy of family values is legitimated. The closing lines of the show's host summarizes these strategies by saying, "If you already have kids, you know what we are talking about, if not, just wait 'till you have kids."

WHEN GOOD VALUES GO BAD: DATING ON TELEVISION

Programs such as *Wait 'Til You Have Kids, Family Challenge,* or even *Family Feud* incorporated important elements of conservative ideology into a seemingly apolitical and benign fictional structure. Whereas such family-focused programs would seem to espouse a rather narrow set of social values, several cultural studies scholars have reminded us that the representations of gender, sexuality, personal relationships, and the family in the Reagan era were always contradictory and often contested.[34] Aniko Bodroghkozy accordingly applies a Gramscian perspective of culture as contestation when she argues:

> although the Reagan and Bush administrations proved fairly successful in asserting their economic agenda and, to a lesser extent, their foreign policy goals, they largely failed to shift social and cultural common sense away from the tolerance and "permissiveness" that were the fallout of the social-change movements of the 1960s.[35]

The discourses of family values and sexual morality form two of the key battle grounds of 1980s' culture. Dating shows emerge as particularly interesting programming forms in this context. They are centrally concerned with issues of heterosexual coupling and the creation of families and accordingly closely relate to key issues of the 1980s and 1990s.

Dating shows gained a large national audience with the premiere of *The Dating Game* on ABC in 1965. ABC followed the initial success of *The Dating Game* with *The Newlywed Game* in the following season. The *Dating Game–Newlywed Game* pairing reminds us that although only one of those two programs is actually involved in creating new couples, both of them are focused on human knowledge, that is, knowledge of relationships and people of the opposite sex.

A variety of relationship-oriented quiz shows premiered or reappeared in the mid-1980s: *Just Men!* (1983), *The Newlywed Game* (1984–1989), and *All about the Opposite Sex* (1990) had as their basic premise that one set of

Figure 5.2. Host Jim Lange posing with two of his assistants on *The Dating Game*. *Courtesy Wisconsin Center for Film and Theater Research.*

contestants predicts responses from contestants of the opposite sex. *Love Connection* (1983–1988), *The Dating Game* (1986–1989), *Matchmaker* (1987–1988), and *Straight to the Heart* (1989) focused on finding a match between two contestants who would then go on a date. The line of relationship-oriented shows with limited success continued in the early 1990s with shows such as *Bedroom Buddies* (1992), *Love at First Sight* (1992), *Love between the Sexes* (1992–1993), and *Studs* (1991–1993). *Singled Out*, which premiered on MTV in the fall 1995 season has been the most successful relationship-oriented show in the 1980s or 1990s. The show's cohost, Jenny McCarthy, even appeared on the cover of *TV Guide*, along with a report of what was competing on *Singled Out* like.[36] Following the success of *Singled Out*, several other human-knowledge shows premiered in the 1996–1997 season on a variety of cable channels: *Bzzz!* (syndicated), *The Newlywed Game* (syndicated), *The Dating Game* (syndicated), *Love Connection* (syndicated reruns on USA), and *The Big Date* (USA).

Even some of the earlier human-knowledge shows such as *The Newlywed Game* or *Love Connection* often dealt with issues of sex and personal relationships ambiguously. On *Love Connection*, a contestant would select one of three potential partners for a date.[37] After the date, the couple would return for another taping of the show and evaluate the quality of their date. These evaluations were often done in separate interviews to ensure that both contestants were as frank as possible about their experiences. Whereas *Love Connection* often showcased a successful date and even gave periodic updates on the new couple (up to the occasional wedding), host Chuck Woolery also delighted in dates gone bad by dragging out the interviews and emphasizing particularly embarrassing details of bad dates.

Bob Eubanks, the regular host of *The Newlywed Game*,[38] similarly has a reputation for calling attention to embarrassing details of the contestants' lives. In an interview, Eubanks explains his strategy to get contestants inadvertently to reveal intimate details of their lives:

> Say the question is, "What's the strangest thing your wife didn't know about you?" And the guy says, "I wear women's underwear at home." I'll say, "I beg your pardon?" I make him say it again. And then he starts to explain. It's that explanation that becomes funny. And then I'll say, "Wait a minute, pal, you're sitting there in a Marine outfit, and you mean to me that you wear your wife's underwear? You're supposed to be defending our country, aren't you?" Then he starts defending himself. Then I say, "Does anybody else know about this?" And he says no. "Well, they do now."[39]

A show such as *The Newlywed Game* uses sexual innuendo and implicit lewdness as a titillating subtext that makes the program more entertaining, but at the same time the primacy of heterosexual relationships is consistently emphasized. Although homosexual relationships were generally excluded from these shows, in principle a mixed-race couple could appear on *The Newlywed Game*. However, in reality, interracial married couples were rarely on the program. The most recent version of *The Dating Game* (syndicated, 1996–2000) has adopted the same rules for issues of race and sexual orientation.

Figure 5.3. Bob Eubanks, host of *The Newlywed Game. Courtesy Wisconsin Center for Film and Theater Research.*

The most prominent 1990s dating show on television, *Singled Out,* consciously evokes the history of dating shows and parodies these shows.[40] Other quiz shows on MTV, such as *Remote Control* (1987–1991) and *Idiot Savants* (1996), have previously parodied traditional quiz shows, for example, by using a set resembling a basement apartment and by humiliating contestants who give wrong answers. Similarly, the element of sexual innuendo and implicit lewdness, which serves as a subtext in earlier human-knowledge shows, is brought to the foreground on *Singled Out*.

Singled Out consists of two separate parts in which either a male or a female contestant (the "picker") picks a date from a pool of about fifty candidates. All of the contestants are between eighteen and twenty-six years old, representing the key sector of MTV's viewership. In the first round, the categories through which the dates are selected often refer to bodily features such as chest size, length of legs, hair color, size of the "package," and so forth. As a result, contestants make selections primarily based on rather superficial preferences. In the second round, the six to ten candidates who remain after the selections of the first round compete with each other in humiliating games, such as barking like a dog or inventing a new dance. Candidates frequently attempt to get the attention of the pickers by making sexual allusions during the competition. In the third round, the three remaining candidates have to match their preferences on dating, sex, consumption, and other lifestyle issues with those of the picker. The candidate closest to the picker's preferences wins a date with him or her. The overt sexual references and the foregrounding of the physical features and sexual prowess of *Singled Out* contestants tend to characterize the process of dating and personal relationships in general as tentative, superficial, and often ridiculous. The star persona of the cohost of *Singled Out*, Jenny McCarthy, provides an additional layer of meaning to the show. A former *Playboy* playmate, she dresses in tight and revealing clothes and often overemphasizes the sexual allusions on the program. Whereas McCarthy frequently pushes some of the male contestants in the dating pool around and insults their appearance and behavior, she also serves as an overdetermined sex object on the program. Her dubious star image thus reinforces the hypersexual character of the show. At the same time, McCarthy's playmate history and behavior is an additional attraction for the main audience for *Singled Out*, young males in their teens and early twenties.

Singled Out parodies earlier dating shows, but the resulting hypersexual excess did little to change the program's basic heterosexual outlook. Only on one occasion did the show stage a special gay/lesbian edition in which the rules stayed exactly the same, except that the pickers got dates of the same sex. This episode was broadcast only in 11 P.M. time slots instead of *Singled Out*'s typical early prime-time slot.

Nevertheless, the taboo of interracial dating that plagued earlier dating shows was often reversed on *Singled Out*. Because the picker does not see the contestants, guessing the race or ethnicity of the candidates in the dating pool was difficult. Additionally, the predetermined categories for selection in the first round of the game were adjusted during the first season of the show to avoid any criteria that might eliminate candidates based on race.

MTV's *Singled Out* is in direct opposition to the legitimation of hetero-sexual marriages and nuclear families The Family Channel advocates. It rel-ativizes the value of personal relationships and refuses to accept the absolute moral values that a show such as *Wait 'Till You Have Kids* espouses. *Singled Out* is as much an ironic comment on other dating shows as it is a dating show itself. Its relativization of the discourse of family values is closely con-nected to liberal, progressive ideologies that do not recognize absolute moral authority. Hunter points out, "moral authority on the progressivist side of the cultural divide tends not to be burdened by the weight of either "natural law," religious prerogative, or traditional community authority."[41] However, the primacy of heterosexual relationships is still in place on *Singled Out*, even though the excess of sexual allusions and the narrow focus on contes-tants' physical qualities caricatures traditional gender roles and sexual behavior patterns.

MTV and The Family Channel have created distinctively different versions of human-knowledge quiz shows. Most of the other 1990s' human-knowledge shows tend to affirm the centrality of personal relationships, but they do not exclusively conceptualize relationships within a patriarchal family. Sexual innuendo and discussions of extramarital sex are acceptable on *The Dating Game*, *The Big Date*, and *Bzzz!*[42] Both on *Bzzz!* and on *The Big Date*, contestants' physical features are frequently emphasized. Contestants regularly wear tight, revealing clothes on both shows, and *Bzzz!* begins by introducing its contestants standing behind a back-lit, semitransparent screen that allows the picker to examine the contours of the contestants' bodies very closely. *The Big Date* also offers contestants selected by a picker to select yet another contestant as a date, and on *Bzzz!* contestants who have already been selected for a date can choose to accept merchandise prizes instead of going on a date. On these shows, personal relationships are characterized by a large degree of instability, which is related to Elizabeth Traube's claim that the discourses of family and sexuality in the 1980s have become destabilized.[43]

THE PATHOLOGY OF DATING

The instability of relationships that characterized 1990s' dating shows contin-ued to be a central feature of a variety of new shows that premiered between the fall of 1998 and 2001. This section focuses on four shows: *Change of Heart*, *Temptation Island*, *Elimidate*, and *Blind Date*.[44] Out of these four, only Fox's *Temptation Island* is a regularly scheduled network program; the other three programs are syndicated and usually broadcast in late-night time slots. An increased sense of ambivalence regarding the viability of stable heterosex-ual relationships characterize all of these programs. Whereas *Elimidate* and *Blind Date* use the fairly standard premise of arranging a date for its contes-

tants, *Change of Heart* and *Temptation Island* vary this formula by pairing couples already in a relationship with potential new partners. *Change of Heart*
only allows couples who do not live together to appear on the show, whereas
Temptation Island features several couples who had been living together.
Temptation Island was heavily criticized after it revealed that one of its couples had not disclosed that they had a child together, and the couple was
eventual dismissed.

   Change of Heart invites couples on the show who have "come to a
crossroads in their relationship." After showcasing the couple's complaints
about their current relationship and their demands for an ideal partner in an
interview at the beginning of the show, *Change of Heart* then sets up each
partner on a date with a potential new mate. In the second half of the show,
both partners are reunited in a studio set and the host questions them about
their experiences. Occasional video clips illustrate the highlights of their
dates. At the end, the people that each partner dated are brought out on
stage and each partner has to make a decision, or, as the program's official
Web site states:

> Following their separate dates, the original couple returns to dis-
> cuss whether they have a future together or if one or both of
> them has [sic] had a "change of heart." The always exciting and
> much anticipated ending of each episode either finds the original
> couple reuniting, with a renewed and revitalized relationship, or
> potentially two new couples heading down the road to
> romance.[45]

Although the programs pretends to operate on the vaguely therapeutic
premise of helping people understand where their relationship is headed, in
reality *Change of Heart* attempts to create or magnify problems in a relationship to ensure conflict. The structure of *Change of Heart* is built toward a
climax—the much-anticipated ending of the program mentioned previously—that almost by definition has to be the couple's end. If the couple
stays together, the program's narrative returns to a distinctly anticlimatic
status quo. Accordingly, the studio audience on *Change of Heart* often cele-
brates spectacular, conflict-ridden breakups enthusiastically. An episode
summary further illustrates this point:

> Jennifer and Kenneth have been together for three years, after he
> stole her from one of his friends! But their relationship (especially
> their sex-life) has seen happier times. It seems like these two
> have gone from being "love bunnies" to something a little more
> platonic! Listen to Kenneth's gripe: "When we first met, we were
> like jackrabbits! She always wanted it. Now, she doesn't want a
> thing. She wants nothing to do with it!" Kenneth's aching for
> more action, but Jennifer gripes that he's too insensitive to her

needs! She thinks that their sex-life might heat up a bit if only he'd show her more affection in public! Tune in Wednesday to see if these two former jackrabbits will stay together or go their separate ways![46]

This description easily foregrounds the conflict potential for this couple and also focuses on their sex life as a prime source for this conflict. Also remarkable is how readily traditional gender roles are integrated into this episode summary. Kenneth is cast in a traditional male role, demanding more sex, whereas Jennifer appears to have the corresponding stereotypical female need for more public displays of affection.

Temptation Island varies the idea of testing a relationship by separating four unmarried couples for two weeks and putting the four men and the four women on opposite ends of a tropical island. The two groups live in separate retreats, where they are exposed to thirteen eligible singles from the opposite sex. The contestants go through a series of dates and social events, eliminating a number of the available singles until they choose the single most attractive for them for a final date. At the conclusion of the multiepisode program, the couples reunite to discuss their experiences and to make a decision about the future of their relationship. The guide to *Temptation Island* describes the show's appeal:

> Four unmarried couples have embarked on an incredible journey. Although they are in long-term relationships, they have traveled to a remote Caribbean island to test their devotion to one another and answer the ultimate question, "Have I found 'The One' or is there someone better out there?"[47]

Similar to *Change of Heart*, *Temptation Island* tries to pass itself off as valid help for the couples' relationships. However, unlike *Change of Heart*, none of the couples in the first installment of *Temptation Island* chose to end their relationship. Host Mark Walberg, who also hosts USA's *The Big Date*, frequently emphasizes that the couples are supposed to make serious choices, undermining the logical structure of *Temptation Island*. The tropical island setting, the sequence of dates in which contestants are involved, and various other events such as pool parties and diving lessons all are arranged to maximize temptation. Walberg's comments at the program's conclusion provides an interesting contrast:

> As we said from the beginning, the journey for our couples has been about choices, choices that they hope will provide the answers to the questions of their hearts.... Tonight, here, they will make their most important choice—whether to continue their lives together as couples or leave Temptation Island alone.

The program's conclusion reemphasizes the drama and seriousness that Walberg's comments try to create. The setting for the finale is on the beach, at night, in front of a campfire. Low-key, dramatic music is playing in the background. Although the program does not actively encourage a couple either to break up or to stay together, the conclusion's solemn mood sets the stage for the couples to continue their relationships. The conversation between Andy and Shannon, one of the four couples, illustrates this point:

MARK WALBERG: Have you thought about what Andy is doing, Shannon could be doing?

ANDY: Shannon and I will go home and we'll disclose everything. Everything that happened, she'll be up front with me and I'll be upfront with her.

WALBERG: Assuming, of course, you guys go home together.

After implying that she had sex with her "dream date," Tom, Shannon declares that she wants to spend the rest of her life with Andy. Both agree to stay together as a couple. Whereas Walberg toys with the notion that one of the couples might break up, the program is designed to accommodate a reunited couple that stays together more easily than a couple that breaks up. However, the overall setup of *Temptation Island* certainly leaves open the opportunity for such a breakup. Because the show needs to maintain suspense we have to expect that at least some couples will break up in future episodes.

Change of Heart and *Temptations Island* still approach relationships with a minimum amount of seriousness; both *Elimidate* and *Blind Date*, however, revel in presenting dates that create conflict and humiliation. Both shows set up singles on dates with people they have not seen before, thus avoiding the danger of being blamed for a broken relationship. *Elimidate* focuses on one main contestant, either male or female, and arranges one date with four singles of the opposite sex. Similar to many other dating shows, the main contestant then goes through a series of events with the other singles to eliminate one contestant per round. The remaining single from three rounds of eliminations is then considered the ideal date for the main contestant. *Elimidate* primarily emphasizes the process of rejecting potential partners, making this process highly public. Video segments showing the competing dates evaluating each other and invariably trying to make negative remarks about their competition comprise a central part of the program. The program produces one couple by the show's end, however, the adversarial selection process comprises the majority of the program.

Blind Date, however, has institutionalized the process of ridiculing contestants even more. Cameras continuously observe the couple as they take part in various activities, some of them physical (workouts, karate lessons, boat rides, dancing), some of them social (dinner, bar). The following provides a description of a typical date:

> Vanessa has two things going for her, bet you can't guess what they are! Her date Randy, who looks like he just got beat up by the Hell's Angels stylists, notices them right away and doesn't stop noticing them all night. Vanessa doesn't seem to mind, ever since she got her uh, new additions, they've become her most lethal weapon. They can make men leap in a single bound, jump over tall buildings, and expose themselves on busy streets. Randy not only spends the entire date drooling over Vanessa and the twins but he also gives her the key to wind him up like the toy he is, and does all that she commands, including dropping his pants on Melrose. To finish the evening, they decide to go hot tubing. And when Vanessa takes her top off, Randy's eyes come out of his head! Did the hot tub work its magic? Or is Randy just another victim of Vanessa and her deadly chest? Tune in and find out![48]

This date included a returning feature on *Blind Date,* the hot tub encounter. Here contestants are given the opportunity to shed most or all of their clothes and display their physical attraction to each other. Not surprisingly, the program showcases good-looking contestants in their early twenties with well-exercised and highly toned bodies. *Blind Date* seems to endorse a philosophy that foregrounds physical appearance over other qualities in a person, although the program also sarcastically comments on that same obsession with physical appearance. As the previous quote demonstrates, significant time is spent commenting on Vanessa's breasts and Randy's reaction to them. The contestants are obviously cast for their physical appearance, yet, ironically, the program seems to distance itself from its own practices. However, the postmodern self-reflexive commentary in which *Blind Date* engages hardly undermines the obsession with physical appearance and sex. This reflexivity is also performed through other techniques. Instant commentary accompanies most actions of the two people on a date. Small pop-up graphics constantly appear on screen, commenting on the contestants' real motivations (for example, seducing their date) or their past relationships. When contestants act particularly awkward or rude, a pertinent, derogatory comment is provided. Although the bodily features of the contestants and their often inane conversations are frequent targets for *Blind Date*'s commentary, the show often focuses on the contestant's personal background:

> Darin is a recently divorced flight instructor, who is very willing to jump back into the game. Sheree is a beauty pageant contestant who wants a man to love her for who she is on the inside, not on the outside....Darin tells her that he has a daughter,

which gives Sheree some doubt about the date. To try something a little different and to keep the date going, they go to build their own miniature dream home at Small Treasures. This gives each a small insight to their personalities. Darin takes Sheree to dinner and begins to find out what she does for a living. The two hit it off so well that it isn't long before Sheree suggests the old hot tub ... this is *Blind Date*![49]

In this excerpt the contestants' preoccupation with physical features is again emphasized alongside the standard hot tub sequence. Interestingly, this episode summary emphasizes the fact that Darin is recently divorced and has a daughter. The fact that the show singles out this particular issue indicates that the irreverence that the show displays toward relationships and sexuality might not be entirely genuine. Rather than having successful dates as its primary goal, *Blind Date* showcases negative dating behavior, and, by extension, behavior in relationships in general.

Blind Date, along with other recent dating shows, creates a new normative behavior model that does not explicitly endorse the sexual politics of the New Right, but instead showcases the seeming absurdity of personal relationships not confined by a restrictive moral agenda. Although no straightforward, positive model of traditional relationships exists, *Blind Date* is structured around the absent norm of heterosexual marriage and the nuclear family.

CONCLUSION

Human-knowledge quiz shows in the 1980s and 1990s exhibit some ambivalence about the validity of categories such as sexuality, family, and relationships, yet they do not fundamentally question the primacy of traditional, heterosexual relationships and patriarchal family structures. The predominance of the 1990s' human-knowledge quiz shows has its roots in the shifts in the U.S. political culture that the New Right initiated in the 1980s. However, shows such as *Singled Out* or *Change of Heart* increasingly relativize the value of personal relationships, refusing to accept the absolutism of conservative morality. At the same time, these shows do not offer any positive alternative for personal relationships. Whereas a show such as *Blind Date* destabilizes heterosexual coupling and personal relationships in general, it is still obsessed with sex as a driving force and maintains a position of compulsory heterosexuality.

Quiz shows in the 1980s and 1990s play an important role in the naturalization of dominant values in U.S. culture. This process of normalizing is accomplished in shows such as *Card Sharks* or *Family Feud* through the use of surveys representing various examples of the ways in which "normal Americans" act and think and, implicitly, how they *should* act and think.

Dating shows present the norm of heterosexual coupling, but they also display the destabilization of this norm that has taken place in the last two decades. The dating shows that appeared between 1998 and 2001 transform the ritual of coupling as it is traditionally enacted into a ritual of dis-coupling. They illustrate the volatile state of relationships while they illustrate the New Right's failure to impose its restrictive politics of family and sexuality.

CHAPTER 6

Interactive Control

Quiz Shows and New Media Technologies

On December 1, 1994, quiz shows became highly visibile on television when the Game Show Network started broadcasting. Backed by Sony Pictures, the Game Show Network features reruns of quiz shows from the 1950s through the 1990s plus several original programs. The ever-expanding spectrum of program choices on cable television, catering to highly specialized and relatively small audiences, facilitated the creation of the Game Show Network. The concept of narrowcasting spawned specialized channels for sports, comedy, auto racing, soap operas, news, home improvement, cooking, and, last but not least, quiz shows. At the same time, executives in the burgeoning cable television industry believed that the public would demand increasing interactive services via cable. As shown previously, the broadcast industry frequently emphasized the ability of quiz shows to elicit special types of "interaction" between the programs and their viewers or listeners, usually termed *audience participation*. Interactive elements subsequently appeared on a variety of cable systems and began to be featured on the Game Show Network. The authors of *The Encyclopedia of TV Game Shows*, some involved with the Game Show Network themselves, emphasize the interactive future of the genre:

> It seems the catch phrase for 1990s television is "interactive" and game shows will be at the head of the pack, along with home shopping channels and pay-per-view feature-film viewing. Interactive television is in its infancy, and it appears to have

great potential for game shows, since it allows for direct viewer participation.[1]

This chapter first reviews cable television's development, especially the discourse of cable as a democratic and pluralistic technology. Next, the chapter considers the possibilities and limitations of interactivity with regard to the Interactive Network, a service which, in the 1990s, offered interactive experiences with various television programs, especially sports and quiz shows. The chapter concludes with a discussion of the way interactive elements have been integrated into quiz shows in the 1990s.

CABLE, TECHNOLOGY AND THE DISCOURSE OF PLURALISM

In the late 1960s, the established system of broadcasting, with three networks providing an almost-exclusive nationwide service and dominating the production process, increasingly came under attack. The Nixon administration (Vice President Spiro Agnew in particular) joined the prevailing criticism of the network broadcasting system because of a perceived liberal bias in the network news operations. A political desire to break the network oligopoly in part motivated many of the regulatory changes in the 1970s. The main efforts in this respect were the Financial Interest and Syndication Rules, the Prime Time Access Rule, and the beginning deregulation of the cable industry. Each of these efforts had a significant impact on the television industry in the following decades.

Especially in the 1980s, the Reagan administration and its conservative supporters defined cable television as a pluralistic technology increasing diversity in the media industry. This discourse of pluralism is also applied to interactive technologies such as QUBE or Interactive Network, which emerge alongside cable television. The ideology of pluralism is seen most distinctly in the development of interactive technologies .

The discourse of cable television and pluralism has its beginnings in the late 1960s and early 1970s, when many diverse groups advocated the development of cable television on a large, nationwide scale. Although some of these groups were working in the interest of the media industry, many other groups were interested in cable primarily for social reasons. Many progressive groups, such as the Americans for Democratic Action (ADA), the American Civil Liberties Union (ACLU), and numerous African-American organizations favored cable television because they believed that it could have a significant, positive social impact and "resolve the power relations among people that caused racism, poverty, and international strife."[2] One of the institutions involved in the debates over cable television, the President's Task Force on Communications Policy, suggested that cable would provide an opportunity for minorities to express themselves and alleviate some of the social tensions of the late 1960s.[3] Similarly,

Ithiel de Sola Pool argues that cable has the potential to increase the diversity of opinion on television if a large population has easy access to cable and can voice its opinion that way.[4]

As Thomas Streeter makes clear, the diverse advocates of cable television created a discourse on cable that displayed a naïve belief in the beneficial social impact of a technology that seemed to exist outside of social, cultural, or institutional forces as an "autonomous entity that had simply appeared on the scene as the result of scientific and technical research."[5] Don Le Duc also connects the belief in the utopian benefits of cable television to a change in the mediated communication process. He argues that cable will result in a "reversal of the traditional roles of mass communications,"[6] so that audience members would not be passive consumers of media messages, but "would participate actively in their selection and dissemination."[7] Similarly, the ADA described cable as a technology that could replace the network television system of "one-way 'broadcasting' to mass 'audiences'" with a system that encourages "active participation."[8] These utopian discussions of cable television, which were closely linked to a severe critique of the established broadcast media, echo previous historic developments, for example, the development of broadcast radio, which concentrated power over the form and content of broadcasting in the hands of a small number of corporate broadcasters. Bertold Brecht discusses early radio from a similar perspective and points out that radio is a distribution medium, that is, a medium that allows only one-way communication.[9] For Brecht radio thus does not live up to its potential as a true communication medium. To fulfill this potential, it would have to let the audience "receive as well as transmit... [and] let the listener speak as well as hear."[10] Brecht's vision of radio is a technology that allows the audience to create and send messages. The ideal of a communication technology that does not limit participation to a reactive relationship has been debated extensively. The utopian discourse of cable television and pluralism connects cable to this ideal.

The FCC ultimately allowed cable television to develop into a nationwide service provider, but defined cable primarily as a commercial system, taking into consideration only a limited amount of progressive thought on cable. The model for cable television that ultimately prevailed is based on the idea that "a system governed by individual choices in the marketplace"[11] can create equal access for all social groups. Le Duc clearly opposes the notion that an increase in the number of available channels also will increase the range of alternative services and the diversity of programs.[12] He claims that examples from early radio, 1950s television, and cable show that marketplace regulation always leads to economic centralization and the limitation of alternative services. Nevertheless, FCC and congressional regulatory policies in the late 1970s and early 1980s eliminated most of the remaining open access requirements for cable television, so that diversity on cable television now relies completely on whatever benevolent power may exist in the marketplace.

Although the access of socially marginal groups to cable television is still limited, Streeter observes that the cable industry has had a limited degree of success in presenting a greater diversity of channels and ideologies on television:

> Channel surfers can now easily hop between the right-wing social conservatism of the Family Channel and the sexual liberalism of a Dr. Ruth Westheimer—perhaps not the best that has been thought and said in either camp, but at least a range of values much broader than was ever common on the politically timid big three networks.[13]

Still, the utopian promise of diversity through the technology of cable has not been realized. This fact is often explained through reference to the high degree of monopolistic control of capitalist enterprises over the television industry, however, the ideological processes that limit diverse expression in the media are often not investigated.[14] What matters is not whether five or fifteen transnational companies control cable television, but rather that the organization of cultural production that these companies represent will limit the range of expression on cable. In other words, the fact that the companies that control cable are firmly rooted in a patriarchal and capitalist culture will set certain limits to cable's range of expression.

INTERACTIVE NETWORK

The *Interactive Network* is a technology that had been advertised intensively in various large television markets throughout the winter of 1994–1995. It enabled television viewers to predict results or single plays in sports events while they are aired and similarly allowed viewers to play along with quiz shows and television dramas. Sacramento-based Interactive Network started limited operations in April 1994 and planned to expand to nationwide coverage in September 1994. However, it gained only 5,000 subscribers in five markets (Chicago, South Bend, Indianapolis, San Francisco, and Sacramento). Despite the backing of large media corporations such as NBC, Tele-communications Inc., Gannett Co., and A. C. Nielsen, Interactive Network never gained enough subscribers to ensure profitability and ceased operating in 1996. Interactive Network filed for Chapter 11 bankruptcy protection in 1998. Its patents are now used in a new interactive television venture called Two Way TV.

Interactive Network used a large, remote control–like input device to record and transmit (through a phone line) individual results to a center where the best participants nationwide and regionally are identified and rewarded with small prizes. A monthly rental fee ($19.95) was assessed for unlimited use of each input device.

This technology offers the opportunity to enhance the involvement—or interaction—of television viewers with some of their favorite television shows. In particular, most of the shows offered for interaction belong to genres usually assumed to create highly involved audiences. Sports fans are often termed "armchair quarterbacks"; similarly, viewers of detective dramas are often called "armchair detectives"; quiz show viewers are always assumed to be attracted to their favorite shows because of the opportunity to compete with contestants from their living room. Interactive Network created new opportunities to get actively involved in popular television programs and to experience a new way of consuming television. Or, as Interactive Network's merchandising catalogue states: "Don't just watch TV, play TV." A November 1993 Interactive Network Member Entertainment Guide describes the opportunities offered:

> Interactive Network has always held a special appeal for sports fans and the reason was never clearer than this month. Major tournaments for three big sports are under way. Football and hockey are joined by basketball as we move deep into the Fall sports season....
>
> Of course, not all IN [Interactive Network] members stick with sports. Some of our most heavily played programs are in the non-sports category. If you're a game show lover, there's a new Family Feud tournament starting this month.
>
> For all our IN Games fanatics, look for the *IN Games Fab Four* tourney. And the *Murder, She Wrote* tournament continues, with a chance to win a Murder Mystery Train Trip leaving from the Denver station![15]

Advertisements for Interactive Network emphasized its potential for the whole family to have fun together, its ability to connect the players to a nationwide network of other participants with similar interests, and its potential to create new forms of interaction between television viewers and television programs. Interactive Network's primary focus on sports and quiz shows supports the conventional wisdom of the broadcast industry that quiz shows invite the use of special participatory features. Despite the utopian potential that seems to exist in interactive technology, most writing in the trade media and in scholarly journals offers a limited definition of *interactivity*: Interactivity is primarily seen as matter of consumer choice, where the viewer or user is only active insofar as he or she chooses from a limited number of preselected commodities or programs. At the same time, scholars such as Bertold Brecht and Raymond Williams discuss communication technology in general and interactive technology in particular as tools that have the potential to enable new forms of democratic interaction.[16] Interactive technology thus seems to engender constant dispute because the potential of interactive technology that some scholars see is only rarely developed in practice. John Caldwell offers a convincing critique of the concept of interactivity, demonstrating that most forms of interactivity exist primarily to offer a limited range of merchandise, games, or cable channels:

> Interactivity [is] not a cybernetic product, but a way for programs to seal a relationship with viewers.... The interactive cybernetic future of the 500-channel environment looks suspiciously like a marketplace, pure and simple.... Interactivity, apparently, means to suture oneself via menus to existing channels or to interactive games, which are not interactive at all.[17]

The notion of suturing the audience to interactive programming is, of course, reminiscent of various audience participation techniques found on radio quiz shows. Using this precedent from radio history, it is not surprising that interactivity is primarily connected to the marketplace. The validation of the common man or the possibility for democratic interaction quickly gives way to consumerism.

The case of Interactive Network raises several interesting questions about interactivity and communication technologies. Generally, we need to consider how communication technology is involved in the construction and maintenance of modern capitalist societies. Understanding future forms of democracy will depend to a significant degree on understanding the relations between power and technology that construct the space of democracy. Locating Interactive Network within the body of theories of globalization and modernity helps to understand communication technology within these macrolevel social considerations. In contrast, recent theoretical and empirical research has attempted to investigate the institutional restrictions that in many ways are imposed on information and communication technologies (ICT) and that shape these technologies in practice. Interactive Network advertising material and user's manuals analyzed from this perspective will thus create a more complex view of the constraints and possibilities for participation in this specific technology.

Interactive Network can then also be situated in the context of the development of broadcast media in the United States. Precedents from the history of the U.S. media system form an important ideological pattern used to define Interactive Network to a significant degree.

MEDIA, MODERNITY, CONTROL

The experience of modernity is frequently seen as closely linked both to modernity's underlying forms of industrial organization and to the new forms of social organization that parallel the emergence of industrialization and modernity. The role that media play in modern and postmodern societies seems to be very central, but is nevertheless often not theorized adequately. Looking at the role of media in modernity can help to explain the utility and the appeal of communication technologies in general and of the Interactive Network in particular.

Anthony Giddens sees the separation of space and time as a central element of modernity. He describes it as the process of disembedding of institutions that increases time-space distanciation. Social activity is taken out of its local contexts and is then "restructur[ed] across indefinite spans of time-space."[18] Globalization in particular (as an important element of modernity) disembeds specific localities from their immediate contexts and reembeds them in potentially worldwide social and spatial relations. Due to the changed character of social relations, modern societies depend significantly on technology to overcome the disembedding tendencies that are a major consequence of modernity. However, Giddens does not elaborate on how "disembedded" communities can be maintained or how communication technologies are involved in these processes. We may reasonably assume that communication technologies are centrally involved in producing some of the problems that modernity generates, while also providing a solution to some of the problems of modernity.

Raymond Williams offers an explanation of the role of communication technology in the development and maintenance of society in modernity.[19] In the highly (physically) mobile world of modernity, Williams sees the communication media as central elements in the creation of unified communities. A paradox that Williams calls *mobile privatization* characterizes modernity: on the one hand, industrialization has increased the mobility of the individual (for example with the automobile), but on the other hand, it has isolated the individual in the privacy of suburban single-family homes. Broadcasting and other communication technologies are part of a solution to this problem because they make exerting control over a dispersed social structure and bringing a picture of the outside world into the home possible. More specifically, Williams sees media systems emerging for the production and reproduction of ideology. Newspapers, for example, are a reaction to "the development of an extended social, economic and political system and a response to a crisis within that system." Media develop as institutions for the "transmission of an ideology."[20] They can be seen as a new form of creating communities, of "social integration and control."[21] Thus, the development of communication technologies can be understood as a complementary development to Giddens's time-space distanciation. They reconnect disembedded institutions and practices so that new forms of social organization can emerge. However, Williams adds the issue of control and ideology as important additional dimension to contemporary thinking about modernity.

Particularly in the context of network broadcasting systems the issue of centralized control over a widely dispersed and potentially individualized audience has to be of fundamental concern.

However, the notion of control is not necessarily clearly defined. Williams thinks of control in terms of an ideology that is produced and disseminated through media technology. In contrast, James Beniger points out that modern mass media are to a significant degree instruments of economic control over audiences.[22] They satisfy the need of bureaucracies (another central element of industrial capitalism) to create a regulated and predictable economic system. Importantly, controlled feedback systems for the mass media are not primarily in the service of the consumer-citizen, but are an important element of bureaucratic control:

> These [film and broadcasting] media were not sufficient to effect true control, however, without a means of feedback from potential consumers to advertisers, thereby restoring to the emergent national and world markets what Durkheim had seen as an essential relationship of the earlier segmental markets: communication from consumer to producer.[23]

For Beniger the media and its related technologies are instruments to control consumption behavior and to monitor audience behavior, whereas Williams emphasizes the ideological aspects of communication technology. Nevertheless, the idea of mobile privatization reminds us that communication technology can serve many interests at once. Consequently, communication technologies are always contested terrain, in theory as well as in practice. They can serve various forms of control, but they can also serve the development of autonomous cultural practices. The ultimate uses and consequences of communication technologies can only be determined in specific historical situations.

All communication technologies, including interactive television systems, have to be seen as a potential that can be used for various forms of centralized control as well as for increasing the agency of the audiences using them. The following sections discuss the possibilities Interactive Network promises and offers.

COMMUNICATION TECHNOLOGY: PRACTICE AND CONSTRAINTS

Although challenging the dominant definitions of new technologies and their uses is always possible, these technologies also tend to impose certain limitations on its potential for being appropriated in practice. Because ownership of new technologies is usually in the hands of capitalist institutions (nations or corporations), one must assume that the owners of these technologies will develop these technologies so that they will predominantly support the interests of their owners. Capitalist ownership of new technologies thus provides a framework from which alternative uses of technology have to start. Importantly, however, ownership frames alternative practices, but it does not have the power to determine them effectively.

An example of this process of framing can be observed in Interactive Network. The hardware and software of this technology are shaped so that television viewing patterns can be regulated: To play Interactive Network games competently and successfully, staying in front of the television set constantly is necessary, as is, consequently, watching the commercials as well. Because Interactive Network is part of a commercial broadcast system and relies on the support of networks and advertisers for its success, a clear interest exists in sustaining this system and in involving the audience more closely in the game as well as the commercials. One of the features that is not fully developed in the Interactive Network system, but that is described in detail in the control unit's owner's guide, is the possibility for interactive advertising:

Interactive Advertising
How would you like to win a vacation while enjoying IN's wide world of games? Get in-depth details on products advertised during the program breaks? Even take advantage of special offers not available anywhere else? Now you can, with IN's next level of advertising—Interactive Ads.
Keep watching your control unit screen during the commercial breaks. Follow the prompts on screen, and use the keyboard to enter your information. You'll be able to:
- Compete in IN's mini-games, like Trivia, for terrific bonus prizes.
- Order special-value merchandise available only to IN members.
- Request details on advertised products. Interactive Network will relay the information you give us directly to the advertiser for fulfillment.
The next time you plug in your phone cord, after interacting with a special advertising segment, your responses will be sent to us along with your scores.[24]

This passage shows clearly that commercial interests motivate Interactive Network and attempt to construct the technology in such a way that its uses are framed to serve the interests of advertiser-supported commercial broadcasting. Consumption clearly drives the audience participation envisioned here. As Caldwell puts it, "the industry creates physical conditions that simultaneously constrain, allow for, and reinforce certain types of viewing."[25] Caldwell clearly sees the existing systems of interactivity as limiting audience practices and as in the service of the commercial interests that control inter-active systems.

Industry practices similar to the ones that Caldwell observes are clearly present in the case of Interactive Network as well. However, Cald-well's position seems to overestimate the power of a technology to determine its uses. Although Interactive Network attempts to create a relatively pow-erful combination of interactive technology and television programs, we cannot assume that every viewer is willing to accept the regulated uses inscribed in this combination of technology. Whereas framing the use of this technology provides a structure for audience behavior, it cannot do so in a deterministic way.

Building on a more complex view of the globalization of media tech-nologies, Ien Ang contrasts hegemony (global domination) and localized practice and uses reception studies to oppose theories of omnipotent media. However, she is not satisfied with a simple statement of the potential for resistance through media consumption and argues that equating an active audience with a powerful audience is not enough.[26] Ang seems to be more interested in following De Certeau's idea that everyday practices have to "make do" with the conditions provided by dominant culture.[27] She is inter-ested in mapping the precise conditions (usually provided by globalized forces) within which the practices of everyday life have to take place. Ang does not conceptualize this relationship as a confrontation, but as a close connection where the hegemonic penetrates popular practice:

> [T]he relationship between the hegemonic and the popular should not be conceived of in terms of mutual exteriority; the hegemonic can be found within the very texture of the popular.[28]

However, Ang ultimately believes that the relationship between the hege-monic and the popular cannot be fully understood in theoretical terms. The diversity of popular practice can be mapped only with ethnographic methods; Ang is arguing for an ethnographic sense of the hegemonic. Most theories of hegemony and practice fail to address the complex relationship between these two elements adequately; therefore, Ang's point is well taken. However, this ethnographic view of cultural process should not replace, but rather complement, theoretical approaches to the same issue.

Particularly some British media scholars have approached the issues of globalization and localized practices in the context of ICT use in family homes in Great Britain. Shaun Moores, for example, is interested in how media technologies connect household members to the outside world.[29] He sees electronic media, especially the established cases of radio and television, as emphasizing the modern dichotomies of public and private and ultimately as instrumental in the restructuring of time-space relations. Television is also regarded as instrumental in articulating a connection between the home and various public spheres "of information and entertainment at a regional, national or transnational level."[30] At the same time, electronic media do not necessarily work in the interest of centralized, national media institutions, as Moores points out.[31] He claims that European satellite systems have weakened the articulation of family and the nation in Great Britain by introducing alternative (European) programming that does not necessarily conform to the British national culture that the national media institutions perpetrate.

However, Moores also points out that the design of a technology and its marketing and promotion attempt to predefine the social uses for which the technology is put. David Morley makes a similar point:

> Consumption practices are working in, through (and occasionally against) the powerful discourses of design, marketing, advertising and education, which have constructed the dominant definitions of these technologies [ICT] and their 'appropriate' uses.[32]

The concept of the *moral economy* of the household that is currently developed in this research tradition is centrally concerned with how a commodity (ICT technology as well as television programs) is bought and incorporated into a household and how it is converted to suit the family's household routines or individual practices.[33] We may assume that communication technologies can be and are regularly converted in their daily use, whereas institutional discourses attempt to define appropriate uses.[34]

Institutional discourses strongly framed Interactive Network. Both the advertising in regular television commercials and fifteen-minute infomercials and the owner's manual provide an important framework for using this technology. The commercials for Interactive Network constantly emphasize the possibility of joining a nationwide network of members to compete on both a regional and national level: "Prove that you know more than other players across the country." Additionally, the Interactive Network logo frequently displayed in the infomercial foregrounds a globe surrounded by circles, emphasizing the potential of Interactive Network to incorporate the whole world. However, in the user's manual and in the "how-to-play" guides that every subscriber receives, any reference to this space-controlling potential of Interactive Network is completely absent, instead emphasizing the rules that need to be followed to interact with a game show, sports program, or drama.

Interactive Network seems to play on the utopian appeal of a technology to enable its users to transcend the time-space distanciation of modernity. As Williams observed, television makes the transcendence of spatial isolation in modernity possible at least on a symbolic level. At the same time television is, of course, also an active element in the increase of mobile privatization. It focuses the life of the individual even more on the isolated suburban home and reduces interaction within a locally based community.

Interactive Network applies essentially the same strategies; it defines leisure as a domestic activity in the family home.

MEDIA, COMMERCIALISM, AND DOMESTICITY

Broadcasting in its current form is often taken for granted. The developments that ultimately defined broadcasting as an advertiser-driven enterprise and as oriented toward a domestic family audience are sometimes assumed to be a natural development of the medium's history. The parallels in the development of radio, network television, and cable television toward commercial structures are striking. As Streeter points out:

> In each case, completely new technologies and/or legal regimes were introduced in ways that wholeheartedly reproduced commercial, legal, and institutional structures on new terrain.[35]

Other forms of alternative broadcasting, for example, nonprofit amateur broadcasting, were eliminated early in the history of broadcasting and were subsequently no longer considered valid alternatives to commercial broadcasting. Even defining the spectrum space as a property is an important act in this context because it makes commodifying the spectrum and letting commercial broadcasters use it exclusively for their own purposes possible.[36] All later attempts to define broadcasting as being in the public interest therefore only can be subordinate to the demands of commercial broadcasting. Susan Smulyan's analysis of the way radio was imagined and promoted as an advertising medium in the 1920s provides a good example for this: Spectrum space as property could be easily converted into a commodity; the main problem then was to attract both advertisers and a regular audience.[37] Radio broadcasters in the 1920s were able to do both; they made radio attractive for advertisers, and they persistently built a (predominantly female) audience with programming that could be integrated easily into the household flow. The continued efforts to locate radio and television quiz shows within the framework of consumption and within definitions of normalized American identity illustrate the ongoing commodification of broadcasting.

The early development of broadcasting thus provides a framework for imagining, regulating, and experiencing communication technologies, which has an impact up to the present. Some important consequences for the role of the audience in contemporary media systems follow from this:

> The economic success of the system rests on a bizarre and methodologically tenuous construction wherein the majority of people involved, the listeners and viewers, are understood not as the free, active, rational individuals of liberal anthropology, but as themselves a form of property, as audiences that are sold to advertisers.[38]

Interactive Network enters this preexisting situation that in turn pre-determines its basic orientation to some extent. Although the membership fees could give some independence to Interactive Network and could thus place it outside the advertiser-dominated media (at least similar to paytelevision channels such as HBO), it is ultimately imagined as completely in the service of traditional broadcast media. It builds mainly on the preexisting commercially structured products of network television and sees its main purpose only in enhancing the experience of several programs that are "made interactive": "Don't just watch TV, play TV." This is, of course, not surprising. As pointed out, the precedents of broadcast media provide a powerful framework within which subsequent technologies are imagined. Interactive Network evidently follows these precedents fully.

Beyond a discussion of the commercial orientation of television, Lynn Spigel shows how the construction of home television viewing in advertisements and magazines was instrumental in demonstrating the global and local connections that the new medium made possible.[39] Alluding to Williams's concept of mobile privatization,[40] Spigel claims that the television set and other communication media were a means by which families were able to distance themselves from the world while connecting to it in a controllable manner. Advertisements in women's magazines suggested that the television set should be surrounded by decorations evoking spatial conquest or other "global imagery." Spigel sees domestic space as utopian in the sense that it provided a safe view of the outside world from within the family home. The utopian appeal of controlling the global from a domestic environment is definitely one reason why Interactive Network alludes to these issues in its advertising. The commercials all show the use of Interactive Network in a domestic environment. Family life is improved as a result of using new domestic technology. The family interaction centers on using of technology and, consequently, Interactive Network is portrayed as nonthreatening. At the same time it is also seen as exciting and utopian because it allows new forms of interaction (particularly across space) to take place. The liberating and utopian aspect of technology is again emphasized in a scene that shows the Interactive Network input device entering a family home like an unidentified flying object (UFO): The living room has drab 1950s' style furniture, the (nuclear) family is dressed similarly, and the whole scene is shot in black and white. In the moment the UFO/input device penetrates the living room, and the whole scene becomes colorized, the setting and clothing change to a contemporary (1990s') style and the family members are spontaneously excited. The technology has the power to enhance the life of the family in modernity and liberate the family from the boredom of conventional media associated with 1950s' television. Importantly, the enhancements to family life portrayed in this scene are all connected to consumerism because most changes taking place in the living room are related to replacing outdated clothes and furnishings with new merchandise. Although these images appear to have a strong utopian appeal, this utopianism is not necessarily matched by the technology itself.

Both Spigel and Smulyan demonstrate that the broadcasting industry made great efforts to focus on the home—the basic unit of consumption in Western culture—as main target for their products. The case of Interactive Network shows that these techniques are almost universally used when introducing new entertainment media. Similar developments became obvious in the more recent marketing of home computers for domestic use. Here a domestic setting offers another market for technology that has not yet been exploited to its fullest potential. In all of these cases, ideological positions (particularly the centrality of the family) seem to coincide with commercial interests. Thus, a strong incentive exists to portray and install Interactive Network as a commercially driven, domestic technology.

INTERACTIVE QUIZ SHOWS

All of the major interactive systems (Full Service Network, Interactive Network, and QUBE) included interactive quiz shows as part of their regular offerings. Similarly, The Family Channel started offering interactive quiz shows in 1993. The first of these shows was *Trivial Pursuit—The Interactive Game*; *Shuffle—The Interactive Game*, *Boggle—The Interactive Game*, and *Jumble—The Interactive Game* replaced it in June 1994. By December 1994, all four of the shows were canceled. The shows were based on popular board games and allowed home audience members only to call a 900 number and play along with the game on the screen via their touch-tone telephone keypad. For each phone call to participate in one of the games a $2.95 fee was charged.

The Game Show Network introduced two interactive shows in 1996, *Game TV* and *Trivia Track*. Neither show has studio contestants; they rely entirely on home audience members who call in and interact with the on-screen hosts. The home contestants are represented through computer graphics, which in the case of *Game TV* take the form of a scoreboard that displays the standings of the two competing contestants. *Trivia Track* uses a computer-generated horse race in which the horses and jockeys stand for the home contestants who answer trivia questions using their telephone keypad. Although these shows allow home audience members to participate in the program, they still closely regulate audience involvement. The representation of contestants is limited to computer graphics and short phone conversations with the hosts; responses are limited to four numbers on a keypad. This form of participation resembles the use of the telephone in quiz shows of the early 1950s such as *Strike It Rich* or *Dr. I.Q.*, but it hardly constitutes a new audience involvement on television. Particularly striking, however, is that the audience once again participates on extremely uneven terms: The television programming is delivered as a text relatively rich in audio and video components, whereas the interaction from the audience can be delivered only via an information-poor audio channel. Audience participation on interactive television services is mostly significant on a symbolic level. The highly reductive version of text-audience relationships that occurs on interactive television does little to address the utopian promises of interactivity.

The unexpected success of *Who Wants to Be a Millionaire*[41] in the summer of 1999 gave quiz shows a new presence on prime-time television and focused significant public attention on the genre. Several other prime-time quiz shows premiered in the fall and spring season, including *Greed* on Fox and a new version of *Twenty-One* on NBC, whereas CBS's planned remake of *The $64,000 Question* never materialized. Although all of these shows invoke the scandalous history of the genre by attempting to imitate the high stakes, style, and structure of the 1950s' big-money quiz shows, *Who Wants to Be a Millionaire*, a remake of a popular British show, was the most successful entry. Several newspaper and magazine articles speculating about the reasons for the sudden success of this show offered *Who Wants to Be a Millionaire*'s connection to its audiences as one explanation for this success. Indeed, the show's use of "lifelines" offers an important opportunity for the contestant and the show as a whole to encourage audience participation and link studio and home audiences to the program. The lifelines provide a contestant with the opportunity to receive help from others in answering a question. One lifeline ("Ask the Audience") allows the contestant to ask the studio audience to answer a question by voting for one of four multiple-choice answers. In a second lifeline ("50/50"), a computer eliminates two of the four multiple-choice answers, leaving the contestant with two answers, one correct and one incorrect. The third lifeline ("Phone a Friend") allows the contestant to call a friend from a predetermined list and ask for assistance in answering the question. Besides offering a limited amount of assistance to a contestant, the lifelines on *Who Wants to Be a Millionaire* also illustrate some of the ways in which the broadcast industry envisions audience participation. The contestant is provided with a connection to a computer, which magically provides assistance, a connection to a community of friendly strangers in the studio, or a connection to one of several familiar people, usually relatives or friends at home. *Who Wants to Be a Millionaire* illustrates some of the fantasies and visions regarding audience participation and interactivity circulating in U.S. culture in general and in the broadcast industry in particular. At the same time, the limits to interaction *Who Wants to Be a Millionaire* imposes are indicative of the shortcomings of interactivity: Interaction with the computer on the 50/50 lifeline is limited to predetermined choices and Phone a Friend relies on preselected friends who cannot see the program unfold live (it is prerecorded and edited). Even Ask the

Audience reduces the interaction between the studio audience and the contestant in *Millionaire*'s hot seat to selecting one of four multiple-choice answers on a keypad.

With the Internet's increasing popularity, interactive television services have all but disappeared. Any interactive involvement with quiz shows is now exclusively located on specialized Web sites featuring versions of broadcast quizzes that allow personal computer users to play adapted versions of their favorite quiz shows at home.

As chapter 2 illustrates, the television industry assumes that quiz shows create a particularly close relationship between text and audience. The quiz show genre was obviously considered well-suited to experiments with interactivity. However, as Caldwell points out, the interaction fostered in interactive cable systems and in the interactive quiz shows which are offered by The Family Channel and the Game Show Network effectively connects the audience to a program, but does not create greater program diversity or opportunities for minorities to participate in cultural production.[42] Interactive systems offer pluralism as a larger array of consumer choices and programming options. The strategies of narrowcasting that characterized the broadcast industry in the 1980s and 1990s informed the design of these systems.

CONCLUSION

In conclusion, another parallel between audience participation on radio quiz shows and interactive television can be drawn: Similar to the broadcast industry in the 1930s and 1940s, institutional instability characterizes the era of cable television and narrowcasting. Network audiences are continuously shrinking and myriad cable channels compete for audience share, which once again has become a fleeting entity. Audience participation facilitated via interactive television is an attempt to restabilize the text-audience relationship. However, the failure of all interactive television systems illustrates that the audience might prefer to imagine a participatory relationship with its quiz shows rather than being forced into specific forms of interaction interactive services prescribe.

CONCLUSION

The Reality of Quiz Shows

Since the premiere of *Survivor* in the summer of 2000, U.S. television has been overrun with a wave of new programming dubbed *reality TV*. It includes talent competitions such as *American Idol*, makeover shows such as *Queer Eye for the Straight Guy* and *What Not to Wear*, programs focused on physical competition such as *Fear Factor*, dating shows such as *Elimidate* and *The Fifth Wheel*, and even the 2003 program *Cupid*, where the ultimate goal is to find a suitable husband for the single woman at the center of the program. In response to this ongoing wave of reality programming, the cable network Bravo launched *The Reality of Reality*, a series that provides a behind-the-scenes look at the world of reality television. One particular episode investigated the history of the "reality genre." *The Reality of Reality* draws numerous parallels between current reality television and television programming of the past fifty years. For example, *Who Wants to Be a Millionaire* is closely related to the 1950s' big-money quiz shows in both visual style and content. *American Idol* is clearly related to earlier programs such as *Star Search*, *The Gong Show*, or, to trace its history back to radio, *Major Bowes' Original Amateur Hour*. Dating shows, of course, also have a long history on U.S. television. The idea of finding a date on television dates back to the little-known *Blind Date* (ABC, NBC, DuMont, 1949–1953) as well as to Chuck Barris's *The Dating Game*, which premiered on ABC in 1965. Finally, *The Reality of Reality* also connects *Fear Factor* to earlier "stunt shows" such as *Truth or Consequences*. Whereas this genealogy of reality television is interesting in itself, it fails to reflect on the fact that *The Gong Show*, *The Dating Game*, and *Truth or Consequences* were actually never known as reality television. The labels offered for such shows are *stunt shows, audience participation*

149

shows, and the generic term *reality*. The genre confusion observed in the context of 1930s' and 1940s' radio has been revived with the rise of the term *reality*. Throughout their history, quiz shows have required contestants to perform physical stunts, tested contestants' knowledge of high culture and trivia, gone on location, and rewarded winning contestants with dates or a career in show business. But they were never called reality shows. The use of the new term *reality* is particularly striking in the case of *Who Wants to Be a Millionaire*. As pointed out, this program is closely related to academic knowledge-based quiz shows such as *Twenty-One*, *The $64,000 Question*, *The $64,000 Challenge*, or *The Big Surprise*. Yet *Millionaire* is often listed as the program that paved the way for the new wave of reality television. The term *reality* simply attaches a new, possibly more attractive, label to several familiar programming forms. The term *reality* might help to set apart a new, supposedly more edgy type of programming from long-running and less high-profile shows such as *The Price Is Right* or *Jeopardy!*. Of course, not all programs currently labeled reality television would have been considered a quiz show in the past. Home improvement programs such as *Changing Rooms*, *Trading Spaces*, and *Weekend Warriors*, as well as make over shows such as *What Not to Wear* or *A Personal Story* might not fit the generic label *quiz show*. However, the bulk of reality television appears to be quiz shows in disguise.

The term *reality* is now applied to a large variety of quiz shows as a retroactive genre designation. The appearance of a new generic label for this genre is not entirely surprising. In the context of the development of radio quiz shows and in the context of the remodeling of the genre in the early 1960s, genre labels are often used interchangeably. The solidification of genre definitions frequently has been performed through the categorizing practices of industry and critics, thereby emphasizing the discursive act of defining generic belonging. As indicated earlier, quiz shows as ritual forms are shaped through the exertion of power, which organizes their production. In specific historical instances, the power of the production side shaped the form of individual programs for specific economic and ideological purposes. The focus on the changing form and content of quiz shows in this book thus highlighted their connection to key changes in the organization of production. In the case of *Vox Pop*, both the form and the definition of the program were manipulated according to the specific economic and cultural role that *Vox Pop* was meant to occupy. These discussions often involved intense power struggles among program owner Parks Johnson, various sponsors, and the networks.

The remodeling of the genre after the quiz show scandals, on the other hand, provides an example of a much more unified and purposeful effort to redefine and restructure the genre. Continuing to produce quiz shows was in the broadcast industry's concrete interest, but encouraging any further association of the genre with the quiz show scandals was not. The name change from *quiz shows* to *game shows* and the changes in program form and scheduling practices illustrate the broadcast industry's concerted effort to change public perception of the genre.

Of course, additional consequences emerge as part of a significant change in the genre. The changes made in 1960s' quiz shows also entailed new assumptions about the appeal of quiz shows for the audience. Quiz shows were specifically restructured to address female home viewers as ideal consumers. New techniques to create forms of personal address and the impression of immediacy likewise helped to discourage any educational pretense in the genre and to naturalize a consumption ethic as a key component of many programs.

The example of the reality show *Survivor*[1] further illustrates the often-arbitrary character of genre designations. A closer look at this program reveals that *Survivor* reproduces the structure of many quiz shows on a larger scale. *Survivor* usually uses an island or a large area of uninhabited landscape as a set. Although this set might appear to be real, untouched, or deserted, a great deal of set design obviously has occurred. For example, the set for the tribal councils on *Survivor: Australian Outback* was built on top of a waterfall and included large rocks assembled to form an enclosed space for the council meetings. This set not only serves a specific function in the show, but it also invokes the exoticism of remote areas or foreign countries in general. Other sets are similarly designed to accommodate the competition in *Survivor*'s reward challenges and immunity challenges. The structure of the overall competition on *Survivor* essentially works to eliminate contestants one by one until the winner of the program has been identified. This structure resembles many other quiz shows, including *The Price Is Right*, where nine contestants go through a series of pricing games until the winner of the final showcase showdown emerges. Granted, the skills to succeed on *Survivor* are different from those needed on *The Price Is Right*, emphasizing physical ability, teamwork, and strategy, but the overall procedures to find a winner bear significant similarities.

Survivor is of course not the only recent program to bring innovations to the quiz show genre. Similar to the changes in 1960s' programs, we can observe that the genre's articulation to key ideologies in U.S. culture is changing. Instead of the consumerism of many earlier programs, shows such as *Fear Factor*, *Boot Camp*, *The Chair*, *The Chamber*, and *Survivor* all put additional emphasis on the contestants' willingness to humiliate themselves and, potentially, to endure significant physical harm. In exchange, the prize money available on these shows has also increased—to sums ranging from $50,000 to $1,000,000 and more. Quiz shows now tend to foreground the contestants' greed, their ruthlessness, and their willingness to do what ever it takes to win. The torture quiz shows mentioned here have an obvious connection to changes in U.S. culture that have occurred since the 1990s. The protection of workers against corporate abuse declined in conjunction with an increasing gap between skilled and unskilled labor. At the same time, state-run welfare systems provide only minimal levels of protection against unemployment or corporate downsizing. As a result, U.S. culture since the 1990s has witnessed an increasing gap among classes along with instability in employment and income level.

The programs mentioned herein reveal that the contestants' willingness to withstand physical or emotional abuse might prove them worthy of a dazzling amount of prize money. However, these programs also illustrate the haphazard character of social mobility. The recent spate of torture quiz shows express the corporate need for a docile workforce psychologically equipped for the shifting demands of corporate culture. We can thus see the emergence of quiz shows that require their contestants to do whatever is necessary to mold them to changing corporate demands in the interest of their personal enrichment.

As illustrated herein, quiz shows are always articulated to very specific ideological formations. Beverly Stoeltje's work explains that changes in the structure of a ritual form reveal changes in the organization of production:

> Significant changes at every stage in the history of a form reveal information about the organization of production.... An examination of the evolution of the form reveals key points in the process of production, the points at which decisions were made affecting the aesthetic organization and access to production, and thus control of meaning.[2]

Empirical evidence from the historical instances covered in this book certainly substantiate Stoeltje's crucial theoretical claims. Just as the recent torture quiz shows articulate the genre to the changing economic and social realities in the United States, the genre has also articulated other ideological formations throughout its history. The unique form and ideology of big-money quiz shows, for example, points to the specific institutional demands that existed in the television industry in the 1950s. The demands on the networks to produce socially relevant, "educational" programming in combination with the basic economic desire to increase audiences led to creating programs with a very narrow set of desirable social and ethnic identities.

The development of new dating shows in the 1980s and 1990s, on the other hand, presents a much more ambivalent attitude toward traditional cultural norms in general and personal relationships in particular. Although ritual genres are specifically structured forms that are usually articulated to dominant cultural formations, it also becomes clear that human-knowledge quiz shows in the 1990s relativize the value of personal relationships and refuse to accept the absolutism of conservative morality. Thus, dating shows such as *Temptation Island* and *Blind Date* are often unable to reproduce a highly normative version of personal relationships. Whereas such programs destabilize parts of the ideology of family values, they still maintain a position of compulsory heterosexuality. At the same time as the contradictory character of the dominant discourse of family values is addressed, the ideal of heterosexuality is nonetheless upheld.

On a theoretical level, the diversity of articulations of the quiz show genre can be explained through the fluctuation of genre affiliations. Quiz shows not only participate in multiple genres, but also display multiple ideological affiliations throughout their history. The necessary surrender of our belief in the absolute rule of the law of genre does, however, mean that we cannot assume that all programs of a specific genre have the same ideological implications. We have to investigate the internal and external organization of individual shows more carefully to address their ideological significance effectively.

The ideological flexibility of ritual genres that both Beverly Stoeltje and Victor Turner[3] observe also establishes quiz shows as an important site where hierarchies of knowledge are expressed and challenged. The ideology of the common man that was at the core of many radio quiz shows expressed the desire for egalitarian forms of cultural expression that informed Depression culture in the United States. However, the dominance of white men and their cultural preferences provided a powerful exclusionary mechanism that sidelined a significant part of the radio public along the lines of race, gender, and ethnicity. Ironically, this preference for white, male culture connects the participatory quiz programs of the radio era to the serene and ceremonious 1950s' big-money quiz shows.

Programs such as *Twenty-One* and *The $64,000 Question* reproduced many of the same exclusionary mechanisms that we had previously witnessed on radio. With regard to the discussion of 1950s' big-money quiz shows, the televisual image of *Twenty-One* winner Charles Van Doren was used to describe the hidden ideological contradictions of big-money quiz shows. The discourse of the common man was used to naturalize the knowledge and values represented on many 1950s' quiz shows. At the same time, the character of Van Doren, a representative of a small elite culture, stood at the center of the egalitarian pretenses of big-money quiz shows, authorizing the same cultural values that the discourse of the common man attempted to obscure.

The rise of new quiz shows in the 1960s, on the other hand, also brought new forms of cultural identification to the forefront. Programs such as *Video Village* and *Let's Make a Deal* specifically target female audiences and position themselves quite differently in the system of cultural hierarchy. Many 1960s' and 1970s' quiz shows focus on everyday knowledge and allow their audiences to interact with programs and hosts in a manner that sets them apart from earlier television quiz shows. However, the television industry often looked down on the female participants and audiences of these programs, which frequently portrayed women as feebleminded and easy prey for advertisers.

From the early 1960s to the late 1990s, quiz shows were almost completely excluded from prime-time television. Quiz shows' position in daytime
television has connected the genre to a low hierarchical position in U.S. culture. Many programs of the 1970s and 1980s eschewed the "academic"
knowledge of big-money quiz shows and instead focused on everyday knowledge. Moreover, human knowledge, that is knowledge of people in general
and knowledge of a specific person, has informed numerous quiz shows in the
1980s and 1990s. This shift away from public and officially sanctioned forms
of knowledge and toward private and unofficial forms of knowledge says a
great deal about the transformations in U.S. political culture. As the private
sphere became the center of intense political debates, official culture—
including the spheres of politics and factual knowledge—continues to
decline. Even *Who Wants to Be a Millionaire,*[4] a prime-time quiz show that frequently showcases academic knowledge, uses a multiple-choice question
format, thereby minimizing the actual knowledge a contestant needs to win a
significant prize.

A final key element that can be observed throughout the history of
quiz shows is their unique relationship to home and studio audiences. Quiz
shows frequently incorporate the audience through a variety of strategies.
At different points in the history of quiz shows audience involvement has
been achieved through telephone conversations between the host and
viewers or through interactive technologies such as Interactive Network,
which allows viewers to respond to menus of questions or options through
remote control devices.

Although quiz shows in the 1940s and 1950s were imagining and
addressing a national community of viewers and thus constituted an unifying
element, quiz shows in the era of narrowcasting are a part of the larger phenomenon of the fragmentation of the national audience. Industry analyst
Ken Auletta connects the rise of narrowcasting to a loss of a sense of community and common values in U.S. culture, while he sees the increase of cultural diversity as a benefit of the decline of network television.[5] Clearly, the
incorporation and representation of the audience in quiz shows does not have
a singular meaning. Nevertheless, we need to acknowledge that the interests
of the broadcast industry clearly drive participation or interactivity in the
genre. Similar to the "mailhooks" Robert Allen described,[6] which soap opera
producers used to elicit viewer responses, sponsors and advertisers foster
audience participation on quiz shows to gain a better understanding of the
audience and provide a model for the relation between text and viewer in
commercial broadcasting.

Interactive technologies enter television at the moment when the
structure of the broadcast industry begins to destabilize. Under the pretense
of providing a tool for diversity or pluralism, the industry is again trying to
create a more stable relationship between audiences and programs. John

Caldwell explicitly describes interactivity in negative terms, claiming that "viewer activity has supported the aims of broadcasters and advertisers from the start."[7] He thus ignores that the viewing or decoding practices of audiences are not necessarily restricted to the intentions of broadcast institutions. The analysis of the idea of audience participation herein confirms Caldwell's argument that viewer activity has its origins in advertisers' desire to control and understand their audiences. However, further analysis of radio programs such as *Vox Pop* and *Information Please* indicates that the cultural effect of audience participation is more complex. The possibility for the audience to renegotiate their relationship with various forms of cultural hierarchy opens up audience participation programs to a variety of negotiated reading positions that are outside the preferred meaning(s) of these programs.

The analysis of audience participation across eras and media brings into focus its dual character as a vehicle for advertisers' economic desires and as a site for audience identification and pleasure. The dual character of quiz shows illustrated throughout this book reconnects *Rules of the Game* with the intellectual project of cultural studies. The quiz show is one of the sites in the sphere of popular media in which a struggle for the meaning of the objects of everyday life occurs. The ongoing struggle for the meaning of quiz shows also serves as a reminder that all totalizing narratives and theories tend to negate the actual complexity of a television genre, even a genre as mundane as the quiz show. Allen's seminal book *Speaking of Soap Operas* in many ways inspired this project. Writing in the early 1980s, Allen rightfully points out that one research tradition that creates reductive explanations for cultural forms such as soap operas (or quiz shows) is empirical mass communication research:

> I believe that the philosophical principles upon which empiricist social science (the foundations of American media research) is based preclude its ever accounting for phenomena that cannot be reduced to the investigatory simplicity of the independent variable in a laboratory experiment.[8]

Whereas critical media studies has greatly expanded since the publication of *Speaking of Soap Operas*, quiz shows in particular still have not received much scholarly attention. I hope that this book is only the starting point for an expansion of humanistic and critical research into the quiz show genre.

Notes

INTRODUCTION: QUIZ SHOWS AND AMERICAN CULTURE

1. Eric Barnouw, *A History of Broadcasting in the United States, Volume III: The Image Empire* (New York: Oxford University Press, 1970), 123.

2. Barnouw, 197–198.

3. John Fiske, *Understanding Popular Culture* (London: Routledge, 1989), 279-280.

4. Susan Smulyan, *Selling Radio: The Commercialization of American Broadcasting, 1920–1934* (Washington, D.C.: Smithsonian Institution Press, 1994), 6.

5. Wayne Munson, *All Talk: The Talk Show in Media Culture* (Philadelphia: Temple University Press, 1993), 76–77.

6. Henri A. Giroux and Roger Simon, "Popular Culture and Critical Pedagogy: Everyday Life as Basis for Curriculum Knowledge," in *Critical Pedagogy, the State, and Cultural Struggle*, ed. Henri A. Giroux and Peter L. McLaren (Albany: State University of New York Press, 1989), 236. See also, Henri A. Giroux and Peter L. McLaren, "Introduction: Media Hegemony: Towards a Critical Pedagogy of Representation," in *Media Knowledge: Readings in Popular Culture*, ed. James Schwoch, Mimi White, and Susan Reilly (Albany: State University of New York Press, 1992), XV–XXXIV. Henri Giroux, Roger I. Simon, et al., *Popular Culture, Schooling, and Everyday Life* (New York: Bergin and Garvey, 1989).

7. Pierre Bourdieu, *Distinction: A Social Critique of the Judgement of Taste* (Cambridge, Mass.: Harvard University Press, 1984); Pierre Bourdieu, *The Logic of Practice* (Stanford, Calif.: Stanford University Press, 1990).

8. Tony Bennett, "Texts, Readers, Reading Formations," *Bulletin of the Midwest Modern Language Association* 16, no. 1, (1983): 3–17.

9. Fiske, *Understanding Popular Culture*.

10. Cf. Nicholas Garnham, "Political Economy and Cultural Studies: Reconciliation or Divorce?" *Critical Studies in Mass Communication* 12, no. 1 (1995): 62–71; Lawrence Grossberg, "Cultural Studies vs. Political Economy: Is Anyone Else Bored with This Debate?" *Critical Studies in Mass Communication*, 12, no. 1 (1995): 72–81.

11. Patrick Hughes, "Producing Audiences: Towards a Political Economy of Subjectivities," *Media International Australia*, 80 (May 1996): 93–98.

12. Munson; Robert C. Allen, *Speaking of Soap Operas* (Chapel Hill: University of North Carolina Press, 1985).

13. John Fiske, *Television Culture* (London: Routledge, 1987), 269.

14. Adam Mills and Phil Rice, "Quizzing the Popular," *Screen Education* 41 (Winter/Spring 1982): 15–25.

15. Roy Rappaport, "Ritual," in *Folklore, Cultural Performances, and Popular Entertainments*, ed. Richard Bauman (New York: Oxford University Press, 1992), 249–60.

16. Victor Turner, "Liminal to Liminoid, in Play, Flow, and Ritual: An Essay in Comparative Symbology," *Rice University Studies* 60, no. 3(1974): 59.

17. Turner, 60.

18. Turner, 71.

19. Beverly Stoeltje, "Festival," in *Folklore, Cultural Performances, and Popular Entertainments*, ed. Richard Bauman, (New York: Oxford University Press, 1992), 261–71.

20. Stoeltje, 262.

21. Mikhail M. Bakhtin, *Rabelais and His World* (Bloomington: Indiana University Press, 1984); Peter Stallybrass and Allon White, *The Politics and Poetics of Transgression*, (Ithaca, N.Y.: Cornell University Press, 1986).

22. Stallybrass and White, 14.

23. Stallybrass and White, 16.

24. Bakhtin.

25. Robert Stam, *Subversive Pleasures: Bakhtin, Cultural Criticism, and Film* (Baltimore, Md.: Johns Hopkins University Press, 1989), 227.

26. Beverly Stoeltje, "The Beauty Contest: Ritualizing the Female Body" paper presented to the Davies Forum, University of San Francisco, San Francisco, Calif., (1997), 5.

27. Stoeltje, "The Beauty Contest," 6.

28. Rick Altman, *The American Film Musical* (Bloomington: Indiana University Press, 1989).

29. Beverly Stoeltje, "Power and the Ritual Genres: American Rodeo," *Western Folklore* 52 (April 1993): 142.

30. Mikhail M. Bakhtin, *The Dialogic Imagination* (Austin: University of Texas Press, 1981).

31. Jacques Derrida, *Acts of Literature* ed. Derek Attridge. (New York: Routledge, 1992).

32. Ien Ang, *Living Room Wars: Rethinking Media Audiences for a Postmodern World* (London: Routledge, 1996).

33. Jean Baudrillard, *In the Shadow of the Silent Majorities, or, the End of the Social and Other Essays* (New York: Semiotext(e), 1983).

34. Mona Sarkis, "Interactivity Means Interpassivity." *Media Information Australia* 69 (1993): 13–16.

35. Raymond Williams, *Television: Technology and Cultural Form*, (Hanover, N.H.: Wesleyan University Press, 1974).

1. WHAT IS A GENRE? QUIZ SHOWS/GAME SHOWS

1. Olaf Hoerschelmann, "Quiz and Game Shows," in *Museum of Broadcast Communications Encyclopedia of Television*, ed. Horace Newcomb (Chicago: Fitzroy Dearborn Publishers, 1997).

2. Rick Altman, *The American Film Musical* (Bloomington: Indiana University Press, 1989); Tzvetan Todorov, *The Fantastic* (Ithaca: Cornell University Press, 1975).

3. Altman, *American Film Musical*, 13.

4. Altman, *American Film Musical*, 13.

5. Rick Altman, *Film/Genre* (London: British Film Institute, 1999).

6. David Schwartz, Steve Ryan, and Fred Wostbrock, *The Encyclopedia of Television Game Shows*, 2nd. ed. (New York: Facts on File, 1995); John Dunning, *Tune in Yesterday: The Ultimate Encyclopedia of Old-Time Radio 1925–1976* (Englewood Cliffs, N.J.: Prentice-Hall, 1976); Jon D.

Swartz and Robert C. Reinehr, *Handbook of Old-Time Radio: A Comprehensive Guide to Golden Age Radio Listening and Collecting* (Metuchen, N.J.: Scarecrow Press, 1993).

7. Michel Foucault, *The History of Sexuality*, Part I (Harmondsworth, Eng.: Penguin, 1978).

8. Patricia O'Brien, "Michel Foucault's History of Culture," in *The New Cultural History*, ed. Lynn Hunt (Berkeley: University of California Press, 1989), 37.

9. "26 Quiz Programs on Air," *New York World Telegram*, not dated (~1939), *Vox Pop* collection, Library of American Broadcasting University of Maryland, College Park, MD, (hereafter cited as Vox), series I, box 20, folder 8.

10. *Major Bowes' Original Amateur Hour*, prod. Lou Goldberg, WHN-New York, NBC, CBS, ABC, 1934–1952.

11. Dunning, 387–89.

12. *Uncle Jim's Question Bee*, sponsored by George Washington Coffee and Lever Brothers, NBC, CBS, 1936–1941.

13. NBC press release, 23 September 1936, Vox, series I, box 3, folder 2.

14. *Vox Pop*, created by Parks Johnson and Jerry Belcher, KTRH-Houston, NBC, CBS, ABC, 1932–1948.

15. David K. Grant, "The Rise of the Audience Participation Program," *Advertising and Selling* (June 1946): 45, 82–86.

16. *Vox Pop 1932 through 1945: The Story of 'The Show That Travels America,'* promotional booklet, not dated (~1945), Vox, series I, box 8, folder: diverse promo.

17. "*Vox Pop 1932 through 1945;" "Vox Pop* on Summer Hiatus after April 22 Show," press release, not dated (~April 1946), Vox, series I, box 20, folder 14; "The Day Quiz Shows Were Born," *Houston Chronicle*, 1 July 1962, TV Pullout, 1–2; Leonard Hall, "Fancy Programs on the Air," *Household Magazine*, April 1939, 30–31; R. B. Sullivan, "They Know the Answers," *Host: The Magazine of Home Entertainment*, Spring 1939, 76.

18. Gregory Lukow and Steven Z. Ricci, "The 'Audience' Goes 'Public': Inter-Textuality, Genre and the Responsibilities of Film Literacy', *On Film*, 12 (1984): 29–36.

19. "*Vox Pop* on the Air," *The Literary Digest*, 5 October 1935, 27; F. Sammis, "The Program on which You Are the Star," *Radio Mirror*, October 1935, 31, 79–80; "*Vox Pop*," *All-Wave Radio* 2, no. 2 (1936): 70–71, 91–92.

20. R. P. Myers to I. E. Showerman, memorandum, 4 April 1940, NBC, box 79, folder 64. NBC Collection on Mass Communications. Wisconsin Historical Society, University of Wisconsin, Madison. (Hereafter cited as NBC).

21. Mikhail M. Bakhtin, *The Dialogic Imagination* (Austin: University of Texas Press, 1981), 428.

22. Sullivan, 18–21, 75–76.

23. Jacques Derrida, "The Law of Genre," in *Acts of Literature*, ed. Derek Attridge (New York: Routledge, 1992), 221–52; also Altman, *Film/Genre*; Steve Neale, *Genre and Hollywood* (Routledge: New York, 2000).

24. Jason Mittell, "A Cultural Approach to Television Genre Theory," *Cinema Journal* 40, no. 3 (Spring 2001): 3–24.

25. Thomas Schatz, *Hollywood Genres: Formulas, Filmmaking, and the Studio System* (New York: Random House, 1981); Will Wright, *Sixguns and Society: A Structural Study of the Western* (Berkeley: University of California Press, 1975).

26. James Carey, *Culture as Communication* (Boston: Unwin Hyman, 1989).

27. Jane Feuer, "Genre Study and Television," in *Channels of Discourse, Reassembled: Television and Contemporary Criticism*, ed. Robert C. Allen (Chapel Hill: University of North Carolina Press, 1992), 138–60.

28. Janet Staiger, *Interpreting Films: Studies in the Historical Reception of American Cinema* (Princeton, N.J.: Princeton University Press, 1992); Feuer, "Genre Study"; Altman, *American Film Musical*; Altman, *Film/Genre*.

29. Altman, *American Film Musical*.

30. Altman, *American Film Musical*, 115.

31. *The Television Audience of Today*, Advertest Research, July 1952, NBC, box 193, folder 23.

32. "Name That Tune," April 1953, NBC, box 397, file 55.

33. "NBC Biography: Jack Barry," 24 July 1956, NBC, box 155, file 3.

34. "What Is an Audience Participation Program?" not dated (~1947), Vox, series I, box 21, folder 35.

35. *The Television Audience of Today*.

36. Altman, *American Film Musical*.

37. Derrida.

38. Schatz; John Cawelti, *Adventure, Mystery and Romance Formula Stones as Art and Popular Culture* (Chicago: University of Chicago Press, 1976); Wright.

39. Carey.

40. Vivian Sobchack, "Genre Film: Myth, Ritual, and Sociodrama," in *Film/Culture*, ed. Sari Thomas (Metuchen, N.J.: Scarecrow Press, 1982), 147–165; Cahiers du Cinéma Collective, "*Young Mr. Lincoln* de John Ford," *Cahiers du Cinéma* 223 (1970): 29–47.

41. Mittell, 18.

42. Beverly J. Stoeltje, "Power and the Ritual Genres: American Rodeo," *Western Folklore* 52 (April 1993): 135–56.

43. Stoeltje, 141.

44. "*Vox Pop* 1932 through 1945."

45. Grant.

46. Parks Johnson's Notebook 1, not dated. Vox, series I, subseries 4, box 2, folder 1.

47. "*Vox Pop* 1932 through 1945."

48. Jason Loviglio, "*Vox Pop*: Network Radio and the Voice of the People," in *Radio Reader: Essays in the Cultural History of Radio*, ed. Michele Hilmes and Jason Loviglio (New York: Routledge, 2002), 99.

49. "What Is *Vox Pop*?" not dated, (~ spring 1940), Vox, series I, box 20, folder 35.

50. Parks Johnson's Notebook 4, not dated (~1940), Vox, series I, box 2, folder 6.

51. Thomas A. DeLong, *Quiz Craze: America's Infatuation with Game Shows* (Praeger: New York, 1991), 138.

52. Nate Tufts to Fred Coll, letter, 7 October 1940, Vox, series I, box 20, folder 32.

53. Nate Tufts to Parks Johnson, letter, 17 October 1940, Vox, series I, box 20, folder 32.

54. J. O. Hidden to T. F. Flanagan, memorandum, 6 September 1940, Vox, series I, box 20, folder 29; J. O. Hidden to T. F. Flanagan, memorandum, 3 January 1941, Vox, series I, box 20, folder 29.

55. Fred Coll to Parks Johnson, letter, 4 June 1946, Vox, series I, box 20, folder 14.

56. Raymond Williams, *Television: Technology and Cultural Form* (Hanover, N.H.: Wesleyan University Press, 1974).

57. Altman, *American Film Musical.*

58. Tony Bennett, "Texts in History: The Determinations of Readings and Their Texts," *Journal of the Midwest Modern Language Association* 18, no. 1 (1985): 1–16.

59. Bennett, 1–16.

60. Stoeltje, 135–56.

61. V. N. Vološinov, *Marxism and the Philosophy of Language* (New York: Academic Press, 1973).

2. A HEART LINE TO AMERICA: CREATING AUDIENCE PARTICIPATION

1. *Pot O' Gold*, prod. James Roosevelt, dir. George Marshall, 1 hr. 26 min., United Artists, 1941, videocassette. *The Jackpot*, prod. Samuel G. Engel, dir. Walter Lang, 1 hr. 25 min., Twentieth Century Fox, 1950, videocassette.

2. J. Fred MacDonald, *One Nation under Television: The Rise and Decline of Network TV*(Chicago: Nelson-Hall, 1994), 28. On the importance of advertising agencies in the production of radio programming; see also, Michele Hilmes, *Hollywood and Broadcasting: From Radio to Cable* (Urbana: University of Illinois Press, 1990), 83.

3. MacDonald, *One Nation*, 23.

4. Robert W. McChesney, *Telecommunications, Mass Media, and Democracy: The Battle for Control of U. S. Broadcasting, 1928–1935* (New York: Oxford University Press, 1994), 224.

5. MacDonald, *One Nation*, 22.

6. Lawrence W. Lichty, "Television in America: Success Story," in *American Media*, ed. Philip S. Cook, Douglas Gomery, and Lawrence Wilson Lichty (Washington, D.C.: Wilson Center Press, 1989), 159–76.

7. Garth Jowett, "Dangling the Dream? The Presentation of Television to the American Public, 1928–1952," *Historical Journal of Film, Radio and Television* 14, no. 2 (1994): 121–45.

8. Cf. Jowett, 122.

9. David Sarnoff, "Tributes Are Paid to NBC Progress at Gala Banquet," *Broadcasting*, 15 November 1936, 13.

10. Jowett, 123.

11. Jowett, 133.

12. Robert E. Sherwood, "Beyond the Talkies—Television," *Scribner's Magazine*, July 1929, 1–2.

13. David Sarnoff, "TV Not to Replace Broadcasting," *Broadcasting*, 15 July 1936, 10.

14. Michele Hilmes, *Radio Voices: American Broadcasting, 1922–1952*, (Minneapolis: University of Minnesota Press, 1997), and Hilmes, *Hollywood*.

15. Hilmes, *Radio Voices*, 82.

16. *Sustaining programming* is programming that the network produces, but does not carry any advertising. It is usually used to fill broadcast time outside of prime time. See Christopher H. Sterling and John M. Kittross, *Stay tuned: A Concise History of American Broadcasting* (Belmont, Calif.: Wadsworth, 1990). *Option time* refers to specific time periods during the day—usually in prime time–when a network has control over the use of the broadcast time of a station. Networks usually use option time to ensure that shows that collect high advertising rates are broadcast nationwide.

17. Cf. James L. Baughman, "The Promise of American Television, 1929-1952," *Prospects: An Annual of American Studies* 11 (1987), 119–34.

18. Gwenyth Jackaway, "Initial Reactions to the Introduction of Television, 1938–1953," in *Communication and Culture: Language, Performance, Technology, and Media: Proceedings from the Sixth International Conference on Culture and Communication*, ed. Sari Thomas and William Evans (Norwood, N.J.: Ablex, 1990), 190–92.

19. Cf. Jason Loviglio, "*Vox Pop*: Network Radio and the Voice of the People," in *Radio Reader: Essays in the Cultural History of Radio*, ed. Michele Hilmes and Jason Loviglio (New York: Routledge, 2002), 89–111.

20. Mel Palmer, "*Vox Pop*–And How!" *Radio Guide*, 5 October 1935, 5.

21. Parks Johnson, memorandum, 30 November 1948, Vox series I, box 1, folder 34.

22. Jack Jamison, "Bystander Beware," *Radio Guide*, 4 July 1936, 43.

23. Warren I. Susman, *Culture as History: The Transformation of American Society in the Twentieth Century* (New York: Pantheon, 1984), 203.

24. "*Vox Pop* 1932–1945: The Story of 'The Show That Travels America,'" VOX, series I, box 8, folder: diverse promo.

25. "Script for *Vox Pop*," 1 January 1934, Vox series I, box 2, folder 13.

26. Loviglio, 92.

27. "Their Studio's on the Street," *Radio Stars*, October 1935, 78. R. E. Eastman to Lee Wailes, memorandum, 25 April 1940, NBC, box 151, folder 39. See also, Fred Sammis, "The Program on which You Are the Star," *Radio Mirror*, October 1935, pp. 31, 79–80.

28. Susman, 200.

29. "*Double or Nothing*," prod. Ken Fickett, Lou Crosby and Diana Bourbon, Mutual, CBS, NBC, 1940–1953.

30. "*Vox Pop*," created by Parks Johnson and Jerry Belcher, KTRH-Houston, NBC, CBS, ABC, 1932–1948.

31. Jerald Manning, "Ready, Wally? Ready Parks? How the *Vox Pop* Boys Run Their Show, and Some Questions for You," *Radio Stars*, November 1936, 60.

32. Loviglio, 95.

33. "What Is *Vox Pop*?" not dated (~1946); Vox, series I, box 20, folder 11.

34. Manning, 24.

35. "Belcher's New Program," not dated (~October 1936), Vox, series I, box 20, folder 6.

36. J. Fred MacDonald, *Don't Touch that Dial: Radio Programming in American Life, 1920–1960* (Chicago: Nelson-Hall, 1979), 47.

37. Jon D. Swartz and Robert C. Reinehr, *Handbook of Old-Time Radio: A Comprehensive Guide to Golden Age Radio Listening and Collecting* (Metuchen, N.J.: Scarecrow Press, 1993), 139–47.

38. MacDonald, *Don't Touch that Dial*, 48.

39. Robert C. Allen, *Speaking of Soap Operas* (Chapel Hill: University of North Carolina Press, 1985).

40. Allen, *Speaking* 115.

41. "*Vox Pop*," *All-Wave Radio*, 2, no. 2 (February 1936): 71.

42. "Now that It Has a Sponsor," *Printer's Ink*, January 1939, 15, 58.

43. "What is an Audience Participation Program?" 27 February 1947; Vox, series I, box 21, folder 35.

44. Parks Johnson, memorandum, 30 November 1948; Vox, series I, box 1, folder 34.

45. David K. Grant, "The Rise of Audience Participation Programs," *Advertising and Selling*, June 1946, 84.

46. Ien Ang, *Desperately Seeking the Audience* (London: Routledge, 1991), 22–23.

47. Bertha Brainard to John Reber, memorandum, 25 June 1936, NBC, box 50, folder 45.

48. Jacob Evans to Jack Herbert, memorandum, 2 April 1953, NBC, John K. Herbert Papers, box 397, folder 55.

49. Irene Beasley, "I Enjoy *Grand Slam* Because...," *Radio and Television Mirror*, June 1950, 42–43, 80.

50. Cf. Loviglio, 108.

51. Seth Geiger and John Newhagen, "Revealing the Black Box: Information Processing and Media Effects," in *Defining Media Studies: Reflections on the Future of the Field*, ed. Mark R. Levy and Michael Gurevitch (Oxford, Eng.: Oxford University Press, 1994), 284–92.

52. Jean Baudrillard, *In the Shadow of the Silent Majorities, or, the End of the Social and Other Essays* (New York: Semiotext(e), 1983), 3–4, 24.

53. Herta Herzog, "Professor Quiz—A Gratification Study," *Radio and the Printed Page*, ed. Paul F. Lazarsfeld (New York: Duell, Sloan & Pearce, 1940), 64–93.

54. Herzog, 64.

55. Herzog, 68–69.

56. John Fiske, *Understanding Popular Culture* (London: Routledge, 1989).

57. Herzog, 70.

58. Cf. Pierre Bourdieu, *Distinction: A Social Critique of the Judgement of Taste* (Cambridge, Mass.: Harvard University Press, 1984).

59. Herzog, 71.

60. Swartz and Reinehr.

61. "*Dr. I.Q.*," NBC, ABC, 1939–1950.

62. "*Information Please*," NBC, CBS, Mutual, 1938–1948.

63. R. B. Sullivan, "They Know the Answers," *Host: The Magazine of Home Entertainment*, Spring 1939, 20.

64. "*What's My Line* Live Announcements for Continuing Use," not dated (~1953); NBC, John Charles Daly Papers, box 8, folder 1.

65. "*Information Please*," memorandum, not dated (~May 1938), NBC, box 61, folder 66.

66. Henry Morton Robinson, "*Information Please*," *Reader's Digest*, January 1939, 65–66.

67. Sullivan, 75.

68. Jowett, 127.

69. Cf. William Boddy, "Building the World's Largest Advertising Medium: CBS and Television, 1940–60," in *Hollywood in the Age of Television*, ed. Tino Balio (Boston: Unwin Hyman, 1990), 63–89.

70. Boddy, 71.

71. "*Information Please*," 15 November 1940, NBC.

72. Jowett.

73. Judy Dupuy, *Television Show Business* (New York: General Electric, 1945), 91, 96.

74. Thomas H. Hutchinson, *Here Is Television: Your Window to the World* (New York: Hastings House, 1946), 154.

75. Hutchinson, 156.

76. *Americana*, Martin Stone Productions, NBC, 1947–1949; *Quiz Kids*, Louis Cowan Productions, NBC, CBS, 1949–1956.

77. Benedict Anderson, *Imagined Communities: Reflections on the Origin and Spread of Nationalism*, rev. ed. (London: Verso, 1991).

78. *Stop the Music*, Louis Cowan Productions, Mark Goodson Productions, ABC, 1949–1956; "*Strike It Rich*," Walt Framer Productions, CBS, 1951–1953; "*Chance of a Lifetime*," Robert Jennings Productions, ABC, 1950–1951.

79. *Chance of a Lifetime*, 5 September 1951.

80. David Schwartz, Steve Ryan, and Fred Wostbrock, *The Encyclopedia of Television Game Shows*, 2nd ed. (New York: Facts on File, 1995), 188.

81. *Break the Bank*, Wolf Productions, ABC, NBC, CBS, 1954–1956; *Name that Tune*, Tel-o-Tune Productions/Harry Salter Productions, NBC, CBS, 1953–1959.

82. Robert C. Allen, "Audience-Oriented Criticism and Television," in *Channels of Discourse, Reassembled: Television and Contemporary Criticism*, ed. Robert C. Allen (Chapel Hill: University of North Carolina Press, 1992), 116.

83. Allen, "Audience-Oriented Criticism," 119.

84. Jowett, 140.

85. Baudrillard, Ang.

86. Susman, 203.

3. BIG MONEY: THE SCANDAL AND QUIZ SHOWS IN THE 1950s

A previous version of this chapter was published as Hoerschelmann, Olaf: "'Beyond the tailfin': Education and the politics of knowledge on big-money quiz shows." *Journal of Communication Inquiry*, vol. 24, no. 2 (April 2000): 177–94.

1. *Champagne for Caesar*, prod. George Moskov, dir. Richard Whorf, 1 hr. 39 min., United Artists, 1950, videocassette.

2. *The $64,000 Question*, prod. Joe Cates and Mert Koplin, CBS, Entertainment Productions Inc., 1955–1958; *The $64,000 Challenge*, prod. Joe Cates and Ed Jurist, CBS, Entertainment Productions, 1956–1958; *Twenty-One*, prod. Howard Merrill and Al Freedman, NBC, Jack Barry and Dan Enright Productions, 1956–1958; *The Big Surprise*, prod. Joe Cates, Seymour Robbie, David Lowe, and Merrill Heatter, NBC, Louis Cowan Productions and Entertainment Productions, 1955–1957.

3. Olaf Hoerschelmann, "The $64,000 Question," in *Museum of Broadcast Communications Encyclopedia of Television*, ed. Horace Newcomb (Chicago: Fitzroy Dearborn Publishers, 1997).

4. Olaf Hoerschelmann, "Quiz and Game Shows," in *Museum of Broadcast Communications Encyclopedia of Television*, ed. Horace Newcomb (Chicago: Fitzroy Dearborn Publishers, 1997).

5. William Boddy, "The Seven Dwarfs and the Money Grubbers: The Public Relations Crisis of U.S. Television in the Late 1950s," in *Logics of Television: Essays in Cultural Criticism*, ed. Patricia Mellencamp (Bloomington: Indiana University Press, 1990), 98–116; Michael R. Real, *Exploring Media Culture* (Thousand Oaks, Calif.: Sage, 1996).

6. Pierre Bourdieu and Loic J. D. Wacquant, *An Invitation to Reflexive Sociology* (Chicago: University of Chicago Press, 1992), 101–2.

7. Pierre Bourdieu, *Distinction: A Social Critique of the Judgement of Taste* (Cambridge, Mass.: Harvard University Press, 1984); Bourdieu and Wacquant.

8. Stephen J. Whitfield, *The Culture of the Cold War* (Baltimore, Md.: Johns Hopkins University Press, 1991), 169–70.

9. Elaine Tyler May, *Homeward Bound: American Families in the Cold War Era* (New York: Basic Books, 1988), 168.

10. Robert A. Divine, *The Sputnik Challenge* (Oxford, Eng.: Oxford University Press, 1993), XVI.

11. Divine, XVI.

12. Barbara B. Clowse, *Brainpower for the Cold War: The Sputnik Crisis and National Defense Education Act of 1958* (Westport, Conn.: Greenwood Press, 1981), 4.

13. Peter B. Dow, *Schoolhouse Politics: Lessons from the Sputnik Era* (Cambridge, Mass.: Harvard University Press, 1991), 19.

14. Clowse.

15. Clowse, 38.

16. Bourdieu and Wacquant, 111.

17. Bourdieu and Wacquant, 112.

18. Whitfield, 177.

19. Raymond Williams, *Marxism and Literature* (Oxford, Eng.: Oxford University Press, 1977), 101–7.

20. Vance Kepley Jr., "From 'Frontal Lobes' to the 'Bob-and-Bob Show': NBC Management and Programming Strategies, 1949–65," in *Hollywood in the Age of Television*, ed. Tino Balio (Boston: Unwin Hyman, 1990), 41–61.

21. Kepley, 49.

22. Pamela Wilson, "NBC Television's 'Operation Frontal Lobes': Cultural Hegemony and Fifties' Program Planning," *Historical Journal of Film, Radio and Television* 15, no. 1 (1995): 83–104.

23. Wilson, 86.

24. Wilson, 92.

25. Michele Hilmes, *Radio Voices: American Broadcasting, 1922–1952* (Minneapolis: University of Minnesota Press, 1997).

26. Michael Curtin, *Redeeming the Wasteland: Television Documentary and Cold War Politics* (New Brunswick, N.J.: Rutgers University Press, 1995), 8.

27. Christopher Anderson, *Hollywood TV: The Studio System in the Fifties* (Austin: University of Texas Press, 1994), 85.

28. William Boddy, "Building the World's Largest Advertising Medium: CBS and Television, 1940–60," in *Hollywood in the Age of Television*, ed. Tino Balio (Boston: Unwin Hyman, 1990), 76.

29. "Responsibility Reports," NBC, Sidney Eiges Papers, box 168, folder 10 (1954); box 171, folder 33–34 (1955).

30. Wilson, 83–104; Laurence Bergreen, *Look Now, Pay Later: The Rise of Network Broadcasting* (Garden City, N.Y.: Doubleday, 1980); William Boddy, "Operation Frontal Lobes versus the Living Room Toy: The Battle over Programme Control in Early Television," *Media, Culture and Society* 9 (1987): 347–68.

31. "Responsibility Reports," NBC, Sidney Eiges Papers, box 168, folder 10 (1954); box 171, folder 33–34 (1955).

32. Wilson, 99.

33. Boddy, "Seven Dwarfs," 106.

34. Wilson, 100.

35. *The $64,000 Question*; *Tic Tac Dough*, prod. Howard Felsher, NBC, Jack Barry and Dan Enright Productions, 1956–1959; *Twenty One*; *The Big Surprise*.

36. Jackson Lears, "A Matter of Taste: Corporate Cultural Hegemony in a Mass-Consumption Society," in *Recasting America: Culture and Politics in the Age of Cold War*, ed. Larry May (Chicago: University of Chicago Press, 1989), 38–57.

37. Lynn Spigel, *Make Room for TV: Television and the Family Ideal in Postwar America* (Chicago: University of Chicago Press, 1992); George Lipsitz, *Time Passages: Collective Memory and American Popular Culture* (Minneapolis: University of Minnesota Press, 1990).

38. Roland Marchand, "Visions of Classlessness, Quests for Dominion: American Popular Culture, 1945–1960," in *Reshaping America: Society and Institutions*, ed. Robert H. Bremmer and Gary W. Reichard (Columbus: Ohio State University Press, 1982), 169.

39. Both of these characterizations refer to popular candidates on *The $64,000 Question*, Redmond O'Hanlon and Gino Prato, and were widely circulated in popular magazines such as *Newsweek* and *Time* as well as in newspapers such as the *New York Times*.

40. "*The $64,000 Question*," not dated (~1957)

41. Tony Bennett, "Texts, Readers, Reading Formations," *Bulletin of the Midwest Modern Language Association* 16, no. 1 (1983): 3–17; Tony Bennett, "Texts in History: The Determinations of Readings and Their Texts," *Journal of the Midwest Modern Language Association* 18, no. 1 (1985): 1–16.

42. Charles Van Doren, "Junk Wins TV Shows," *Life*, 23 September 1957, 137–48.

43. "TV's biggest find!", *TV Guide* 21 January 1956, 4–7.

44. Jack Gould, "Man in the Street: The Public Can Often Outshine TV Stars," *New York Times*, 14 August 1955, 11.

45. R. Gehman, "How to Think Big," *Cosmopolitan*, December 1955, 81.

46. "*The $64,000 Question*," *Newsweek*, 5 September 1955, 41–45.

47. Real, 228.

48. Bourdieu, *Distinction*.

49. Hilmes.

50. Hilmes, 76.

51. Boddy, "Seven Dwarfs," 104.

52. Bourdieu and Wacquant.

53. See for example, David Schwartz, Steve Ryan, and Fred Wostbrock, *The Encyclopedia of Television Game Shows*, 2nd. ed. (New York: Facts on File, 1995); J. Fred MacDonald, *One Nation under Television: The Rise and Decline of Network TV*(Chicago: Nelson-Hall, 1994); Thomas A. DeLong, *Quiz Craze: America's Infatuation with Game Shows* (New York: Praeger: 1991).

4. DEALING WITH CHANGE: THE EVOLUTION OF QUIZ SHOWS IN THE 1960s

1. *Quiz Show*, prod. and dir. Robert Redford, 2 hr. 13 min., Wildwood Enterprises and Baltimore Pictures, 1994, videocassette.

2. "Hardly a Scratch in TV's Image," *Broadcasting*, 2 November 1959, 41.

3. "TV Begins Scrubbing Its Tarnish," *Broadcasting*, 26 October 1959, 41.

4. Forrest F. Owen, "Why Kill Good Quizzes with the Bad?" *Broadcasting*, 16 November 1959, 31.

5. "Congress Quizzing on TV Quizzes," *Broadcasting*, 3 August 1959, 37–38.

6. "The Resurgence of Television Game Shows," *Broadcasting*, 6 November 1961, 60.

7. "Why the 'Quiz-Panel' Shows Are TV Staples," *Sponsor*, 4 July 1959, 36–37, 76–77.

8. "Daytime Net TV Show Rates," *Sponsor*, 21 November 1960, 36–37.

9. "Game Shows Making Strong Comeback," *Broadcasting*, 24 July 1961, 62–63.

10. Henry Jenkins, *Textual Poachers: Television Fans and Participatory Culture* (New York: Routledge, 1992), 224.

11. "Game Shows Making Strong Comeback," 62.

12. "Game Shows Making Strong Comeback," 62.

13. Michel Foucault, *The History of Sexuality Part I*, (Harmondsworth, Eng.: Penguin, 1978).

14. David Schwartz, Steve Ryan, and Fred Wostbrock, *The Encyclopedia of TV Game Shows*, 2nd ed.,(New York: Facts on File, 1995).

15. Julie D'Acci, "Nobody's Woman? *Honey West* and the New Sexuality," in *The Revolution Wasn't Televised: Sixties Television and Social Conflict*, ed. Lynn Spigel and Michael Curtin (New York: Routledge, 1997), 73–94.

16. Olaf Hoerschelmann, "*Jeopardy!*," in *Museum of Broadcasting Communications Encyclopedia of Television*, 2nd ed., ed. Horace Newcomb (New York: Taylor and Francis, 2004).

17. Schwartz, Ryan, and Worstbrock, 97.

18. Beverly Stoeltje, "Power and the Ritual Genres: American Rodeo," *Western Folklore* 52 (April 1993): 142.

19. Victor Turner, "Liminal to Liminoid, in Play, Flow, and Ritual: An Essay in Comparative Symbology," *Rice University Studies* 60, no. 3 (1974): 53–92; Beverly Stoeltje, "The Beauty Contest: Ritualizing the Female Body," paper presented to the Davies Forum, University of San Francisco, San Francisco, Calif., 1997; Stoeltje, "Power and the Ritual Genres."

20. Christopher H. Sterling and John M. Kittross, *Stay Tuned: A Concise History of American Broadcasting* (Belmont, Calif.: Wadsworth, 1990), 328–33.

21. Kenneth J. Bindas and Kenneth J. Heineman, "Image Is Everything? Television and the Counterculture Message in the 1960s," *Journal of Popular Film and Television* 22, no. 1 (1994): 24.

22. Thomas Frank, *The Conquest of Cool: Business Culture, Counterculture, and the Rise of Hip Consumerism* (Chicago: University of Chicago Press, 1997), 119.

23. Bindas and Heineman; Aniko Bodroghkozy, "*The Smothers Brothers Comedy Hour* and the Youth Rebellion," in *The Revolution Wasn't Televised: Sixties Television and Social Conflict,* ed. Lynn Spigel and Michael Curtin (New York: Routledge, 1997), 201–19.

24. Jackson Lears, *Fables of Abundance: A Cultural History of Advertising in America* (New York: Basic Books, 1994).

25. Wendy Selby, "Social Evil or Social Good: Lotteries and State Regulation in Australia and the United States," in *Gambling Cultures: Studies in History and Interpretation,* ed. Jan McMillen (London: Routledge, 1996), 65–85; Jan McMillen, "Understanding Gambling: History, Concepts and Theories," in *Gambling Cultures: Studies in History and Interpretation,* ed. Jan McMillen (London: Routledge, 1996), 6–42.

26. McMillen, "Understanding Gambling."

27. Selby, 79.

28. Lears; McMillen, "Understanding Gambling."

29. *Video Village,* prod. Merrill Heatter–Bob Quigley Productions, CBS, 1960–1962.

30. "Game Shows Making Strong Comeback," 62–63.

31. Jefferson Graham, *Come on Down!!!: The TV Game Show Book* (New York: Abbeville Press, 1988), 142–43.

32. Graham, 39–42.

33. Lynn Spigel and Michael Curtin, "Introduction," in *The Revolution Wasn't Televised: Sixties Television and Social Conflict*, ed. Lynn Spigel and Michael Curtin (New York: Routledge, 1997), 1–18.

34. Frank, 19.

35. Pamela Wilson, "NBC Television's 'Operation Frontal Lobes': Cultural Hegemony and Fifties' Program Planning," *Historical Journal of Film, Radio and Television* 15, no. 1 (1995): 100.

36. Frank, 105.

37. Andreas Huyssen, "Mass Culture as Woman: Modernism's Other," in *Studies in Entertainment*, ed. Tania Modleski (Bloomington: Indiana University Press, 1986), 191.

38. "Seven Men Capture the Most Responsive Audience in Daytime Television!" *Broadcasting*, 6 June 1960, 14–15.

39. "TvB Digs Up New Data on Daytime TV," *Sponsor*, 1 August 1960, 69.

40. "Cracking the Supermarkets," *Sponsor*, 7 August 1961, p. 31; "When Will Radio/TV Crack the Supers?" *Sponsor*, 31 July 1961, 27–30, 49–50.

41. *Shopping Spree*, prod. Bill Derman and Joe Landis, NBC, 1962. 1962.

42. *Seven Keys*, prod. Wellington Productions, ABC, 1961–1964.

43. "Supermarket Sweep," prod. Talent Associates, ABC, 1965–1967.

44. See for example, Mary Ann Doane, *The Desire to Desire: The Woman's Film of the 1940s* (Bloomington: Indiana University Press, 1987).

45. Lynne Joyrich, "All that Television Allows: TV Melodrama, Postmodernism, and Consumer Culture," in *Private Screenings: Television and the Female Consumer*, eds. Lynn Spigel and Denise Mann (Minneapolis: University of Minnesota Press, 1992), 242.

46. Susan Douglas, "Will You Love Me Tomorrow? Changing Discourses about Female Sexuality in the Mass Media, 1960–1968," in *Ruthless Criticism: New Perspectives in U.S. Communication History*, eds. William S. Solomom and Robert W. McChesney (Minneapolis: University of Minnesota Press, 1993), 353.

47. Raymond Williams, *Marxism and Literature* (Oxford, Eng.: Oxford University Press, 1977), 128–135.

48. George Lipsitz, "Who'll Stop the Rain: Youth Culture, Rock 'n' Roll, and Social Crises," in *The Sixties: From Memory to History*, ed. David Farber (Chapel Hill: University of North Carolina Press, 1994), 206–34; Bodroghkozy, 201–19; Elaine Tyler May, *Homeward Bound: American Families in the Cold War Era* (New York: Basic Books, 1988).

49. May.

50. Lipsitz, 216.

51. Wayne Munson, *All Talk: The Talk Show in Media Culture*. (Philadelphia: Temple University Press, 1993), 43.

52. Jane Feuer, "The Concept of Live Television: Ontology as Ideology," in *Regarding Television*, ed. E. Ann Kaplan (Los Angeles: American Film Institute, 1983), 14.

53. David Barker, "The Emergence of Television's Repertoire of Representation, 1920–1935," *Journal of Broadcasting and the Electronic Media*, 35, no. 3 (1991); 311.

54. Laura Mulvey, "Visual Pleasure and Narrative Cinema," *Screen*, 16, no. 3 (1975): 17.

55. Michele Hilmes, "The Television Apparatus: Direct Address," *Journal of Film and Video*, 37, no. 4 (1985); 28.

56. Margaret Morse, "Talk, Talk, Talk—The Space of Discourse in Television," *Screen* 26, no. 2 (1985); 2–15.

57. Tony Verna: Live TV: An Inside Look at Directing and Producing (Boston: Focal Press, 1987), 197.

58. Walter Benjamin: *The World of Art in the Age of Mechanical Reproduction* (New York: Schocken Books, 1969).

59. Robert Vianello, "The Power Politics of 'Live' Television," *Journal of Film and Video* 38, no. 3 (Summer 1985): 37.

60. *Let's Make a Deal*, prod. Stefan Hatos–Monty Hall Production, Ron Greenberg–Dick Clark Productions, ABC, NBC, syndicated, 1963–1986, 1990–1991. The pilot for *Let's Make a Deal* is available at the UCLA Film and Television Archives.

61. *Let's Make a Deal*, pilot, UCLA Film and Television Archive.

62. Bakhtin.

63. Bodroghkozy.

64. Bodroghkozy, 211–12.

65. Cf. May.

66. Schwartz, Ryan, and Wostbrock, 110.

67. Graham, 176.

68. Graham, 37–38.

69. *The Price Is Right*, prod. Jay Wolpert, Barbara Hunter, Phillip Wayne, Roger Dobkowitz, CBS, 1972–present. My discussion of *The Price Is Right* relates to the CBS daytime version.

70. David Marc and Robert J. Thompson, *Prime Time, Prime Movers* (Boston: Little, Brown, 1992), 256.

71. Graham, 185.

72. "When Will Radio/TV Crack the Supers?" *Sponsor*, 31 July 1961, 49.

73. "The Price of Color TV Is Right," *Sponsor*, 20 February 1960, 19.

74. Victoria E. Johnson, "Citizen Welk: Bubbles, Blue Hair, and Middle America," in *The Revolution Wasn't Televised: Sixties Television and Social Conflict*, ed. Lynn Spigel and Michael Curtin (New York: Routledge, 1997), 279.

75. Kenneth J Bindas and Kenneth J. Heineman, "Image Is Everything? Television and the Counterculture Message in the 1960s," *Journal of Popular Film and Television* 22, no. 1 (1994): 22.

76. Jackson Lears, *Fables of Abundance: A Cultural History of Advertising in America* (New York: Basic Books, 1994), 258.

5. DATING GAMES: PLAYING RELATIONSHIPS IN 1980s AND 1990s TELEVISION

1. *Confessions of a Dangerous Mind*, prod. Andrew Lazar and Jeffrey Sudzin, dir. George Clooney, 1 hr. 53 min., Miramax and Artisan Entertainment, 2002, VHS. The film is based on the book *Confessions of a Dangerous Mind. An Unauthorized Autobiography* by Chuck Barris (New York: St. Martin's Press, 1984).

2. *The Dating Game*, prod. Chuck Barris Productions, ABC, syndicated, 1965–1974, 1978–1980, 1986–1989; *The Newlywed Game*, prod. Chuck Barris Production, Barris Industries, ABC, syndicated, 1966–1980, 1985–1989, 1993–present; *Three's a Crowd*, prod. Chuck Barris Productions, syndicated, 1979–1980; *Treasure Hunt*, prod. Chuck Barris Productions, syndicated, 1981–1982; *$1.98 Beauty Show*, prod. Chuck Barris Productions,

syndicated, 1978–1979; *The Gong Show*, Chuck Barris–Chris Bearde Productions, NBC, syndicated, 1976–1980, 1988–1989.

3. John Fiske, *Television Culture* (London: Routledge, 1987), 269.

4. See for example, Thomas Frank, *The Conquest of Cool: Business Culture, Counterculture, and the Rise of Hip Consumerism* (Chicago: University of Chicago Press, 1997); Stephen Fox, *The Mirror Makers: A History of American Advertising and Its Creators* (New York: Vintage Books, 1984); Aniko Bodroghkozy, *Groove Tube: Sixties Television and the Youth Rebellion* (Durham, N.C.: Duke University Press, 2001).

5. *High Rollers*, prod. Merrill Heatter–Bob Quigley Productions, Merril Heatter Productions/Century Tower Productions/Orion Television, NBC, syndicated, 1974–1980, 1987-1988.

6. *Card Sharks*, prod. Mark Goodson-Bill Todman Productions, NBC, CBS, syndicated, 1978-1981, 1986–1989.

7. *Family Feud*, prod. Mark Goodson–Bill Todman Productions, Mark Goodson Productions, ABC, CBS, syndicated, 1976–1985, 1988–1995, 1999–present.

8. Warren I. Susman, *Culture as History: The Transformation of American Society in the Twentieth Century* (New York: Pantheon, 1984), 212.

9. Bodroghkozy, 249.

10. Ken Auletta, *Three Blind Mice* (New York: Vintage Books, 1992); Michael Curtin, *Redeeming the Wasteland: Television Documentary and Cold War Politics* (New Brunswick, N.J.: Rutgers University Press, 1995).

11. David Harvey, "Flexibility: Threat of Opportunity," *Socialist Review* 21, no. 2 (1991) 65–77; Michael Curtin, "On Edge: Culture Industries in the Neo-Network Era," in *Making and Selling Culture*, ed. Richard Ohmann, Gage Averill, Michael Curtin, David Shumway, and Elizabeth G. Traube (Hanover, N.H.: Wesleyan University Press, 1996), 181–202.

12, J. Fred MacDonald, *One Nation under Television: The Rise and Decline of Network TV* (Chicago: Nelson-Hall, 1994), 227.

13. Douglas Kellner, *Television and the Crisis of Democracy* (Boulder Colo.: Westview Press, 1990), 64.

14. Larry Grossberg, *We Gotta Get Out of This Place: Popular Conservatism and Postmodern Culture* (New York: Routledge, 1992), 250–52.

15. James Davison Hunter, *Culture Wars: The Struggle to Define America* (New York: Basic Books, 1991); Elizabeth G. Traube, *Dreaming*

Identities: Class, Gender, and Generation in 1980s Hollywood Movies (Boulder, Colo.: Westview Press, 1992); Grossberg.

16. Stephen Macedo, "Introduction," in *Reassessing the Sixties: Debating the Political and Cultural Legacy*, ed. Stephen Macedo (New York: Norton, 1997), 9–18; Grossberg; Hunter.

17. Alan Wolfe, "Politics by Other Means." *New Republic*, 11 November 1991, 39.

18. Grossberg; Hunter.

19. Macedo.

20. Hunter, 177–78.

21. Hunter, 179.

22. Hunter, 180.

23. Traube, 129.

24. Hunter, 122.

25. Jane Feuer, *Seeing through the Eighties: Television and Reaganism* (Durham, N.C.: Duke University Press), 34.

26. MacDonald, 230–33.

27. MacDonald, 232.

28. MacDonald.

29. Kellner; Traube.

30. Ella Taylor, *Prime-Time Families: Television Culture in Postwar America* (Berkeley: University of California Press, 1989); Traube.

31. Feuer.

32. Hunter, 122.

33. *Wait 'Til You Have Kids*, prod. Jay Wolpert Enterprises, Family Channel, 1996–1997.

34. Feuer; Traube.

35. Bodroghkozy, 249.

36. Mark Schwed, "MTV's Miss Matchmaker," *TV Guide*, 8 June 1996: 22–24; Anna David and Jim Juvonen, "'Singled' File," *TV Guide* 8 June 1996: 26–29.

37. *Love Connection*, prod. Lorimar Television, Telepictures Corporation, 1981-1993.

38. *The Newlywed Game*.

39. Jefferson Graham, *Come on Down!!! The TV Game Show Book* (New York: Abbeville Press, 1988), 109.

40. *Singled Out*, prod. MTV Productions, MTV, 1995–1997.

41. Hunter, 126.

42. *The Dating Game; The Big Date*, USA Networks, 1995–1996; *Bzzz!* prod. Ralph Edwards/Stu Billett Productions, Tribune Entertainment, WGN, 1996–2000.

43. Traube.

44. *Change of Heart*, prod. Telepictures Distribution, Warner Brothers, syndicated, 1998–present; *Temptation Island*, prod. Twentieth Century Fox, Chum Television, syndicated, 2001–present; *Elimidate*, prod. Telepictures productions, syndicated, WB, 2001–present; *Blind Date*, prod. Bobwell Production, Goldcoast Entertainment, syndicated, 1999–present.

45. Warner Brothers Studios, "*Change of Heart*," http://changeofheart. warnerbros.com (accessed November 10, 2001).

46. Warner Brothers Studios, "*Change of Heart*" This Week," http:// changeofheart.warnerbros.com/html/this Week.html (accessed November 10, 2001).

47. Fox Broadcasting Company, "*About Temptation Island*: Rules," http://www.fox.com/temptation2/about/rules.htm (accessed November 10, 2001).

48. NBC-Universal, "*Blind Date* Episode Guide: Vanessa and Randy," http://www.blinddatetv.com (accessed November 10, 2001).

49. NBC-Universal, "*Blind Date* Episode Guide: Darin and Sheree," http://www.blinddatetv.com (accessed November 10, 2001).

6. INTERACTIVE CONTROL: QUIZ SHOWS AND NEW MEDIA TECHNOLOGIES

1. David Schwartz, Steve Ryan, and Fred Wostbrock, *The Encyclopedia of Television Game Shows*, 2nd ed. (New York: Facts on File, 1995), xxiv.

2. Thomas Streeter, "Blue Skies and Strange Bedfellows: The Discourse of Cable Television," in *The Revolution Wasn't Televised: Sixties*

Television and Social Conflict, eds. Lynn Spigel and Michael Curtin (New York: Routledge, 1997), 227.

3. Streeter, "Blue Skies," 234.

4. Ithiel de Sola Pool, *Technologies of Freedom* (Cambridge, Mass.: Harvard University Press, 1983), 158.

5. Streeter, "Blue Skies," 224.

6. Don Le Duc, *Cable Television and the FCC: A Crisis in Media Control* (Philadelphia: Temple University Press, 1973), 16.

7. Le Duc, 14.

8. Streeter,"Blue Skies," 230.

9. Bertold Brecht, "The Radio as an Apparatus of Communication," in *Brecht on Theatre: The Development of an Aesthetic*, ed. and trans. John Willet (New York: Hill and Wang, 1964, orig. 1932),52.

10. Brecht, 52.

11. Pool, 166.

12. Le Duc.

13. Streeter, "Blue Skies," 236.

14. Streeter, "Blue Skies"; Thomas Streeter, "The Cable Fable Revisited: Discourse, Policy, and the Making of Cable Television," *Critical Studies in Mass Communication*, 4 (1987): 174–200.

15. Interactive Network, "Competition Guidelines," Interactive Network, Member Entertainment Guide, 1 November 1993, 17.

16. Brecht; Raymond Williams, *Television: Technology and Cultural Form* (Hanover, N.H.: Wesleyan University Press, 1974).

17. John Thornton Caldwell, *Televisuality: Style, Crisis, and Authority in American Television* (New Brunswick, N.J.: Rutgers University Press, 1995), 260.

18. Anthony Giddens, *The Consequences of Modernity* (Stanford, Calif.: Stanford University Press, 1990), 21.

19. Williams.

20. Williams, 15.

21. Williams, 17.

22. James R. Beniger, *The Control Revolution* (Cambridge, Mass.: Harvard University Press, 1986), 20.

23. Beniger, 20.

24. Interactive Network, *Operating System 1.8 Upgrade Guide* (Mountain View, Calif.: Interactive Network, 1993), 5.

25. Caldwell, 262.

26. Ien Ang, "Culture and Communication: Towards an Ethnographic Critique of Media Consumption in the Transnational Media System," *European Journal of Communication* 5, no. 2–3 (1990): 239–60.

27. Michel De Certeau, *The Practice of Everyday Life* (Berkeley: University of California Press, 1984).

28. Ang, 248.

29. Shaun Moores, *Interpreting Audiences: The Ethnography of Media Consumption* (London: Sage, 1993), 70.

30. Shaun Moores, "Television, Geography and 'Mobile Privatization,'" *European Journal of Communication* 8, no. 3 (1993), 365.

31. Moores, "Television, Geography," 368.

32. David Morley, "Where the Global Meets the Local: Notes from the Sitting Room," *Screen* 32 no. 1 (1991): 4.

33. For Example, Roger Silverstone, Eric Hirsch, and David Morley, "Information and Communication Technologies and the Moral Economy of the Household," in *Consuming Technologies: Media and Information in Domestic Spaces*, ed. Roger Silverstone and Eric Hirsch (London: Routledge, 1992), 15–31.

34. Graham Murdock, "Communications and the Constitution of Modernity," *Media, Culture and Society* 15, no. 4 (1993): 521–39.

35. Thomas Streeter, "Selling the Air: Property and the Politics of U.S. Commercial Broadcasting," *Media, Culture and Society* 16, no. 1 (1994): 110.

36. Streeter, "Selling."

37. Susan Smulyan, "Radio Advertising to Women in Twenties America: 'A Latchkey to Every Home,'" *Historical Journal of Film, Radio and Television* 13, no. 3 (1993): 299–314.

38. Streeter, "Selling" 111.

39. Lynn Spigel, *Make Room for TV: Television and the Family Ideal in Postwar America* (Chicago: University of Chicago Press, 1991), 99–135.

40, Williams.

41. *Who Wants to Be a Millionaire*, prod. Michael Davies and Paul Smith, dir. Mark Gentile, ABC, Buena Vista Television, Celador, Valley Crest Productions, 1999–present.

42. Caldwell.

CONCLUSION: THE REALITY OF QUIZ SHOWS

1. *Survivor*, prod. Mark Burnett, CBS, Castaway Television Productions, Survivor Entertainment Group, 2000–present.

2. Beverly Stoeltje, "Power and the Ritual Genres: American Rodeo," *Western Folklore* 52 (April 1993): 142.

3. Stoeltje, Victor Turner, "Liminal to Liminoid, in Play, Flow, and Ritual: An Essay in Comparative Symbology," *Rice University Studies* 60, no. 3 (1974).

4. *Who Wants to Be a Millionaire*, prod. Michael Davies and Paul Smith, dir. Mark Gentile, ABC, Buena Vista Television, Celador, Valley Crest Productions, 1999–present.

5. Ken Auletta, *Three Blind Mice* (New York: Vintage Books, 1992).

6. Robert C. Allen, *Speaking of Soap Operas* (Chapel Hill: University of North Carolina Press, 1985).

7. John Thornton Caldwell, *Televisuality: Style, Crisis, and Authority in American Television* (New Brunswick, N.J.: Rutgers University Press, 1995), 261.

8. Allen, 7.

Bibliography

Abrahams, Roger D. "Enactment-Centered Theory." In *Frontiers of Folklore*, ed. William R. Bascom, 85–117. Boulder, Colo: Westview Press, 1977.

Abt, Vicki. "The Role of the State in the Expansion and Growth of Commercial Gambling in the USA." In *Gambling Cultures: Studies in History and Interpretation*, ed. Jan McMillen, 179–98. London: Routledge, 1996.

Allen, Robert C. "Audience-Oriented Criticism and Television." In *Channels of Discourse, Reassembled: Television and Contemporary Criticism*, ed. Robert C. Allen, 101–37. Chapel Hill: University of North Carolina Press, 1992.

———. *Speaking of Soap Operas*. Chapel Hill: University of North Carolina Press, 1985.

Altman, Rick. *The American Film Musical*. Bloomington: Indiana University Press, 1989.

———. *Film/Genre*. London: British Film Institute, 1999.

———. "A Semantic/Syntactic Approach to Film Genre." In *Film Genre Reader*, ed. Barry Keith Grant, 26–40. Austin: University of Texas Press, 1986.

———. "Television/Sound." In *Studies in Entertainment: Critical Approaches to Mass Culture*, ed. Tania Modleski, 39–54. Bloomington: Indiana University Press, 1986.

Alvey, Mark. "The Independents: Rethinking the Television Studio System." In *The Revolution Wasn't Televised: Sixties Television and Social Conflict*, eds. Lynn Spigel and Michael Curtin, 139–58. New York: Routledge, 1997.

Anderson, Benedict. *Imagined Communities: Reflections on the Origin and Spread of Nationalism* (Rev. Ed.). London: Verso, 1991.

Anderson, Christopher. *Hollywood TV: The Studio System in the Fifties*. Austin: University of Texas Press, 1994.

Anderson, Kent. *Television Fraud: The History and Implications of the Quiz Show Scandals*. Westport, Conn.: Greenwood Press, 1978.

Ang, Ien. *Living Room Wars: Rethinking Media Audiences for a Postmodern World*. London: Routledge, 1996.

———. *Desperately Seeking the Audience*. London: Routledge, 1991.

Auletta, Ken. "The Magic Box." *New Yorker*, 11 April 1994, 40–45.

———. *Three Blind Mice*. New York: Vintage Books, 1992.

Bakhtin, Mikhail Mikhailovich. *Rabelais and His World*. Bloomington: Indiana University Press, 1984.

———. *The Dialogic Imagination*. Austin: University of Texas Press, 1981.

Barker, David. " 'It's Been Real': Forms of Television Representation." *Critical Studies in Mass Communication* 5 (1988): 42–56.

———. "Television Production Techniques as Communication." In *Television: The Critical View*, ed. Horace Newcomb, 87–100. New York: Oxford University Press, 1994.

Barnouw, Erik. *A History of Broadcasting in the United States*. vol. 1, *To 1933: A Tower in Babel*. New York: Oxford University Press, 1966.

———. *A History of Broadcasting in the United States*. Vol. 2, *1933–1953: The Golden Web*. New York: Oxford University Press, 1968.

———. *A History of Broadcasting in the United States*. Vol. 3, *From 1953: The Image Empire*. New York: Oxford University Press, 1970.

Baudrillard, Jean. *In the Shadow of the Silent Majorities, or, the End of the Social and Other Essays*. New York: Semiotext(e), 1983.

Baughman, James L. "The Promise of American Television, 1929–1952." *Prospects: An Annual of American Studies* 11 (1987): 119–34.

Bauman, Richard. " 'I'll Give You Three Guesses': The Dynamics of Genre in the Riddle Tale." In *Untying the Knot: On Riddles and Other Enigmatic*

Modes, eds. Galit Hasan-Rokem and David Shulman, 62–77. New York: Oxford University Press, 1996.

Becker, Lee B. "Audience Reactions to Interactive Cable: An Update on the Columbus, Ohio, Qube System." *Rundfunk Und Fernsehen* 30, no. 1 (1982): 5–13.

Bennett, Tony. "Texts in History: The Determinations of Readings and Their Texts." *Journal of the Midwest Modern Language Association* 18, no. 1 (1985): 1–16.

———. "Texts, Readers, Reading Formations." *Bulletin of the Midwest Modern Language Association* 16, no. 1 (1983): 3–17.

Bergreen, Laurence. *Look Now, Pay Later: The Rise of Network Broadcasting*. Garden City, N.Y.: Doubleday, 1980.

Berthold, Michael C. "*Jeopardy!*, Cultural Literacy, and the Discourse of Trivia." *Journal of American Culture* 13, no. 1 (1990): 11–17.

Bindas, Kenneth J., and Kenneth J. Heineman. "Image Is Everything? Television and the Counterculture Message in the 1960s." *Journal of Popular Film and Television* 22, no. 1 (1994): 22–37.

Bocock, Robert. *Ritual in Industrial Society: A Sociological Analysis of Ritualism in Modern England*. London: George Allen and Unwin, 1974.

Boddy, William. "Building the World's Largest Advertising Medium: CBS and Television, 1940–60." In *Hollywood in the Age of Television*, ed. Tino Balio, 63–89. Boston: Unwin Hyman, 1990.

———. *Fifties Television: The Industry and Its Critics*. Urbana: University of Illinois Press, 1990.

———. "Operation Frontal Lobes versus the Living Room Toy: The Battle over Programme Control in Early Television." *Media, Culture and Society* 9 (1987): 347–68.

———. "The Seven Dwarfs and the Money Grubbers: The Public Relations Crisis of U.S. Television in the Late 1950s." In *Logics of Television: Essays in Cultural Criticism*, ed. Patricia Mellencamp, 98–116. Bloomington: Indiana University Press, 1990.

Bodroghkozy, Aniko. "*The Smothers Brothers Comedy Hour* and the Youth Rebellion." In *The Revolution Wasn't Televised: Sixties Television and Social Conflict*, ed. Lynn Spigel and Michael Curtin, 201–19. New York: Routledge, 1997.

Bolen, Darrell W. "Gambling: Historical Highlights and Trends and Their Implications for Contemporary Society." In *Gambling and Society*, ed.

William R. Eadington, 7–38. Springfield, Il: Charles C. Thomas Publisher, 1976.

Bourdieu, Pierre. *Distinction: A Social Critique of the Judgement of Taste.* Cambridge, Mass.: Harvard University Press, 1984.

———. *The Logic of Practice.* Stanford, Calif.: Stanford University Press, 1990.

Bourdieu, Pierre, and Loïc J. D. Wacquant. *An Invitation to Reflexive Sociology.* Chicago: University of Chicago Press, 1992.

Brecht, Bertold. "The Radio as an Apparatus of Communication." In *Brecht on Theatre: The Development of an Aesthetic,* ed. and trans. John Willet, 51–53. New York: Hill and Wang, 1964.

Brooks, Tim, and Earle Marsh. *The Complete Dictionary to Prime Time Network TV Shows 1946–Present* (4th ed.). New York: Ballantine Books, 1988.

Brown, Ben. "Trouble in Paradise." *American Film* 7, no. 9 (1982): 61–62.

Cahiers du Cinéma Collective. "*Young Mr. Lincoln* De John Ford." *Cahiers Du Cinéma* 223 (1970): 29–47.

Caldwell, John Thornton. *Televisuality: Style, Crisis, and Authority in American Television.* New Brunswick, N.J.: Rutgers University Press, 1995.

Carey, James. *Culture as Communication.* Boston: Unwin Hyman, 1989.

Carey, John, and Pat Quarles. "Interactive Television." In *Transmission,* ed. Peter D'Agostino, 105–17. New York: Tanam Press, 1985.

Cawelti, John. Adventure, Mystery and Romance: Formula Stories as Art and Popular Culture. Chicago: University of Chicago Press, 1976.

"CBS to Eliminate All Shows Relying on 'Lavish Prizes.'" *Advertising Age,* 19 October 1959, 1, 8.

Ciardi, J. "Exit a Symbol." *Saturday Review,* 21 November 1959, 27–28, 59.

Clowse, Barbara Barksdale. *Brainpower for the Cold War: The Sputnik Crisis and National Defense Education Act of 1958.* Westport, Conn.: Greenwoods, 1981.

"Congress Quizzing on TV Quizzes." *Broadcasting,* 3 August 1959, 37–38.

"Contradictions Emerging on Future of Interactive TV." *Cable Age* 1, no. 1 (1981): 58–60.

"Cracking the Supermarkets." *Sponsor,* 7 August 1961, 30–31, 60.

Curtin, Michael. "On Edge: Culture Industries in the Neo-Network Era." In *Making and Selling Culture*, ed. Richard Ohmann, Gage Averill, Michael Curtin, David Shumway, and Elizabeth G. Traube, 181–202. Hanover, N.H.: Wesleyan University Press, 1996.

———. *Redeeming the Wasteland: Television Documentary and Cold War Politics*. New Brunswick, N.J.: Rutgers University Press, 1995.

D'Acci, Julie. "Nobody's Woman? *Honey West* and the New Sexuality." In *The Revolution Wasn't Televised: Sixties Television and Social Conflict*, ed. Lynn Spigel and Michael Curtin, 73–94. New York: Routledge, 1997.

David, Anna, and Jim Juvonen. "'Singled' File." *TV Guide* 8 June 1996, 26–29.

"Daytime Net TV Show Rates." *Sponsor*, 21 November 1960, 36–37.

"Daytime TV Gets a Face-Lifting." *Sponsor*, 4 September 1961, 25–28, 44.

DeLong, Thomas A. *Quiz Craze: America's Infatuation with Game Shows*. New York: Praeger, 1991.

Deming, Robert H. "The Television Spectator-Subject." *Journal of Film and Video* 37, no. 3 (1985): 48–63.

Derrida, Jacques. *Acts of Literature*. New York: Routledge, 1992.

Divine, Robert A. *The Sputnik Challenge*. Oxford: Oxford University Press, 1993.

Dombrink, John. "Gambling and the Legalisation of Vice: Social Movements, Public Health and Public Policy in the United States." In *Gambling Cultures: Studies in History and Interpretation*, ed. Jan McMillen, 43–64. London: Routledge, 1996.

Douglas, Susan. "Will You Love Me Tomorrow? Changing Discourses about Female Sexuality in the Mass Media, 1960–1968." In *Ruthless Criticism: New Perspectives in U.S. Communication History*, ed. William S. Solomom and Robert W. McChesney, 349–73. Minneapolis: University of Minnesota Press, 1993.

Dow, Peter B. *Schoolhouse Politics: Lessons From the Sputnik Era*. Cambridge, Mass.: Harvard University Press, 1991.

Dunning, John. *Tune in Yesterday: The Ultimate Encyclopedia of Old-Time Radio 1925–1976*. Englewood Cliffs, N.J.: Prentice-Hall, 1976.

Dupuy, Judy. *Television Show Business*. New York: General Electric, 1945.

Dyer, Richard. "Entertainment and Utopia." In *Genre: The Musical*, ed. Rick Altman, 175–89. London: Routledge and Kegan Paul, 1981.

Eco, Umberto. *The Role of the Reader: Explorations in the Semiotics of Texts.* Bloomington: Indiana University Press, 1979.

Ellis, John. *Visible Fictions: Cinema, Television, Video.* London: Routledge and Kegan Paul, 1982.

Fabe, Maxene. *TV Game Shows.* Garden City, N.Y.: Doubleday, 1979.

Feuer, Jane. "The Concept of Live Television: Ontology as Ideology." In *Regarding Television*, ed. E. Ann Kaplan, 12–22. Los Angeles: American Film Institute, 1983.

———. "Genre Study and Television." In *Channels of Discourse, Reassembled: Television and Contemporary Criticism*, ed. Robert C. Allen, 138–60. Chapel Hill: University of North Carolina Press, 1992.

———. *Seeing through the Eighties: Television and Reaganism.* Durham, N.C.: Duke University Press, 1995.

Fiske, John. "British Cultural Studies and Television." In *Channels of Discourse, Reassembled: Television and Contemporary Criticism*, ed. Robert C. Allen, 284–326. Chapel Hill: University of North Carolina Press, 1992.

———. "The Discourses of TV Quiz Shows, or School + Luck = Success + Sex." In *Television Criticism: Approaches and Applications*, ed. Leah Vande Berg and Lawrence Wenner, 445–62. New York: Longman, 1990.

———. *Media Matters: Everyday Culture and Political Change.* Minneapolis: University of Minnesota Press, 1994.

———. *Power Plays, Power Works.* London: Verso, 1993.

———. *Television Culture.* London: Routledge, 1987.

———. *Understanding Popular Culture.* London: Routledge, 1989.

———. "Women and Quiz Shows: Consumerism, Patriarchy and Resisting Pleasures." In *Television and Women's Culture: The Politics of the Popular*, ed. Mary Ellen Brown, 134–43. London: Sage, 1990.

Foucault, Michel. *The History of Sexuality, Part I.* Harmondsworth, Eng.: Penguin, 1978.

"Fresh New Programs for '62–'63." *Broadcasting* 61, no. 19 (1961): 31–36.

"Game Shows Making Strong Comeback." *Broadcasting*, 24 July 1961, 62–63.

Gamson, Joshua. *Freaks Talk Back: Tabloid Talk Shows and Sexual Nonconformity.* Chicago: University of Chicago Press, 1998.

Garnham, Nicholas. "Political Economy and Cultural Studies: Reconciliation or Divorce?" *Critical Studies in Mass Communication* 12, no. 1 (1995a): 62–71.

———. "Reply to Grossberg and Carey." In *Critical Studies in Mass Communication* 12, no. 1 (1995b): 95–100.

Gehman, R. "How to Think Big." *Cosmopolitan*, December 1955, 76–81.

Giroux, Henry A., and Peter L. McLaren. "Introduction: Media Hegemony: Towards a Critical Pedagogy of Representation." In *Media Knowledge: Readings in Popular Culture, Pedagogy, and Critical Citizenship*, ed. James Schwoch, Mimi White, and Susan Reilly, XV–XXXIV. Albany: State University of New York Press, 1992.

Giroux, Henry A., and Roger Simon. "Popular Culture and Critical Pedagogy: Everyday Life as Basis for Curriculum Knowledge." In *Critical Pedagogy, the State, and Cultural Struggle*, ed. Henry A. Giroux and Peter McLaren, 236–52. Albany: State University of New York Press, 1989.

Giroux, Henry A., Roger I. Simon, and Contributors. *Popular Culture, Schooling, and Everyday Life.* New York: Bergin and Garvey, 1989.

Gitlin, Todd. *The Sixties: Years of Hope, Days of Rage.* New York: Bantam Books, 1987.

Glynn, Kevin. *Tabloid Culture: Trash Taste, Popular Power, and the Transformation of American Television.* Durham, N.C.: Duke University Press, 2000.

Gould, Jack. "Man in the Street: The Public Can Often Outshine TV Stars." *New York Times*, 14 August 1955, sec. II, 11.

———. "A Plague on TV's House. Rigged Quiz Shows Viewed as Symptom of the Age, with Many Guilty Parties." *New York Times*, 12 October 1959, 39.

Graham, Jefferson. *Come on Down!!!: The TV Game Show Book.* New York: Abbeville Press, 1988.

Grossberg, Lawrence. "Cultural Studies vs. Political Economy: Is Anyone Else Bored with This Debate?" *Critical Studies in Mass Communication* 12, no. 1 (1995) 72–81.

———. *We Gotta Get Out of This Place: Popular Conservatism and Postmodern Culture.* New York: Routledge, 1992.

Hall, Stuart. "Encoding/Decoding." *Culture, Media, Language,* ed. Stuart Hall, Dorothy Hobson, A. Lowe, and Paul Willis, 128-39. London: Hutchinson, 1980.

———. "On Postmodernism and Articulation: An Interview with Stuart Hall." *Journal of Communication Inquiry* 10, no. 2 (1986): 45–60.

———. "Signification, Representation, Ideology: Althusser and the Post-Structuralist Debates." In *Critical Perspectives on Media and Society,* ed. Robert K. Avery and David Eason. New York: Guilford Press, (1991): 88–113.

"Hardly a Scratch in TV's Image." *Broadcasting,* 2 November 1959, 41–46.

Hartley, John. "Encouraging Signs: Television and the Power of Dirt, Speech, and Scandalous Categories." In *Interpreting Television: Current Research Perspectives,* ed. Willard D. Rowland Jr. and Bruce Watkins, 119–41. Beverly Hills, Calif.: Sage, 1984.

Harvey, David. "Flexibility: Threat of Opportunity." *Socialist Review* 21, no. 2 (1991): 65–77.

Heckscher, August. "The Quality of American Culture." In *Goals for Americans: Programs for Action in the Sixties,* ed. Presidents Commission on National Goals, 126–46. Englewood Cliffs, N.J.: Prentice-Hall, 1960.

Herman, Robert D. "Motivations to Gamble: The Model of Roger Caillois." In *Gambling and Society,* ed. William R. Eadington, 207-17. Springfield, Il.: Charles C. Thomas Publisher, 1976.

Herzog, Herta. "Professor Quiz—A Gratification Study." In *Radio and the Printed Page,* ed. Paul F. Lazarsfeld, 64–93. New York: Duell, Sloan and Pearce, 1940.

Hilmes, Michele. *Hollywood and Broadcasting: From Radio to Cable.* Urbana: University of Illinois Press, 1990.

———. *Radio Voices: American Broadcasting, 1922–1952.* Minneapolis: University of Minnesota Press, 1997.

———. "The Television Apparatus: Direct Address." *Journal of Film and Video* 37, no. 4 (1985): 27–36.

Hoerschelmann, Olaf. "Beyond the Tailfin: Education and the Politics of Knowledge on Big Money Quiz Shows." *Journal of Communication Inquiry* 24, no. 2 (April 2000): 177–94.

———. "The $64,000 Question." In *Museum of Broadcasting Communications Encyclopedia of Television,* ed. Horace Newcomb, 700–1. Chicago: Fitzroy Dearborn, 1997.

——. "Quiz Shows/Game Shows." In *Museum of Broadcasting Communications Encyclopedia of Television*, ed. Horace Newcomb, 600–5. Chicago: Fitzroy Dearborn, 1997.

Holbrook, Morris. *Daytime Television Gameshows and the Celebration of Merchandise: The Price Is Right*. Bowling Green, Ohio: Bowling Green State University Press, 1993.

"How NBC TV Games Forced CBS Switch." *Sponsor*, 27 February 1961, 36–37, 54.

"How Viewing Differs by Age and Sex." *Sponsor*, 5 June 1961, 45.

Hughes, Patrick. "Producing Audiences: Towards a Political Economy of Subjectivities." *Media International Australia* 80, (May 1996): 93–98.

Huizinga, Johan. *Homo Ludens: A Study of the Play-Element in Culture*. Boston: Beacon Press, 1955.

Hunter, James Davison. *Culture Wars: The Struggle to Define America*. New York: Basic Books, 1991.

Hutchinson, Thomas H. *Here Is Television: Your Window to the World*. New York: Hastings House, 1946.

Huyssen, Andreas. "Mass Culture as Woman: Modernism's Other." In *Studies in Entertainment*, ed. Tania Modleski, 188–207. Bloomington: Indiana University Press, (1986).

Jackaway, Gwenyth. "Initial Reactions to the Introduction of Television, 1938–1953." In *Communication and Culture: Language, Performance, Technology, and Media: Proceedings from the Sixth International Conference on Culture and Communication*, ed. Sari Thomas and William Evans, 187–97. Norwood, N.J.: Ablex, 1990.

Jauss, Hans Robert. *Toward an Aesthetic of Reception*. Minneapolis: University of Minnesota Press, 1982.

Jenkins, Henry. "Dennis the Menace, 'the All-American Handful.'" In *The Revolution Wasn't Televised: Sixties Television and Social Conflict*, ed. Lynn Spigel and Michael Curtin, 119–35. New York: Routledge, 1997.

——. *Textual Poachers: Television Fans and Participatory Culture*. New York: Routledge, 1992.

Jewell, Richard B. "Hollywood and Radio: Competition and Partnership in the 1930s." *Historical Journal of Film, Radio and Television* 4, no. 2 (1984): 125–41.

Johnson, Victoria E. "Citizen Welk: Bubbles, Blue Hair, and Middle America." In *The Revolution Wasn't Televised: Sixties Television and Social Conflict*, ed. Lynn Spigel and Michael Curtin, 265–85. New York: Routledge, 1997.

Jowett, Garth. "Dangling the Dream? The Presentation of Television to the American Public, 1928–1952." *Historical Journal of Film, Radio and Television* 14, no. 2 (1994): 121–45.

Joyrich, Lynne. "All that Television Allows: TV Melodrama, Postmodernism, and Consumer Culture." In *Private Screenings: Television and the Female Consumer*, ed. Lynn Spigel and Denise Mann, 227–51. Minneapolis: University of Minnesota Press, 1992.

Karp, Walter. "The Quiz Show Scandal." *America Vistas 1877 to Present*, 6th ed., ed. Leonard Dinnerstein and Kenneth T. Jackson, 317–34. Oxford, Eng.: Oxford University Press, 1991.

Kellner, Douglas. "Cultural Studies, Multiculturalism and Media Culture." In *Gender, Race and Class in Media*, ed. Gail Dines and Jean M. Humez, 5–17. Thousand Oaks, Calif.: Sage, 1995.

———. *Television and the Crisis of Democracy*. Boulder, Colo.: Westview, 1990.

Kepley Jr., Vance "From 'Frontal Lobes' to the 'Bob-and-Bob' Show: NBC Management and Programming Strategies, 1949–65." In *Hollywood in the Age of Television*, ed. Tino Balio, 41–61. Boston: Unwin Hyman, 1990.

Kerr, Clark. "An Effective and Democratic Organization of the Economy." In *Goals for Americans: Programs for Action in the Sixties*, ed. Henry M. Wriston, Frank Pace Jr., Erwin D. Canham, James B. Conant, Colgate W. Darden, Crawford H. Greenewalt, Alfred M. Gruenther, Learned Hand, Clark Kerr, James R. Killian Jr., and George Meany, 148–61. Washington, D.C.: Prentice-Hall, 1960.

Kozloff, Sarah. "Narrative Theory and Television." In *Channels of Discourse, Reassembled: Television and Contemporary Criticism*, ed. Robert C. Allen, 67–100. Chapel Hill: University of North Carolina Press, 1992.

Le Duc, Don. *Cable Television and the FCC: A Crisis in Media Control*. Philadelphia: Temple University Press, 1973.

———. "Deregulation and the Dream of Diversity." *Journal of Communication* 32, no. 4 (1982): 164–78.

Lears, Jackson. *Fables of Abundance: A Cultural History of Advertising in America*. New York: Basic Books, 1994.

————. "A Matter of Taste: Corporate Cultural Hegemony in a Mass-Consumption Society." In *Recasting America: Culture and Politics in the Age of Cold War*, ed. Larry May, 38–57. Chicago: University of Chicago Press, 1989.

Levine, Lawrence W. *Highbrow/Lowbrow: The Emergence of Cultural Hierarchy in America.* Cambridge, Mass.: Harvard University Press, 1988.

Lichty, Lawrence W. "Television in America: Success Story." In *American Media*, ed. Philip S. Cook, Douglas Gomery, and Lawrence Wilson Lichty, 159–76. Washington, D.C.: Wilson Center Press, 1989.

Lipsitz, George. "Who'll Stop the Rain: Youth Culture, Rock 'n' Roll, and Social Crises." In *The Sixties: From Memory to History*, ed. David Farber, 206–34. Chapel Hill: University of North Carolina Press, 1994.

Livingstone, Sonja, and Peter Lunt. *Talk on Television: Audience Participation and Public Debate.* London: Routledge, 1994.

"Lots more spot carriers in '61." *Sponsor*, 27 February 1961, 33–36.

Loviglio, Jason. "Vox Pop: Network Radio and the Voice of the People." In *Radio Reader: Essays in the Cultural History of Radio*, ed. Michele Hilmes and Jason Loviglio, 89–112. New York: Routledge, 2002.

MacDonald, J. Fred. *Don't Touch that Dial: Radio Programming in American Life, 1920–1960.* Chicago: Nelson-Hall, 1979.

————. *One Nation under Television: The Rise and Decline of Network TV.* Chicago: Nelson-Hall, 1994.

Macedo, Stephen. "Introduction." In *Reassessing the Sixties: Debating the Political and Cultural Legacy*, ed. Stephen Macedo, 9–18. New York: Norton, 1997.

Marc, David, and Robert J. Thompson. *Prime Time, Prime Movers.* Boston: Little, Brown, 1992.

Marchand, Roland. *Advertising the American Dream: Making Way for Modernity, 1920–1940.* Los Angeles: University of California Press, 1985.

————. "Visions of Classlessness, Quests for Dominion: American Popular Culture, 1945–1960." In *Reshaping America: Society and Institutions*, ed. Robert H. Bremmer and Gary W. Reichard, 163–90. Columbus: Ohio State University Press, 1982.

May, Elaine Tyler. *Homeward Bound: American Families in the Cold War Era.* New York: Basic Books, 1988.

McChesney, Robert W. *Telecommunications, Mass Media, and Democracy: The Battle for Control of U.S. Broadcasting, 1928–1935.* New York: Oxford University Press, 1994.

McMillen, Jan. "Understanding Gambling: History, Concepts and Theories." In *Gambling Cultures: Studies in History and Interpretation,* ed. Jan McMillen, 6–42. London: Routledge, 1996.

Mills, Adam, and Phil Rice. "Quizzing the Popular." *Screen Education* 41 (Winter/Spring 1982): 15–25.

Mittell, Jason. "A Cultural Approach to Television Genre Theory." *Cinema Journal* 40, no. 3 (Spring 2001): 3–24.

Moores, Shaun. *Interpreting Audiences: The Ethnography of Media Consumption.* London: Sage, 1993.

Morley, David. *Family Television.* London: Comedia, 1986.

———. *The "Nationwide" Audience.* London: British Film Institute, 1980.

———. *Television, Audiences, and Cultural Studies.* London: Routledge, 1992.

Munson, Wayne. *All Talk: The Talk Show in Media Culture.* Philadelphia: Temple University Press, 1993.

Munting, Roger. *An Economic and Social History of Gambling in Britain and the USA.* Manchester, Eng.: Manchester University Press, 1996.

Neale, Steve. *Genre and Hollywood.* New York: Routledge, 2000.

"Network Programming Trends: How Audiences Divide Their Time Among Network Show Types." *Sponsor,* 1 August 1960, 118.

"New Goodson-Todman Game: Diversify." *Broadcasting,* 30 January 1961, 44–46.

"The New TV Season: How Do Ad Men Rate It Over-all?" *Printer's Ink,* 10 November 1961, 11–12.

Newcomb, Horace. "On the Dialogic Aspects of Mass Communication." *Critical Perspective on Media and Society,* ed. Robert K. Avery and David Eason, 69–87. New York: Guilford Press, 1991.

———. "The Opening of America: Meaningful Difference in 1950s Television." In *The Other Fifties: Interrogating Midcentury American*

Icons, ed. Joel Foreman, 103–23. Urbana: University of Illinois Press, 1997.

Newcomb, Horace, and Paul Hirsch. "Television as Cultural Forum." In *Interpreting Television*, ed. W. Rowland and B. Watkins. Newbury Park, Calif.: Sage, 1984.

Norbeck, Edward. "The Anthropological Study of Human Play." *Rice University Studies* 60, no. 3 (1974): 1–8.

Nussbaum, Martha C. "Women in the Sixties." In *Reassessing the Sixties: Debating the Political and Cultural Legacy*, ed. Stephen Macedo, 82–101. New York: Norton, 1997.

O'Brien, J. "A Congressman Speaks: Networks Must Clean House or Congress Will." *TV Guide* 7, no. 45 (1959): 5–7.

Olson, Scott R. "Meta-Television: Popular Postmodernism." *Critical Studies in Mass Communication* 4 (1987): 284–300.

Owen, Forrest F. "Why Kill Good Quizzes with the Bad?" *Broadcasting*, 16 November 1959, 31.

"The Price of Color TV Is Right." *Sponsor*, 20 February 1960, 19.

"Programmers Pick TV Favorites." *Broadcasting*, 24 July 1961, 19–21.

"Quiz question: How Will the Investigation of One of Television's Programming Staples Affect Its Future?" *Television Age* 22 September 1958, 29–33, 104.

Radway, Janice. *Reading the Romance: Women, Patriarchy, and Popular Literature*. Chapel Hill: University of North Carolina Press, 1991.

Rappaport, Roy. "Ritual." In *Folklore, Cultural Performances, and Popular Entertainments*, ed. Richard Bauman, 249–60. New York: Oxford University Press, 1992.

Real, Michael R. *Exploring Media Culture*. Thousand Oaks, Calif.: Sage, 1996.

"The Resurgence of Television Game Shows." *Broadcasting*, 6 November 1961, 60.

Ritchie, Michael. *Please Stand By: A Prehistory of Television*. Woodstock, N.Y.: Overlook Press, 1994.

Rosenberg, Bernard. "Mass Culture in America." In *Mass Culture: The Popular Arts in America*, ed. Bernard Rosenberg and David Manning White, 3–12. New York: Free Press, 1957.

Sarkis, Mona. "Interactivity Means Interpassivity." *Media Information Australia* 69 (1993): 13–16.

Sarnoff, David. "Tributes Are Paid to NBC Progress at Gala Banquet." *Broadcasting*, 15 November 1936, p. 13.

———. "TV Not to Replace Broadcasting." *Broadcasting*, 15 July 1936, 10.

Schatz, Thomas. *Hollywood Genres: Formulas, Filmmaking, and the Studio System.* New York: Random House, 1981.

Schwartz, David, Steve Ryan, and Fred Wostbrock. *The Encyclopedia of TV Game Shows*, 2nd. ed. New York: Facts on File, 1995.

Schwed, Mark. "MTV's Miss Matchmaker." *TV Guide*, 8 June 1996, 22–24.

Schwoch, James, Mimi White, and Susan Reilly. *Media Knowledge: Readings in Popular Culture, Pedagogy, and Critical Citizenship.* Albany: State University of New York Press, 1992.

Seiter, Ellen, Hans Borchers, Gabriele Kreutzner, and Eva-Maria Warth. "'Don't Treat Us Like We're So Stupid and Naive': Towards an Ethnography of Soap Opera Viewers." In *Remote Control: Television, Audiences, and Cultural Power*, ed. Ellen Seiter, Hans Borchers, Gabriele Kreutzner, and Eva-Maria Warth, 223–47. London: Routledge, 1989.

Selby, Wendy. "Social Evil or Social Good: Lotteries and State Regulation in Australia and the United States." In *Gambling Cultures: Studies in History and Interpretation*, ed. Jan McMillen, 65–85. London: Routledge, 1996.

"Seven Men Capture the Most Responsive Audience in Daytime Television!" *Broadcasting*, 6 June 1960, 14–15.

Shaw, Punch. "Generic Refinement on the Fringe: The Game Show." *Southern Speech Communication Journal* 52 (1987): 403–10.

Sherwood, Robert E. "Beyond the Talkies-Television." *Scribner's Magazine* July 1929, 1–2.

"The $64,000 Question." *Newsweek*, 5 September 1955, 41–45.

Slack, Jennifer Daryl. "The Theory and Method of Articulation in Cultural Studies." In *Stuart Hall: Critical Dialogues in Cultural Studies*, ed. David Morley and Kuan-Hsing Chen, 112–27. London: Routledge, 1996.

Smith, James F. "When It's Bad It's Better: Conflicting Images of Gambling in American Culture." In *Gambling Cultures: Studies in History and Interpretation*, ed. Jan McMillen, 101–15. London: Routledge, 1996.

Smulyan, Susan. "Radio Advertising to Women in Twenties America: A Latchkey to Every Home!" *Historical Journal of Film, Radio and Television* 13, no. 3 (1993): 299–314.

———. "The Rise of the Radio Network: Technological and Cultural Influences on the Structure of American Broadcasting." *Prospects: An Annual of American Studies* 11 (1987): 105–17.

———. *Selling Radio: The Commercialization of American Broadcasting, 1920–1934.* Washington, D.C.: Smithsonian Institution Press, 1994.

Sobchack, Vivian. "Genre Film: Myth, Ritual, and Sociodrama." In *Film/Culture*, ed. Sari Thomas, 147–65. Metuchen, N.J.: Scarecrow Press, 1982.

Sotirin, Patty. "On Resistance: Extending Laclau's Theory of Articulation As Analogical." Paper presented at the International Communication Association Conference, Albuquerque, N.M.; *Philosophy of Communication Division*, 27 May 1995.

Spigel, Lynn. *Make Room for TV: Television and the Family Ideal in Postwar America.* Chicago: University of Chicago Press, 1992.

Spigel, Lynn, and Michael Curtin. "Introduction." In *The Revolution Wasn't Televised: Sixties Television and Social Conflict*, ed. Lynn Spigel and Michael Curtin, 1–18. New York: Routledge, 1997.

Staiger, Janet. *Interpreting Films: Studies in the Historical Reception of American Cinema.* Princeton, N.J.: Princeton University Press, 1992.

Stallybrass, Peter, and Allon White. "Bourgeois Hysteria and the Carnivalesque." In *The Cultural Studies Reader*, ed. Simon During, 284–94. London: Routledge, 1993.

———. *The Politics and Poetics of Transgression.* Ithaca, N.Y.: Cornell University Press, 1986.

Stam, Robert. *Subversive Pleasures: Bakhtin, Cultural Criticism, and Film.* Baltimore, Md.: Johns Hopkins University Press, 1989.

Steigerwald, David. *The Sixties and the End of Modern America.* New York: St. Martin's Press, 1995.

Sterling, Christopher H., and John M. Kittross. *Stay Tuned: A Concise History of American Broadcasting.* Belmont, Calif.: Wadsworth, 1990.

Stoeltje, Beverly J. "The Beauty Contest: Ritualizing the Female Body." Paper presented to the Davies Forum, University of San Francisco, San Francisco, Calif., 1997.

———. "Festival." In *Folklore, Cultural Performances, and Popular Entertainments*, ed. Richard Bauman, 261–71. New York: Oxford University Press, 1992.

———. "Power and the Ritual Genres: American Rodeo." *Western Folklore* 52 (April 1993): 135–56.

Stone, Joseph, and Tim Yohn. *Prime Time and Misdemeanors: Investigating the 1950s TV Quiz Scandal—A D.A.'s Account*. New Brunswick, N.J.: Rutgers University Press, 1992.

Streeter, Thomas. "Blue Skies and Strange Bedfellows: The Discourse of Cable Television." *The Revolution Wasn't Televised: Sixties Television and Social Conflict*, ed. Lynn Spigel and Michael Curtin, 221–42. New York: Routledge, 1997.

———. "The Cable Fable Revisited: Discourse, Policy, and the Making of Cable Television." *Critical Studies in Mass Communication* 4 (1987): 174–200.

———. *Selling the Air: A Critique of the Policy of Commercial Broadcasting in the United States*. Chicago: University of Chicago Press, 1996.

———. "Selling the Air: Property and the Politics of U.S. Commercial Broadcasting." *Media, Culture & Society* 16, no. 1 (1994): 91–116.

Susman, Warren. "Did Success Spoil the United States? Dual Representations in Postwar America." In *Recasting America: Culture and Politics in the Age of Cold War*, ed. Larry May, 19–37. Chicago: University of Chicago Press, 1989.

———. *Culture as History: The Transformation of American Society in the Twentieth Century*. New York: Pantheon, 1984.

Sutton-Smith, Brian. "Play as Adaptive Potentiation." In *Studies in the Anthropology of Play: Papers in Memory of B. Allan Tindall*, ed. Phillips Stevens Jr., 232–37. West Point, N.Y.: Leisure Press, 1976.

Swartz, Jon David, and Robert C. Reinehr. *Handbook of Old-Time Radio: A Comprehensive Guide to Golden Age Radio Listening and Collecting*. Metuchen, N.J.: Scarecrow Press, 1993.

"Symptoms of a Sickness." *New York Times*, 3 November 1959, 30.

Tafler, David. "Boundaries and Frontiers: Interactivity and Participant Experience—Building New Models and Formats." In *Transmission: Toward a Post-Television Culture*, 2nd ed., ed. Peter D'Agostino and David Tafler. Thousand Oaks, Calif.: Sage, 1995.

Taylor, Ella. *Prime-Time Families: Television Culture in Postwar America.* Berkeley: University of California Press, 1989.

Tedlow, Richard S. "The TV Quiz Show Scandals of the 1950s." In *America Vistas 1877 to Present*, 4th ed., ed. Leonard Dinnerstein and Kenneth T. Jackson, 310–24. Oxford, Eng.: Oxford University Press, 1983.

"TIO's First Year: An Appraisal." *Broadcasting*, 26 September 1960, pp. 27–30.

Todorov, Tzvetan. *The Fantastic.* Ithaca, N.Y.: Cornell University Press, 1975.

Traube, Elizabeth G. *Dreaming Identities: Class, Gender, and Generation in 1980s Hollywood Movies.* Boulder, Colo.: Westview Press, 1992.

Tudor, Andrew. "Genre." In *Film Genre Reader*, ed. Barry Keith Grant, 3-10. Austin: University of Texas Press, 1986.

Turner, Victor. "Liminal to Liminoid, in Play, Flow, and Ritual: An Essay in Comparative Symbology." *Rice University Studies* 60, no. 3 (1974): 53–92.

"TV Begins Scrubbing Its Tarnish." *Broadcasting*, 26 October 1959, 41–46.

"TV's Biggest Find!" *TV Guide* 21 January 1956, 4–7.

"TV Violence? Now It's in Rivalry among Nets." *Advertising Age* 13 (February 1961): 1, 132.

"TvB Digs Up New Data on Daytime TV." *Sponsor*, 1 August 1960, 36–37, 69.

"The Ultimate Responsibility." *Time*, 16 November 1959, 74–80.

Van Doren, Charles. "'Junk Wins TV Shows.'" *Life*, 23 September 1957, 137–48.

Vianello, Robert. "The Power Politics of 'Live' Television." *Journal of Film and Video* 37, no. 3 (1985): 26–40.

Vološinov, Valentin. *Marxism and the Philosophy of Language.* New York: Academic Press, 1973.

Watson, Mary Ann. *The Expanding Vista: American Television in the Kennedy Years.* New York: Oxford University Press, 1990.

Weinberg, Meyer. *TV in America: The Morality of Hard Cash.* New York: Ballantine Books, 1962.

Welch, Patrick E. "The Quiz Program: A Network Staple." *Journal of Broadcasting* 11, no. 4 (1958): 311–18.

"When Will Radio/TV Crack the Supers?" *Sponsor,* 31 July 1961, 27–30, 49–50.

White, Mimi. "Ideological Analysis and Television." In *Channels of Discourse, Reassembled: Television and Contemporary Criticism,* ed. Robert C. Allen, 161–202. Chapel Hill: University of North Carolina Press, 1992.

Whitfield, Stephen J. *The Culture of the Cold War.* Baltimore, Md.: Johns Hopkins University Press, 1991.

"Why the 'Quiz-Panel' Shows Are TV Staples." *Sponsor,* 4 July 1959, 36–37, 76–77.

Williams, Mary Rose, and Enrique D. Rigsby. "The Non-Discursive Rhetoric of Television: Spinning the Wheel with Pat and Vanna." In *Television Criticism: Approaches and Applications,* ed. Leah Vande Berg and Lawrence Wenner, 463–79. New York: Longman, 1990.

Williams, Raymond. *Marxism and Literature.* Oxford, Eng.: Oxford University Press, 1977.

———. *Television: Technology and Cultural Form.* Hanover, N.H.: Wesleyan University Press, 1974.

Willis, Paul. *Common Culture: Symbolic Work at Play in the Everyday Cultures of the Young.* Boulder, Colo.: Westview Press, 1990.

Wilson, Pamela. "NBC Television's 'Operation Frontal Lobes': Cultural Hegemony and Fifties' Program Planning." *Historical Journal of Film, Radio and Television* 15, no. 1 (1995): 83–104.

Wolfe, Alan. "Politics by Other Means." *New Republic,* 11 November 1991, 39–40.

Wright, Will. *Sixguns and Society: A Structural Study of the Western.* Berkeley: University of California Press, 1975.

Zahradnik, Rich. "Interactive Services: Telephone Now Completes the Circuit." *Channels of Communication* (1984): 24.

Index